"If you want to limit your reading on this topic to just one book, this should be it. . . . An astute observer and clear communicator of matters pertaining to real estate, mortgages and home ownership, Tom Kelly was one of the first to recognize the many ways that reverse mortgages can help seniors live more comfortably. This book is so useful and pragmatic that anyone trying to fully understand a reverse mortgage should read it . . ."

—*Peter H. Bell, President, National Reverse Mortgage*
Lenders Association, Washington, D.C.

"The New Reverse Mortgage Formula" is an important book for any senior or boomer seeking to better understand financing options that solve the retirement, health care or aging-in-place puzzles. With his usual style, Tom Kelly has again succeeded at providing consumers with a valuable, easy to read resource that simply translates the often confusing world of financial services into a road map for financial security . . ."

—*Jim Mahoney, Chief Executive Officer, Financial Freedom*
Senior Funding Corporation, Irvine, California

"Newspaper readers and radio listeners around the country have benefited from Mr. Kelly's topics and opinions for years. He is an excellent communicator and one of the few journalists who continually puts the consumer first . . ."

—*Alan Tonnon, attorney, author and charter member*
of the Washington Real Estate Commission

"There is no more precious asset than your own home. Home holds your memories, your garden, your pets, friends and family—and most importantly your sense of independence. Tom Kelly clearly outlines how to assure you can stay in your home and receive income as well. Whether you are currently a senior or senior caregiver, looking for options—or you are planning for your own senior years—this is the one book to read, and reread often . . ."

—*Laura Phillips Bennett, President,*
Bennett & Company Marketing

The New Reverse Mortgage Formula

How to Convert Home Equity into Tax-Free Income

TOM KELLY

WILEY
John Wiley & Sons, Inc.

This book is printed on acid-free paper. ∞

Published by John Wiley & Sons, Inc., Hoboken, New Jersey.
Published simultaneously in Canada.

For general information on our other products and services please contact our Customer Care Department within the United States at (800) 762-2974, outside the United States at (317) 572-3993 or fax (317) 572-4002.

Wiley also publishes its books in a variety of electronic formats. Some content that appears in print may not be available in electronic books. For more information about Wiley products, visit our web site at www.Wiley.com.

Library of Congress Cataloging-in-Publication Data:

Kelly, Tom.
The new reverse mortgage formula : how to convert home equity into tax-free income/Tom Kelly.
p. cm.
Includes index.
ISBN 0-471-67956-9 (pbk. : alk. paper)
1. Mortgage loans, Reverse—United States.   2. Home equity conversion—United States.
3. Retirement income—United States.   I. Title: How to convert home equity into tax-free income.
II. Title.

HG2040.5.U5K46 2004

332.7'22—dc22   2004058894

Printed in the United States of America

10 9 8 7 6 5 4 3 2 1

CONTENTS

Tom Kelly is a nationally syndicated newspaper feature writer and radio talk show host. He served the *Seattle Times* readers for 20 years—several as real estate editor—and his work now appears in the *Los Angeles Times,* the *Houston Chronicle,* the *St. Louis Post Dispatch,* the *Oakland Tribune, The Kansas City Star, The Sacramento Bee, The News Tribune* in Tacoma, Washington, *The Reno Gazette-Journal, The Courier-Journal* in Louisville, Kentucky, *The Tennesseean* in Nashville, plus more than two dozen other newspapers.

In 2004, Tom's award-winning radio show *Real Estate Today* began its eleventh year on 710 KIRO-AM, the CBS affiliate in Seattle and the state's largest station. The show is syndicated by Business Talk Radio to approximately 40 domestic markets and airs on 450 stations in 160 foreign countries via Armed Forces Radio.

He is the coauthor of *How a Second Home Can Be Your Best Investment* written with John Tuccillo, former chief economist for the National Association of Realtors.

His latest venture, another radio program—*Transitions: New Perspectives on Aging*—targets the questions, sources, and issues of persons over 55 and their adult children.

Tom and his wife, Jodi, an associate dean and professor at Seattle University, have four children and live on Bainbridge Island, Washington.

ACKNOWLEDGMENTS

This book is dedicated to our four children—Charley, Mikal, Andy, and Chris. These terrific people continually delighted us as youngsters and now light up our home with their laughter and ideas each time they return. Perhaps if our house isn't still leveraged to the hilt as a result of their higher education, we will be able to leave them something when we eventually move.

To the many individuals from academia, home building, mortgage lending, tax, and accounting that have aided me for years in my newspaper writing and radio work and who also provided creative insights and useful information for this effort. I have called upon them often, and their patience, interest, and kindness have been extraordinary. Leading this list are Richard Garrigan, Sarah Hulbert, Lee McCutcheon, Mike Broderick, Heather Papineau, Joanne Elizabeth Kelly, Peter Bell, Darryl Hicks, Frank Piemonte, Glenn Petherick, Rob Keasal, John Tuccillo, Jim Mahoney, Tom Scabareti, Jeff Taylor, John Mlekush, Barbara Stucki, Laura Bennett, Kevin Hawkins, Sharon Brooks, and Rajiv Nagaich. Special thanks also must go to Mike Hamilton, senior editor, who not only recognized the need for a book on this topic but also the timing of its delivery. I also am grateful to the numerous mortgage borrowers, and their loan representatives, for sharing their stories. Some of the borrowers requested their names be changed, yet their stories are very real.

Comedian Jay Leno periodically hosts a segment on *The Tonight Show* entitled "Jaywalking." During the popular feature, Leno interviews everyday people on the street, asking them to answer common questions or define specific words and phrases. Most don't have a clue.

Mention the words *reverse mortgage* to homeowners and the scene is similar. Most folks envision the sinister Snidely Whiplash chugging down the road in his black sedan, twirling his well-waxed mustache, and drooling over the prospect of informing the desperate occupants that he now holds the parchment deed to the cherished homestead they've nurtured for decades. Bring up the concept of a reverse mortgage in the presence of adult children, and they see their inheritance sinking faster than their beloved technology stocks during the tech wreck of 1999 to 2002.

In fact, Dante would have a field day explaining the perceptions now harbored by many consumers surrounding the most misunderstood financing option in today's money world: "Folks, a long time ago, you sold your home to the devil (your lender) for a little cash during your lifetime. Now it's time to pay up . . . and get out!"

What, exactly, is this financial tool that sparks so many question marks and exclamation points? In a capsule, a reverse mortgage is a special type of home loan that lets a homeowner, age 62 or older, convert a portion of the funds built up over years of payments and appreciation into cash. In essence, the cash flow is reversed. Instead of you making payments to the bank, the bank makes payments to you. But unlike a traditional home equity loan or second mortgage, no repayment is required until the borrower no longer uses the home as his or her principal residence. You do not need to repay the loan as long as you or one of the borrowers continues to live in the house and keeps the taxes and insurance current.

You can never owe more than your home's value. The home does not have to be sold to pay off the loan. The consumer (or the heirs) can pay off the reverse mortgage and keep the home. The proceeds from reverse mortgages are tax-free and do not affect Social Security or Medicare benefits. However, the funds received from a reverse mortgage may affect eligibility for certain kinds of government assistance, such as Medicaid or Supplemental Social Security Income, unless the payments are structured so that what you receive is spent in the month it is received.

Borrowers can use the funds for any purpose: home modification to help age in place, supplemental income, health care, retirement of existing mortgages and debt, drug prescriptions, and travel. Reverse mortgage motives have begun to range from absolute need to unexpected pleasure.

Mom, you don't have to pay up until you move out. Kids, if Mom dies, you'll have to pay what's owed. But guess what . . . ? Some of that outstanding debt is going to be offset by the home's appreciation. Have you checked what the family home is worth now compared to seven years ago? Even if Mom throws her mortgage in reverse and slams the accelerator to the floor, you still will probably end up with a tidy sum.

This book will explain how the *new reverse mortgage*—while still expensive—can provide a critical revenue stream for millions of elderly homeowners, offer a key financial strategy to the enormous group of Baby Boomers marching toward the traditional retirement years, and supply a viable solution to the coming health care crisis in the United States. The concept might not be for everyone, but it can be a valuable option, especially for seniors who want to stay in their homes yet have no other means of paying their monthly bills. The cost of the loan can be extremely expensive if the homeowner receives relatively small monthly payments and plans to stay in the home a short time, but for people planning to live in their homes many years, the loan can become very attractive, as we'll explore in Chapter 2.

However, steep costs are typically weighed only by the wealthy or elders with other viable alternatives. Extremely needy, often desperate seniors digest those costs en route to the only avenue that will solve their financial troubles or enable them to stay in their home.

"When people say reverse mortgages are too expensive, I bite my lip, count to 10 and ask 'compared to what?' " said Jeff Taylor, Wells Fargo Home Mortgage vice president and national director of the Senior Products Group. "Is it more expensive than selling the home, paying the closing costs, the real estate commission and then moving Mom to a new neighborhood and into an expensive assisted living or nursing home she doesn't want to be in?"

According to the U.S. Bureau of the Census and the National Center for Health Statistics, the older population—persons 65 years of age and older—numbered 35 million in 2000, and most of them would like to stay in their homes as long as possible. This age group represented 12.4

percent of the population—about one in every eight Americans. In addition, the number of Americans ages 45 to 64—who will reach 65 over the next two decades—increased 34 percent from 1990 to 2000. Every day, the 50+ population is growing by 10,000 people, and this trend is expected to continue for the next 20 years. Right now, an American turns 50 every seven seconds.

According to the Bureau of the Census, senior citizens in this country have approximately $2 trillion in home equity. This book will target these consumers plus their children—the 75 million Baby Boomers—who are now asking financial and lifestyle questions on behalf of their parents and who also will consider a reverse mortgage as a viable solution in their lives. Secondarily, this book will be of use to those in the real estate, legal, health care, and financial industries who will assist these huge senior-Boomer groups—the largest, healthiest, and wealthiest segments ever encountered on the American growth landscape. Because the market is so large, professionals are looking for any information they can use in helping family, friends, and customers to age in place.

"Some people will say reverse mortgages are absolutely too expensive, while others will tell you they are the greatest deal on earth. What all the years of talking to seniors about reverse mortgages has taught me is that you can show somebody what something costs, but you cannot tell them what it's worth to them," said Ken Scholen, who founded the nonprofit National Center for Home Equity Conversion (NCHEC) in Madison, Wisconsin, in 1981 to better educate consumers on reverse mortgages and other alternatives. Scholen, who has never acted as a mortgage lender, still serves as NCHEC director and coordinates AARP's reverse mortgage program and counseling service along with Bronwyn Belling, a long-time reverse mortgage specialist.

"Seniors who are at a financial crossroads have many decisions to make," Scholen said. "They should find out what they can get for their house and seriously consider selling. They can move to a less expensive house or area . . . go and see for themselves what they thought it would be. For most people, this process reinforces the strong tie to what they have now. When you look at other places, you get a better idea of what you value now."

It's time to make some decisions—for both seniors and their adult children who will soon be making the same decisions for themselves. This book is an attempt to spark that process.

Proof that evolution can go in reverse.
—ANONYMOUS

Throwing Your Mortgage Into Reverse

Exploring the Reality behind the Perception

What many people have now— house, neighborhood, friends, church, club—is exactly what they'd like to keep. Unfortunately many of them simply don't know how, or where, to look to find the funds to help them age in place. And, the immediate key for the present group of seniors is supplementing income for everyday expenses while affording long-term care. The two represent the most delicate balance in this country today—if you spend for one, you simply don't get the other. The need for long-term care will generate a rush of reverse mortgage applications for decades to come. A reverse mortgage may not be the only avenue taken to offset the costs of retirement living, discussed in Chapter 6, but many analysts believe it could easily emerge as the secret sauce.

Dr. Barbara Stucki, a Bend, Oregon, researcher and consultant, completed a study for the National Council on the Aging (NCOA) that supports tapping into home equity via a reverse mortgage as the critical financing vehicle to help seniors afford long-term care services at home. Stucki, former senior policy analyst for the American Council of Life Insurance and an AARP employee, was the project manager and lead author of *National Blueprint for Increasing the Use of Reverse Mortgages for Long-Term Care.* The NCOA, with the support of the Centers for Medicare and Medicaid Services (CMS) and the Robert Wood Johnson Foundation, sought to find a way to increase the use of home equity to fund long-term care services and insurance, thereby curtailing the financial disaster predicted for Medicare and Medicaid.

"There is simply no other pot of funds sitting around that is going to solve the long-term care situation in this country other than home equity," Stucki said. "I just don't see any other way—unless people simply want to dig deep down and pay out of their pockets. The idea is to use your home to stay at home."

That's why the appeal of reverses will become even greater as the population ages. In Chapter 1, we will explore the huge potential market and show why the use of these built-up equity funds will be as varied as the population segments considering their use. In Chapter 9, we will examine how today's reverse mortgage has come a long way from the first reverse loans that contained no consumer safeguards while often providing the underwriting lender a huge portion of the home's future value. Since 1989 when the U.S. Department of Housing and Urban Development (HUD) first launched a pilot program that would insure reverse mortgages, the vehicle has been refined and improved to a point where reverses are readily accepted in the secondary mortgage market.

In laymen's terms, Wall Street has taken notice. There's a market for these packages as investment instruments in conventional corporate structures. Fannie Mae, the biggest player in America's secondary mortgage market, is eager to get its hands on every reverse mortgage available. In fact, it even buys every reverse mortgage that HUD insures. The huge, stodgy, conventional mortgage mom spreading her wings to encompass the poor, ragamuffin, government outcast? Did hell freeze over while we were all refinancing our conventional mortgages? A few short years ago, the chance of Fannie Mae buying government loans was about as slim as the New York Yankees fan club inviting Boston Red Sox season ticket holders to a Sunday afternoon picnic.

Consumers can choose how to receive the money from a reverse mortgage. The options, outlined in Chapter 3, include a lump sum, fixed monthly payments for life, a line of credit, or a combination of the above. The most popular option—chosen by more than 60 percent of borrowers—is the line of credit, which allows consumers to draw on the loan proceeds at any time. The size of the reverse mortgage depends on age at application, loan type, home value, and—sometimes—location. In general, the older the consumer, the more valuable the home, and the lesser the amount owed, the larger the reverse mortgage will be.

The costs associated with getting a reverse mortgage, explained in Chapter 2, include the origination fee (which can be financed as part of the mortgage), an appraisal fee, and other charges similar to those costs for regular mortgages. One of the most confusing fees involved is the mortgage insurance premium. Seniors are usually flabbergasted when they find the amount is 2 percent of the appraised value of their home. Couple that cost with a loan origination fee and standard closing costs, and a borrower can easily spend $6,000 to borrow $319 a month for life. Why, you ask, should a senior who owns his or her home free and clear have to pay for mortgage insurance? Unlike typical mortgage insurance that protects the lender if the borrower defaults, mortgage insurance on a reverse mortgage ensures the borrower (or the borrower's estate) will never owe more than the value of the home. That means other assets will never be used to repay the mortgage if the home's value turns out to be less than the loan balance. The new reverse mortgage is a non-recourse loan, and the mortgage insurance guarantees that component.

Three reverse mortgage products are available to consumers in the United States and one product in Canada, all explained in Chapter 3. In the United States, the most popular reverse mortgage is the federally insured FHA Home Equity Conversion Mortgage (HECM). The other major product is the Home Keeper reverse, developed in the mid-1990s by Fannie Mae. Financial Freedom Senior Funding Corporation offers a jumbo private reverse mortgage product, designed to accommodate seniors living in higher-priced homes. This is the Cash Account Plan. The HECM and Home Keeper products are available in every state, while Financial Freedom's product is offered in most states and the District of Columbia. In Canada, the reverse mortgage product offered nationwide is the Canadian Home Income Plan (CHIP).

Before we get started on the likely candidates for reverses, let's take a peek at the basics and supply some answers to many of the nuts-and-bolts questions that consumers first raise regarding reverses:

Does the bank take my house? The reverse mortgage lender, like any lender, rarely, if ever, takes the title to the property. A reverse mortgage loan is the same as a forward, or conventional, mortgage loan: There's a lien on the property until the loan is repaid. When the amount owed is repaid (at death or relocation in a reverse mortgage) the lender is paid the amount of the lien. Banks don't really want your house: They want to lend you money, not act as a landlord and real estate property manager.

What's the difference between a home equity loan and a reverse mortgage? A reverse mortgage is a home equity loan without a payment. You do not repay the loan as long as the home remains your principal residence. Your income and credit rating is not considered when qualifying for the loan. There is no requirement that you requalify each year.

With a home equity loan, you must make regular payments to repay the loan. These payments begin as soon as the loan is originated. To qualify for such a loan, you must earn a monthly income great enough to make those payments. If you fail to make the monthly payments, the lender can foreclose, and you can be forced to sell your home. In addition, you may be required to requalify for a home equity loan each year. If you do not requalify, the lender may require you to pay the loan in full immediately. So while both the reverse mortgage and the home equity loan enable you to turn the equity in your home into spendable dollars, there are some important differences between the two types of mortgages.

Who helps to clarify the reverse process? All potential borrowers must first meet with an independent reverse mortgage counselor before filling out an application. The counselor's job is to educate and inform consumers about the various reverse programs and the alternative options available. This required counseling session is at no cost to the borrower and can be done in person or over the telephone.

How much money can be borrowed? The reverse mortgage loan amount is based on the home value, the number and age of the homeowner(s), and the current interest rate. The maximum allowable home value varies depending on the program selected. The FHA program has limits depending upon county.

Will my heirs owe anything if I die? You, or your heirs, will never owe more than your property is worth. Upon your death, the loan balance consisting of principal paid to you or on your behalf, plus any accrued interest, becomes due and payable. Your estate/heirs may choose to repay the loan by selling the property or they may want to pay it off by other means so they can keep the home. If the loan should exceed the value of your property, your estate will owe no more than the value of the property; the mortgage insurance will cover any balance due to the lender. No additional financial claims may be made against your heirs or estate.

Can I be forced to sell if property values decline? As long as you continue to occupy the property as your principal residence, you cannot be forced to sell or vacate the property. That's still true even if the total amount you owe on this loan exceeds the value of the property or if the fixed term over which you received monthly payments has expired. No deficiency judgment may result from your loan. Mortgage insurance covers any further obligation to the lender.

If my home appreciates in value during the mortgage term, who will be entitled to that appreciation? The new reverse mortgage does not provide the lender with an equity share in the appreciation of your home. Any money remaining after the mortgage is paid belongs to you or, upon your death, to your estate. You or your estate is legally required to pay back to the lender only the outstanding balance due.

What if I decide to sell my home? If you choose to sell your home, the outstanding balance becomes due and payable to the mortgage lender. Any proceeds left over once the loan is paid belong to you.

Can I sell my home to my children and continue to live in it? If you sell your home to your children or any other individual (or simply give them title), the loan will become due and payable. After the loan is repaid, any arrangement for your continued occupancy of the property must be made with the new owners.

Must I pay off any loans or liens against the property? Reverse mortgages require that all prior loans and liens be paid off so that the reverse mortgage loan is in first place, or in first lien, position. Many times, the proceeds from the reverse mortgage can pay off the underlying loans. An elder does not have to own the home free and clear to obtain a reverse mortgage.

More questions will be answered in later chapters. It's time to explore the groups and individuals who will be considering reverse mortgages. Chapter 1 will show you why the numbers, reasons, and backgrounds will change over time.

The mortgage is still in our name, but increasingly, the house is theirs.
One diaper, one vote.
—FRED G. GOSMAN

Who Are These Guys?

Understanding the Scope of the Reverse Mortgage Market

This chapter will explore why a significant percentage of older homeowners, plus their children—the 75 million baby boomers who are now asking financial and lifestyle questions for their parents—will consider a reverse mortgage as a viable opportunity in their life. While aging in place—including home maintenance, medical costs and property taxes—will be the primary reason for tapping into home equity for decades to come, there are many other underestimated needs and wants that will quickly race to the front burner once a greater number of consumers digest the relatively new reverse mortgage programs and the predicted health care debacle. Travel, investments, longed-for toys, and even new home purchases will be popular choices under the reverse mortgage umbrella.

According to the U.S. Bureau of the Census and the National Center for Health Statistics, the older population—persons 65 years of age and older—numbered 35 million in 2000 and represented 12.4 percent of the population—about one in every eight Americans. Nearly 80 percent of the nation's seniors own their own homes and 73 percent of those are owned free and clear of any mortgages, amounting to nearly $1.9 trillion in home equity. In addition, Americans over the age of 85 currently comprise the fastest growing segment of the older population. In 2000, an estimated 2 percent of the population was age 85 and older. By 2050, the percentage in this age group is projected to increase to almost 5 percent of the U.S. population. The size of this age group is especially important for the future of the U.S. health care system, because these individuals tend to be in poorer health and require more services than the younger old. Projections by the U.S. Census Bureau suggest that the population age 85 and older could grow from about 4 million in 2000 to 19 million by 2050. Some researchers predict that death rates at older ages will decline more rapidly than reflected in the Census Bureau's projections, which could result in faster growth of this population.[1]

"You have 5,500 people turning 65 every day," said Cheryl Chapin, national sales manager for the senior products group at Wells Fargo. "When you consider the vast number of people who will be eligible for this product in the next few years, the market is going to be huge."

There's a snowball already rolling down the hill. . . . The number of Americans aged 45–64—who will reach 65 over the next two decades—increased 34 percent from 1990–2000. Every day, the 50+ population is growing by 10,000 people, and this trend is expected to continue for the

---

[1] Kenneth Manton, Burton Singer, Richard Suzman (Eds), *Forecasting the Health of Elderly Populations.* New York: Springer-Verlag, 3–35.

next 20 years. Right now, an American turns 50 every seven seconds. (See Figure 1.1.) In addition to being the largest and healthiest group ever to come down the American housing pipeline, the Baby Boomers will also be the wealthiest bunch with approximately two-thirds of their assets in home equity. And, as we explain later in this chapter, they are going to stay put for entirely different reasons than their parents. The pressure on the baby boomer households to generate income and maintain lifestyle in the traditional retirement years will take on a new focus.

Just how big could the reverse market easily become? Approximately $74 billion by 2015, according to Wells Fargo projections. Jim Mahoney, a veteran in reverse lending, heads the Irvine, California–based Financial Freedom Senior Lending Corp., a subsidiary of IndyMac Bank. He believes the word is just beginning to spread regarding the nonrecourse component of the loan.

Figure 1.1 Senior Snapshot

Generation	Birth Years	Age Today
GI	1901–1924	79–102
Silent	1925–1942	61–78
Boom	1943–1960	43–60

- Someone in the United States turns 50 every 7 seconds.
- Between 1996 and 2010 the number of adults over age 65 will increase by 6 million, up 16 percent.
- Over two-thirds of the people who have ever turned 65 in the history of the world are alive today.
- Never before has America had this many 85-year-olds.

Source: Strauss & Howe
Brooks Adams Research

"But our biggest challenge continues to be education," Mahoney said. "We constantly battle the idea some people have that we are going to take the house. A reverse mortgage is simply a lien—just like any other mortgage. Our progress, though, is obvious. We moved from a cottage industry to a real force in all 50 states."

While the numbers bring immense reverse mortgage possibilities, the impact on the housing industry in general is especially significant. The challenge now for federal and state legislators, health care providers, building contractors, nursing home operators, and others dealing with aging issues is clearly staring them in the face: What happens if these huge groups *do not* stay in their homes, or age in place? Where would we put them and how could we possibly fund such volume? Toss in the idea that people are living 30 years longer than they did 40 years ago and the potential shelter/care components become enormous. In a capsule, the bigger-picture dilemma is three-pronged: the number of people entering the senior age bracket, the speed in which retirement residences and assisted living centers can be built, and the enormous funding needed to care for the occupants. As we discuss in Chapter 7, the country's predisposition toward nursing homes and the funneling of Medicare and Medicaid funds clearly must change. The bitterly ironic piece is Americans would rather stay at home, and very few vehicles, other than lawsuits, are enabling them to do so. Reverse mortgages have surfaced as an attractive—and perhaps necessary—option.

Who should not, or cannot, get a reverse mortgage? It depends on the homeowner's borrowing philosophy and need of funds. Sometimes there is not enough equity in the home to merit the costs of the loan. Sarah Hulbert, vice president and national director for Seattle Mortgage (now doing business in many states as Reverse Mortgage of America), one of the top three national reverse mortgage originators along with

Wells Fargo and Financial Freedom, said more seniors would have access to a greater portion of their home equity if a single national loan limit were approved. Now, the U.S. Department of Housing and Urban Development, which insures the most popular reverse program, ties loan limits to average household incomes in specific areas. Those limits can hinder persons with more expensive homes in less expensive areas. For example, on July 28, 2004, the maximum loan limit in King County, Washington, was $262,295 while across Puget Sound in Kitsap County the limit dropped to $199,500.

"The goal in all we do is to provide seniors with a greater access to funds," Hulbert said. "But if a senior has an expensive house with a lot of equity in a rural area, that person would be really restricted in the amount he or she could borrow. The reverse mortgage often would not provide them with the money they really need—yet the equity is clearly there."

In 1990, the traditional stories of white-collar and blue-collar folks retiring at age 65 and looking forward to a life of golf, fishing and pottery-making were still very common and expected. These folks were eager to join the "make do" generation that survived the Depression and World War II in a relatively risk-free retirement where the biggest threat to their well being usually occurred during the annual Thanksgiving Day flag football game with their suddenly huge grandkids. Now, pushed along by reduced pension plans, higher health care expenses, lost retirement savings due to corporate shenanigans and the "tech wreck" of once high-flying Internet companies, many U.S. elders are seeking ways of supplementing their incomes merely to meet their monthly bills. Some prolong their working years because they must; others continue in the workforce because they simply enjoy what they do and fear the lull of slowing down. They've seen their buddies become bored, stymied, and often ill due to a lack of challenging projects.

"We were often left with the tag line 'yes, but . . . you didn't live during the Depression.' " said Richard Garrigan, author and professor of finance emeritus at DePaul University in Chicago. "And after a short pause that was followed by 'and I hope you don't have to.' They are very opposed to risk-taking because of where they have been. And how can you blame them, even today? Sometimes I don't know if we are living in America or Scamerica. I'm lucky in that I'm 66, still have most of my marbles and have a background in finance. What about some of the older folks who never had to take care of the household finances, never really worried about writing important checks and just raised the kids?

"There are still a lot of people who'll say they don't have much to leave to the kids, but I don't think some families sit down and think this thing out."

Let's look at today's and tomorrow's elders and explore not only the common reasons for each group's potential interest in reverse mortgages but also their specific motivations.

Generations Have Common Needs, Specific Uses

In the book *Generations: The History of America's Future 1584–2069*, authors William Strauss and Neil Howe describe a generation as a cohort, or cluster of people born approximately during the same 20-year time period. Strauss and Howe contend that because people form values from common historical events, experiences, and influences, we can understand and often anticipate how a specific generation will think and respond. The following generational explanations will shed some light on how and why certain groups are prime candidates for reverse mortgages. Other researchers have grouped specific segments using different years as guidelines, so there will be overlaps and underlaps in the Strauss and Howe sampling when measured side by side with other data. Here are the capsule descriptions from *Generations* along with brief explanations of how each cohort thinks and operates:

The GI Generation (born 1901–1924)

Members of the GI Generation developed a special and good kid reputation as the beneficiaries of new playgrounds, scouting clubs, vitamins, and child-labor restrictions. They came of age with the sharpest rise in schooling ever recorded. As young adults, their uniformed corps patiently endured the Depression and heroically conquered foreign enemies. In a midlife subsidized by the GI Bill, they built gleaming suburbs, invented miracle vaccines, plugged missile gaps, and launched moon rockets. Their unprecedented grip on the U.S. presidency (1961–1992) began with a New Frontier, a Great Society, and Model Cities, but wore down through Vietnam, Watergate, deficits, and problems with "the vision thing." As senior citizens, they safeguarded their own entitlements but with little influence over culture and values. (See Figure 1.2.) *Representative members:* John Kennedy, Ronald Reagan, Walt Disney, Judy Garland, John Wayne, Ann Landers, Walter Cronkite.[2]

The GI Generation had to make do during the Depression and World War II, and that philosophy still influences its conduct today. Members of this group often are reluctant to spend money on themselves in order to make their lives more comfortable. They definitely subscribed to a

---

[2] William Strauss, Neil Howe, *Generations: The History of America's Future 1584–2069.*

Figure 1.2 The GI Generation

- **Approximate size: 63 million**
- **Born: 1901–1924 (age 79–102)**
- **First retired: 1966**
- **Peak retired: 1987**
- **Self Image: Heroic and patriotic**
- **Famous GIs: Katharine Hepburn, John Wayne, Jimmy Stewart, Walt Disney, Billy Graham**

About the GIs

- **The GI generation held the White House for 32 years and gave us seven presidents—Kennedy, Johnson, Nixon, Ford, Carter, Reagan and Bush—more than any other generation.**
- **They believe: "We have done the work of democracy every day." This is the "We've earned it" generation of retirees.**
- **The GI generation desired fun, activities, elegance, luxury.**

Source: Strauss & Howe
Brooks Adams Research

pay-it-off philosophy, especially when it came to the roof over their heads. Very few purchased long-term care insurance and are thus footing the bill for home care assistance. The GI's unwritten goal was to retire without a mortgage, and not achieving this goal often was seen, and felt, as a huge and depressing failure. Many of them don't see any reason to dive into their financial assets and would rather leave it for their kids even though their children are in a far better financial place than they are.

Susan Mack, an occupational therapist and president of Homes for Easy Living Universal Design Consultants in Murrietta, California, a company specializing in home modifications for persons with special needs, said she is constantly frustrated by the GIs' frugal mind-set.

"We'd go to great lengths to explain to these people and to their adult children when they come out of the hospital that it's important to modify their home to make it safer for them, but they wouldn't spend the money," Mack said. "They would go home and compromise their quality of life and put themselves in jeopardy of having another disability because they wouldn't put in a grab bar or they wouldn't install a walk-in shower. The amazing thing was that they began consoling me, instead of me consoling them. They'd say 'Susan, honey, don't worry. I'll be just fine. I'll make do.' "

According to the Princeton, New Jersey–based SRI Consulting Business Intelligence, the amount of household debt for people over 65 nearly tripled between 1992 and 2000. Many seniors simply haven't saved enough for retirement: 44 percent of retirees age 60 or older (overlap with the Silents) have saved $75,000 or less; eleven percent have saved nothing at all. Forty-four percent cite Social Security as their primary source of income.[2]

Biggest lure to a reverse mortgage: These reasons can be grouped in to the need for basic living necessities, plus property taxes, which have been compromised by rising health care costs; supplements to dwindling financial portfolios, home modifications, travel, and money to assist in the costs of raising grandchildren. *Led to participate:* They recently discovered availability of the reverse. Often, the only funds available to remain in the home, make needed repairs. They have been convinced to "live a little" by adult children, willingness to help out, surprised by current value of home brought by appreciation.

[2] Ibid

The Silent Generation (born 1925–1942)

The Silent Generation grew up as the suffocated children of war and the Depression. They came of age just too late to be war heroes and just too early to be youthful free spirits. Instead, this early marrying "lonely crowd" became the risk-averse technicians and professionals as well as the sensitive rock-'n'-rollers and civil-rights advocates of a post-crisis era in which conformity seemed to be a sure ticket to success. Midlife was an anxious passage for a generation torn between stolid elders and passionate juniors. Their political ascendancy in the mid-1970s coincided with fragmenting families, cultural diversity, institutional complexity, and prolific litigation. They are now redefining elderhood as a time for reconnecting with family, experimenting with new roles, and shedding the stodgy GI senior citizen moniker. Their hip style and reputation for indecision continues to give them a poor reputation for national leadership and is likely to make them the first generation in U.S. history never to produce a president. (See Figure 1.3.) *Representative members:* Colin Powell, Alan Greenspan, Woody Allen, Martin Luther King Jr., Sandra Day O'Connor, Gloria Steinem, Elvis Presley.[3]

William Manchester, the famous biographer, once commented that this group of people was "withdrawn, cautious, unimaginative, indifferent, unadventurous and silent." The generation's name also picked up steam when it was used in a *Time* cover story in 1951. This risk-averse group made some wise investments and typically saved more than other cohorts. According to the U.S. Census Bureau, the number of households headed by people age 60 and up with an income of at least $100,000 jumped 27 percent, to two million, between 1998 and 2002.

---

[3] Ibid

Figure 1.3 The Silent Generation

- Approximate size: 49 million
- Born: 1925–1942 (age 61–78)
- First retired: 1989
- Peak retires: 2008
- Self Image: Seeking to contribute
- Famous Silents: Woody Allen, Marilyn Monroe, Jesse Jackson, James Dean, Elvis Presley

About the Silents

- Only generation in American history to be smaller than the one before and the one after
- Never gave us a president; went from GIs to Boomers with Clinton
- Still seeking to contribute
- Korean War generation—last to get a monument
- Fiercely individual
- See themselves as real people—warts and all
- Confusing consumers—clip coupons and buy Cadillacs
- Affluent, but do not afford themselves luxury; want comfort and value

Source: Strauss & Howe
Brooks Adams Research

They, and others, are taking cash and indulging their youthful fantasies—perhaps for the first time. Harley-Davidson reports that customers of ages 65 to 74 tripled between 2000 and 2003. Other members of this generation now find themselves as grandparents—and as their grandchildren's primary caregivers. A skipped generation household is now defined as a grandparent and grandchild living with no parent in the home. In 2000, 5.8 million grandparents (60 percent over the age of 60) lived with grandchildren younger than age 18.

"A lot of these people just don't see themselves as retiring," said Donna Butts, executive director of Generations United, a national organization in Washington, D.C., specializing in intergenerational strategies. "They raised their own kids, now they are raising another set. It comes with obvious financial risks and their income will continue to be a challenge."

Biggest lure to a reverse mortgage: Health-conscious group plans to live longer, spending for education, travel, second homes, and long-term care insurance now plus drawing reverse funds later to age in place. Have begun to see power of home appreciation as potential back up to their retirement nest egg. Risk-averse mentality will keep them weighing costs more than Boomers. Silents will keep reverse cash in hand just in case something comes up. *Led to participate:* Special occasion, family reunion, coveted toy, "something they've always wanted to do." Strong sense of contributing—to children's weddings, grandchildren's education, people in dire straights.

The Boom Generation (born 1943–1960)

Members of the Boom Generation grew up as indulged youths during an era of community-spirited progress. These kids were the proud creation of postwar optimism, Dr. Spock rationalism, and *Father Knows Best* family order. Upon coming of age, however, Boomers loudly proclaimed their antipathy to the secular blueprints of their parents; they demanded inner visions over outer visions and self-perfection over thing-making or team-playing. The Boom awakening climaxed with Vietnam War protests, the 1967 Summer of Love, inner-city riots, the first Earth Day, and Kent State. In the aftermath, Boomers appointed themselves arbiters of the nation's values and crowded conspicuously into such culture careers as teaching, religion, journalism, marketing, and the arts. During the 1990s, entering midlife, they trumpeted values, touted a "politics of meaning," and waged scorched-earth culture wars. Now on the verge of elderhood, Boomers are rejecting the old notion of retirement in part because many have not saved enough to afford it. In old age, they look to be much more influential in the culture than in the economy or politics—much the opposite of the GIs who raised them. *Representative members:* George W. and Laura Bush, Bill and Hillary Clinton, Bill Bennett, Steven Spielberg, Meryl Streep, Spike Lee, Bill Gates, Doctor Laura Schlessinger.[4]

Figure 1.4 The Boom Generation

- **Approximate size: 79 million**
- **Born: 1943–1960 (age 43–60)**
- **First retires: 2008**
- **Peak retires: 2026**
- **Self Image: Purifiers**
- **Famous Boomers: Joe Namath, George W. Bush, Bill Gates, Martha Stewart, David Letterman**

About the Boomers

- **Largest generation in American history**
- **Last generation who had stay-at-home Moms**
- **Labeled more than any others: Sixties, Dr. Spock, Woodstock, Vietnam, Love, Pepsi**
- **Will redefine how to retire, age and die**
- **Value creativity, fiercely loyal to family**
- **America's most furious and violent youth upheaval of the twentieth century**
- **Sought a new, self-dictated religion through drugs, transcendental means**
- **Rage cooled**

Source: Strauss & Howe
Brooks Adams Research

[4] Ibid

Baby Boomers—the largest, healthiest, and wealthiest group ever appearing on the U.S. growth landscape—never met a loan they didn't like. The reverse mortgage will simply be an extension of the status quo. After leveraging appreciation and location in their starter and move-up homes to pay for cars, college tuitions, and trips, their eventual retirement home probably will hold most of the equity in their lives. Their last home will not be terribly modest because of this cohort's desire to entertain. Some members will purchase long-term care insurance in their earning years, allowing for more cash to be spent on more gadgets. While some analysts say the Boomers will gain wisdom with age and curb their spending ways down the road, others won't be persuaded. How they will behave continues to confound researchers.

"Baby Boomers are famous for believing one thing and then behaving totally different from what they think they do," said Eric Snider, who has a doctorate in social psychology and serves as Shea Homes' marketing director for Trilogy, the homebuilding company's upscale active adult communities. "They have retreated to their homes and away from society. Yet, that is not their reality at all."

According to a study Snider conducted for Shea, the Walnut, California–based company that specializes in upscale homes in North Carolina, Arizona, California, Washington, and Colorado, that's one of the reasons why homes have exploded in the past 50 years from an average of 953 square feet to 2,200 square feet. At the same time, the size of the family has declined dramatically.

"When you ask Boomers about age-restricted communities, they initially say, 'I'm not going to live in one of those,' " Snider said. "But when you look at the characteristics of the community, it gives them exactly what they are looking for: exclusivity, amenities and personal experiences. Boomers are all about personal experiences."

In a 2004 economic study prepared by the Urban Institute for AARP (formerly the American Association of Retired Persons), authors Barbara Butrica and Cori Uccello contend that Boomers will amass more wealth in real terms at retirement than will the two previous generations.[5] Median household wealth at age 67 will grow from $448,000 among current retirees to $600,000 among Boomers. Income at retirement is consistent with trends in wealth at retirement, the study shows. Projected household income at age 67 will increase from $44,000 among current retirees to $65,000 among boomers. As with wealth, there will be income disparities among older and younger Boomers. Nonretirement income is expected to decline between older and younger Boomers.

However, other researchers, including Larry Cohen, director of the Princeton, New Jersey–based Consumer Financial Decisions, wonder if Boomers, given their spending history, will ever get to the traditional retirement years with any real assets.

"As the cohort responsible for the explosion of credit use in the 1980s and 1990s, Boomers are hardly likely to forgo immediate gratification in their later years," Cohen said. "The trend among seniors will only be exacerbated when the Boomers enter retirement age. The convenience of credit card use with the occasional slip into revolving along with leveraging their assets for around the world tours or trips into space mean that the more responsible Boomers will have credit insurance to

---

[5] Barbara Butrica and Cori Uccello, *How Will Boomers Fare at Retirement?*, AARP, March 2004.

cover their inevitable demise. The rest, who are not so wealthy that they simply can afford that type of lifestyle, may wind up bequeathing their debt as their legacy instead of the trillions that they inherited."

Biggest lure to a reverse mortgage: Spend and borrow, spend and borrow. . . . Boomers, who will work into their 70s, will continue to do both. Why expect change when they've changed the world around them every step of the way? Long-term health insurance policies purchased earlier in their lives will leave the idea that more home equity will be available for their consuming habits. They were the main group burned by the high-technology crash, yet still gambled. *Led to participate:* Reverse was simply part of their plan. They will keep the home separate and independent from what they will leave their children—which might be only a bed and a desk.

Now that we have considered the primary candidates for a reverse mortgage, let's explore how much cash they will be able to borrow and how much cash it will cost them to borrow it. Chapter 2 will provide some of the nuts and bolts of the complex reverse mortgage vehicle.

Literature was formerly an art and finance a trade.
Today, it is the reverse.
—JOSEPH ROUX

How Much Can I Borrow... and What Will It Cost?

Reverse Mortgage Amounts Tied to Age, Location, and Home Value

Several years ago, there was a popular television commercial preaching the importance of properly maintaining your automobile to better improve the chances of enjoying a top-performing, long-lasting vehicle. The mechanic's message was simple: If you spent a minimal amount of money on regularly scheduled oil changes you would not have to foot the huge bill for a complete engine overhaul.

"You can pay me now," the mechanic announced, "or you can pay me later."

Reverse mortgage options are no exception. Similar to a "forward," or traditional mortgage, if the interest rate on a reverse mortgage seems low, the fees most likely will be higher. Conversely, if the fees are low, or none at all, the interest rate undoubtedly will be higher than on other loans in the same category.

In this chapter, we will consider the hard costs involved in a reverse mortgage and also explore some of the soft costs that do not show up on any spreadsheet or disclosure form. For homeowners over age 62 with considerable assets other than the equity in their home or for those people whose goal is to leave all of the equity in their home to their children, reverse mortgage costs may not make sense. Or, if taking money out of the home, especially after it's completely paid off, is adverse to one's investment philosophy, it's unlikely even an attractive program would alter that mind-set. However, before cashing your stock, paying the capital gains tax, and handing the remainder to the kids for the down payment on their first home or other expenditures, take a peek at using the reverse mortgage as an alternative financing plan. Once a stock is cashed, it's gone. Some of the costs of the reverse mortgage and funds extended to the kids could be recovered in future appreciation as you remain in the home.

"A lot of the people in the reverse mortgage age lived through the Depression era," said Rachel Brichan who focuses on jumbo reverse mortgages for the Irvine, California–based Financial Freedom. "To them, you were expected to have the house paid off by the time you retired. Somehow you felt like a failure if you didn't. It's hard for them to break through that mentality, but it's becoming more of a financial question now because of what their homes are worth."

On the other side of the housing ledger are the "absolute need" households where the cost of obtaining a reverse mortgage cannot be measured simply by the interest rate and fees charged on a line of credit. That's what Wells Fargo's Jeff Taylor was referring to in the Introduction of this book when he responds, "Compared to what?" when faced with defending the seemingly high cost of reverse mortgages. If you sell your home and pay the closing costs, could you find another home with the same amenities and friendly neighborhood as your present home? What price do you assign to relieving the anxiety of a maxed-out credit card? How do you quantify the ability to purchase needed medications?

Obviously, we cannot predict when we are going to die. However, try to take a shot at guessing how long you will stay in your home. Unless you are in a desperate situation and really need cash, it probably will not make sense to obtain a reverse mortgage if you are going to stay fewer than four years. That's because of the fees involved. If you plan to stay longer, and a growing number of people plan to do so, the reverse mortgage could be a viable option.

But What Will It Be Worth If You Stay?

What financial planners and accountants often underestimate is the ability of the homeowner to retain home appreciation during the term of the reverse mortgage. Three-bedroom, two-bath homes containing 1,250 square feet in Westchester, California, near the Los Angeles International Airport, were selling for $385,000 in 2000 yet were back on the market in 2004 at $545,000—and heading higher. While these soaring home prices are the biggest challenge to first-time buyers in this country, the increased values could be a boon to elders who couldn't care less how much their home is now worth—they simply want to stay in it. By pulling out some of the newfound equity, seniors can live more comfortably while leaving much of the home's value to their estate, usually their children. Some of these people, needing to pay bills or longing for a vacation, are saying, "Kids, we intend to leave you the $385,000 the home was worth in 2000, but we'd like to spend the difference." By spending it via a reverse mortgage, elders continue the potential for home appreciation, thereby offsetting the amounts they spend.

If you consider the astonishing appreciation of homes in California, Florida, and New York—three of the four states that contain the most persons over the age of 65 in the United States—and compare the recent appreciation rates to the numbers used to calculate the future value on the nation's most popular reverse mortgage, a huge difference surfaces.

For example, according to the National Association of Realtors, the median selling price of a single-family home in New York rose more than 32 percent from May 2003 to May 2004. During the same period, prices rose 20 percent in Florida and 26.5 percent in California. Home prices in Texas, the fourth state with a huge senior population, remained flat. The national median existing-home price was $183,600 in May 2004, up 10.3 percent from May 2003 when the median price was $166,400. (The median is a typical market price where half of the homes sold for more and half sold for less.) However, the standard appreciation index used on the FHA Home Equity Conversion Mortgage (HECM) remained at 4 percent. It has not changed. Granted, one year does not make a cycle, but the annual leaps in home values stated above are not unprecedented. Even if home appreciation slows considerably in the states with greatest senior population, the amount of money remaining after utilizing a reverse mortgage would be far greater than the HECM estimates.

Let's suppose Betty Booper lost her job as a commercial radio voice, had little income, yet her home, worth $150,000, was completely paid off. She did not want to relocate and eventually wanted to leave something for her one daughter, Susie. Betty, age 64, took out a reverse mortgage and was eligible to get $83,100 in one lump. After closing costs of $7,800 and servicing fee set-aside costs of $4,887, she was handed a lump-sum payment of $70,413 that she used to purchase radio equipment for a home studio. After 10 years, Betty was a star. She wanted to move to the bright lights of New York. Over the past 10 years, some of the homes in Betty's area increased 12 percent a year, but hers increased 8 percent a year. (See Figure 2.1.) Betty sold the home for its fair market value of $311,845 and paid off the loan balance of $158,471, leaving $153,374 to Susie—more than the value of the home when Betty was in desperate straits 10 years ago. Betty also made no mortgage payments for 10 years. The amount of equity that Betty could borrow at the start of the loan nearly doubled over the 10-year term.

Were the loan fees expensive? In the first two years, absolutely, because they would have cost 10.32 percent had Betty sold. In fact, the fees would have been even higher had Betty not chosen a lump-sum payout at the beginning. If Betty had selected one monthly check for life, her fees during the first one to two years of the loan would have been 59.51 percent. (See Appendix, Sample 1.) That's because Betty's $432.16 monthly check totals only contributed $14,096 to the loan balance. When you factor up-front fees of $7,800, Betty had better stay in the home a long time to make those monthly payments worthwhile. Again, fees are also relative to the program chosen.

On the lump-sum program, however, Betty's total annual loan cost after the 10-year period was 5.71 percent. Was Betty's home appreciation rate

Figure 2.1 Federal Housing Administration Home Equity Conversion Mortgage (HECM)

Amortization Schedule—Annual Projections

Borrower Name/Case	Betty Booper—Total Draw	Refinance: No	
Age of Youngest Borrower: 64		Initial Property Value:	$150,000
Expected Interest Rate:	6.250%	Beg. Mortgage Balance:	$78,212
Maximum Claim Amount:	$150,000	Initial Line of Credit:	$0.00
Initial Principal Limit:	$83,100	Monthly Payment:	$0.00
Initial Draw:	$70,412.06	Monthly Servicing Fee:	$30.00
Financed Closing Costs:	$7,800		

NOTE: Actual interest charges and property value projections may vary from amounts shown. Available credit will be less than projected if funds withdrawn from line of credit.

		Annual Totals				End of Year				
Yr	Age	SVC Fee	Payment	MIP	Interest	Loan Bal	Line of Credit	Prin Limit	Property Value @4%	Property Value @8%
1	64	360	0	404	5,055	84,031	0	88,886	156,000	156,000
2	65	360	0	434	5,430	90,255	0	95,075	162,240	168,480
3	66	360	0	466	5,831	96,913	0	101,694	168,729	181,958
4	67	360	0	501	6,260	104,034	0	108,775	175,478	196,515
5	68	360	0	538	6,720	111,651	0	116,349	182,497	212,236
6	69	360	0	577	7,211	119,799	0	124,450	189,797	229,215
7	70	360	0	619	7,736	128,514	0	133,115	197,389	247,552
8	71	360	0	664	8,298	137,835	0	142,384	205,285	267,357
9	72	360	0	712	8,899	147,806	0	152,298	213,496	288,745
10	73	360	0	763	9,542	158,471	0	162,902	222,036	311,845
11	74	360	0	818	10,229	169,878	0	174,245	230,918	336,792
12	75	360	0	877	10,965	182,080	0	186,377	240,154	363,736
13	76	360	0	940	11,751	195,131	0	199,354	249,761	392,835
14	77	360	0	1,007	12,593	209,091	0	213,235	259,751	424,261

Figure 2.1 *(Continued)*

Total Annual Loan Cost Rate

Appreciation Rate	Disclosure Period (Yrs.)			
	2	10	20	28
0%	10.32%	5.70%	3.48%	2.47%
4%	10.32%	5.70%	5.08%	4.88%
8%	10.32%	5.70%	5.08%	4.88%

too high to be realistic? Perhaps, but the expected interest rate, 6.25 percent, also was calculated at a higher than normal level. The intangible variable was Betty's need to get back on her feet and the ability to stay—and work—at home. How do you assign an interest rate, or loan fee, when there is no other way out? Plus, she left a considerable amount of money to Susie, again showing that seniors can spend all, or part, of their home's future appreciation and still leave the kids something.

While the housing market has set record levels for sales activity in every year from 1996 to 2004, it will undoubtedly slow. That frenetic pace cannot be expected to continue indefinitely because the housing industry runs in cycles and interest rates fluctuate. But experts don't see any huge chuckholes in the road for home appreciation. There are simply no major negative indicators on the horizon.

Dr. James F. Smith, a professor of finance at the Kenan-Flagler Business School at the University of North Carolina at Chapel Hill, has been one of the country's top forecasters of interest rates and housing markets. In 2003, Smith believes, the country entered a period similar to the one we experienced from 1953 to 1965 when productivity was relatively high and inflation was never considered a major factor.

"It would take a horrible spike in inflation for interest rates to throw the housing markets out of sync," Smith said. "I really don't see that happening. You've got every bank in this country trying to stamp out or keep inflation low."

Smith served as the chief economist for the one-million-member National Association of Realtors and for the Society of Industrial and Office Realtors. He held leading economic and research positions with Union Carbide, Wharton Econometric Forecasting Associates in Philadelphia, and Sears, Roebuck and Co. He also served as a senior economist to the Board of Governors of the Federal Reserve System in Washington, D.C., and as a full-time consultant to the President's Council of Economic Advisers where he formalized the process of developing economic forecasts for the Reagan Administration.

"Housing values will continue strong because of the number of people who really want to buy a home," Smith said. "You have to understand the huge immigrant population that will help to drive the housing ladder. You might see a couple of time blips, but housing will absolutely remain strong and continue to gain in value."

Real estate prices don't crash like stocks do when the bull runs out of steam. Home prices move up and down but within a lesser range than stocks. And, in most markets in this country, homes will be worth considerably more 11 years down the road—the length of the average reverse mortgage.

"Our average reverse mortgage runs about 11.2 years," said Lee McCutcheon of Seattle Mortgage. "Unless there is a medical emergency, a reverse mortgage should not be viewed as a short-term fix."

The amount of cash proceeds received in a reverse mortgage is based on a formula using age, home value, location, and interest rates as factors. Let's take a quick look at how each affects the amount borrowed.

- *Rate*   The lower the interest rate, the larger the reverse mortgage. This is because a current variable-rate interest benchmark is used to determine the initial size of a reverse mortgage. Because interest rates have been historically low since 2000, the combination of low rates and high home values made it an optimal time for seniors to obtain or refinance a reverse mortgage. The ability to get larger reverse mortgages recedes when interest rates rise.

- *Age*   The older the borrower at the time the reverse mortgage closes, the larger the share of home equity he or she can borrow against. This is because remaining life expectancy decreases with age. The younger the borrower, the larger the percentage of home equity that is reserved to ensure future payment of the accrued interest on the loan. In the case of a couple seeking an HECM, the loan size is based on the age of the youngest borrower.

- *Appraised value*   The higher the value of the home, the more a senior can borrow.

- *Location (HECM only)*   The FHA single-family loan limit for the particular area where the home is located affects the size of the reverse mortgage that a borrower can get. The FHA loan limit varies by county and typically changes annually in an attempt to keep pace with rising home prices. Loan ceilings are lower for nonmetropolitan and rural areas and higher for more expensive metropolitan areas. Some counties have FHA limits between these two extremes. However, once the value of a home exceeds the FHA loan limit for the area, the size of the HECM can't get any larger. What would significantly improve the product is a single national limit, enabling homeowners with expensive homes in low-cost regions to tap as much equity as those elders in high-cost areas of the country. The ability to borrow should not be curtailed by geographic location.

One common misperception of prospective borrowers is that they can qualify for a reverse mortgage equal or close in size to the value of their home, or at least the local FHA loan limit. This isn't the case. The actual loan amount will be equal to a smaller amount than these two figures, but still a substantial fraction of the home's value, in order to ensure that there will likely be sufficient equity left in the home when the loan comes due to ensure full repayment.

A very rough rule of thumb to estimate your maximum reverse mortgage loan amount is to use your age minus five years as the percentage you can take from your net equity. For example, if you are a 75-year old person with a $200,000 home owned free and clear in a midexpense area of the country, the maximum reverse mortgage line of credit you could expect to receive would be 70 percent of $200,000, or $137,000 before closing costs. And, because of the complex formula of most of the reverse mortgage products, Mom and Dad probably will be unable to tap all of the equity in the family home anyway.

The size of a reverse mortgage is also affected by the type of loan chosen. In addition to the HECM, which accounted for 90 to 95 percent of all reverse mortgages made in 2004, there are two other reverse mortgage products. One is the Fannie Mae Home Keeper loan, available in every state. The other is Cash Account, a proprietary jumbo reverse mortgage product developed by Financial Freedom Senior Funding

Corp., Irvine, California. Available in a majority of states, the Cash Account is usually taken out on more expensive homes because it permits a much larger reverse mortgage than HECM or Home Keeper. The borrower has several choices on how to receive the funds from a reverse mortgage. The proceeds can be taken as a lump sum, line of credit, fixed monthly payment, or a combination. For most lines of credit, an added benefit is that the unused amount of the line of credit grows automatically each year based on a formula. In some cases, the credit line grows at a rate half a percentage point higher than the interest rate on the loan.

Here is a capsule of the three programs for a $200,000 home that is owned free and clear. (See Figure 2.2.) Financial Freedom's Cash Account is more suitable for more expensive homes, as discussed in Chapter 3. While there are many reverse mortgage calculators available on the Internet, one of the better ones can be accessed by clicking on the calculator at www.financialfreedom.com. Follow the steps and enter the basic information requested. The calculator will provide you with the amounts you can expect from the major programs and their options. Where you live is critical to the FHA HECM product. More age and price profiles, along with complete amortization schedules, are included in the appendix.

Remember, seniors can outlive the value of their home without being forced to move. The homeowner cannot be displaced and forced to sell the home to pay off the mortgage, even if the principal balance grows to exceed the value of the property. If the value of the house exceeds what is owed at the time of the homeowner's death, the rest goes to the estate.

Figure 2.2 Reverse Mortgage Programs			

Mr. Fred Fairway, Age 75
Redmond, WA, 98052

Home Value—$200,000	FHA/HUD HECM	Fannie Mae Home Keeper	Financial Freedom Cash Account
Cash Available			
	$122,528	$73,808	$58,324
Or Monthly Income			
	$822	$638	N/A
or Line of Credit			
	$122,528	$73,808	$58,324
Annualized Growth Rate	4.12%	N/A	5.00%
Creditline Value In 5 Years	$149,904	$73,808	$74,438
Creditline Value In 10 Years	$183,398	$73,808	$95,004
or Any Combination of the Above			

For example: 50 percent cash, 25 percent monthly check, 25 percent line of credit

Source: Financial Freedom Senior Funding

Standard Costs of Reverse Mortgages

Let's look at the standard costs for the most popular reverse mortgage products. Many of the same costs that a borrower pays to obtain a home purchase loan, or to refinance their existing mortgage, also apply to reverse mortgages. You can expect to be charged an origination fee, up-front mortgage insurance premium (for the FHA Home Equity Conversion Mortgage, or HECM), an appraisal fee, and certain other standard closing costs. In most cases, these fees and costs are capped and may be financed as part of the reverse mortgage. Some proprietary loans have no fees, which we discuss in detail in Chapter 3.

Interest Charges

In a traditional, forward mortgage, the borrower starts with little equity in the home and a large loan balance. The reverse mortgage big picture begins the opposite way: The equity portion makes up most of the home's value and the debt portion, if any, is very small. The reverse mortgage borrower receives money from the equity in his or her home in the form of a line of credit, monthly check, lump sum, or a combination of the above (discussed in Chapter 3). Because there are no monthly payments required on the reverse mortgage, the loan balance increases as funds are received and interest accrues on the loan balance. Therefore, the loan balance increases and the equity in the home decreases during the term of the reverse mortgage. The line of credit is different, in that interest is not charged until the funds are actually used. The borrower's remaining credit line grows over time.

"This is what I believe to be the remarkable feature of the reverse mortgage," said DePaul University's Richard Garrigan. "No other mortgage that I know allows this type of growth in a line of credit. It's going to make a lot of people feel better about paying the fees to obtain the reverse mortgage."

The interest rate on the reverse mortgage is determined either at the time of application or at the time the loan closes, whichever is lower. There are interest rate ceilings, or "caps," on how much the interest rate can increase. The net amount of equity in the home spent during the term of a reverse mortgage eventually will be determined by the fluctuation of the interest rate, length of the loan term, appreciation gained, and the spending habits of the borrower. A change in interest rate does not affect the amount or the number of loan advances a borrower receives, but it does cause the loan balance to grow at a faster or slower rate. Homes in extremely popular markets could see a majority of the reverse mortgage funds spent replaced by appreciation while homes in flat or depreciating markets would have little, if any, equity remaining after the reverse mortgage is settled. Under no circumstances would the borrower, or the estate, owe more than the value of the home when the borrower moves out of the home. This is what is known as a *nonrecourse loan*.

Tax Ramifications

The interest that has accrued on the reverse mortgage is not deductible until paid. Remember, the homeowner makes no payments during the term of the reverse mortgage. Therefore, the homeowner usually deducts the accrued interest in the tax year that the homeowner moves out, sells, or refinances the home. If the homeowner dies before the reverse mortgage debt is settled, the interest deduction will be a "deduction in respect of a decedent" and will be treated by the estate or someone who receives the house outside of probate in the same manner as it would have in the hands of the decedent. Because the home is part of the estate, it gets a new stepped-up basis equal to fair market value at the time of the homeowner's death. Therefore, its sale usually does not produce a taxable gain.

The timing of the sale of the home, and subsequent tax deduction from the reverse mortgage, can also be important to consumers. For example, if an elder takes a rather large draw from an ordinary individual retirement account, the home could be sold in the same year to help offset the taxable income from the IRA. The mortgage interest deduction from the reverse mortgage could help reduce, or eliminate, the possibility of paying income tax on the IRA.

Mortgage Insurance Premium

The most confusing fee involved in a reverse mortgage is the mortgage insurance premium. Seniors are usually flabbergasted when they find the amount is 2 percent of the appraised value of their home or maximum claim value, whichever is less. There also is an ongoing annual premium equal to 0.5 percent of the loan balance. Couple that cost with a loan origination fee and standard closing costs, and a borrower can easily spend $6,000 to borrow $319 a month for life.

Why should a senior who owns his or her home free and clear have to pay for mortgage insurance? Unlike typical mortgage insurance that protects the lender if the borrower defaults, mortgage insurance on a reverse mortgage ensures the borrower (or the borrower's estate) will never owe more than the value of the home. That means other assets will never be used to repay the mortgage if the home's value turns out to be less than the loan balance. That's why the new reverse mortgages are known as nonrecourse loans.

The American Homeownership and Economic Opportunity Act, signed by President Clinton in 2000, waived the 2 percent HECM reverse mortgage insurance fee if the proceeds are used to buy long-term health care insurance.

The U.S. Department of Housing and Urban Development's assistant secretary for housing oversees all FHA programs in his role as federal housing commissioner. Because an FHA product (HECM) is by far the most popular reverse mortgage program, the commissioner is the most powerful person in the reverse mortgage category. John Weicher, appointed to the position in 2001, was asked to tackle some of the most-asked questions about the need for mortgage insurance for HECMs in an exclusive interview conducted in July 2004.

Q: *How many HECMs have needed the aid of mortgage insurance because the value of the property was lower when the reverse mortgage term ended?*

A: If we assume that the lender needed mortgage insurance because the property had not appreciated sufficiently to repay the full indebtedness, then 726 lenders have needed to file a claim to recover a shortfall following the sale of the property through May 31, 2004. In cases where the loan is deemed due and payable (usually upon the death of the borrower), the lender must acquire title either through foreclosure or deed in lieu of foreclosure. The lender then sells the property and files a claim for the shortfall subject to HUD's claim requirements. If the property has not been sold by the lender's deadline, the claim is calculated using the appraised value of the property.

Q: *How many HECMs needed the aid of mortgage insurance because the senior outlived the value of the property?*

A: Again we must make an assumption that a claim will be necessary because the mortgagor (or his or her heir) has sold the property and the value of the property was less than the indebtedness. A claim will be filed following HUD's claim requirements to pay the lender the shortfall. As of May 31, there were 68 claims of this type filed with HUD. A different scenario may have also resulted in the need for a mortgage insurance claim to be filed. Where the mortgagor has chosen a tenure (or modified tenure) plan, payments will be made as long as the mortgagor lives in the home. As the maximum claim amount is based primarily upon the value of the home (assuming that the value of the home does not exceed the FHA loan limit for the jurisdiction), the lender will assign the loan to HUD and file an insurance claim when the total of payments exceeds the value of the home. In those cases, the mortgagor took a risk in that he or she could receive more in the accrued monthly benefits than would have been received in the outright sale of the home. The insurance premiums cover that risk. In essence, the mortgagor continues to receive payments from HUD following assignment as long as the mortgagor continues to live in the property. This is considered as an optional assignment to HUD, of which there have been 2,793 through May 31, 2004.

Q: *Will there ever be a time when the borrower will receive a mortgage insurance refund on a reverse mortgage, perhaps like HUD's old Distributive Share Program?*

A: No. Even though the reverse mortgage program has a positive economic value, *FHA* is introducing changes to the program, such as allowing refinancing that will reduce this overall economic value. Therefore, FHA must retain all premium income to ensure that the economic value of the program remains positive.

Q: *How critical is mortgage insurance to the future of reverse mortgages?*

A: Mortgage insurance is critical to the future of reverse mortgages. Mortgage insurance provides protection to investors and creates liquidity in the market. Without mortgage insurance, originators of reverse mortgages would have great difficulty in identifying investors to participate in the program.

Origination Fee

The origination fee covers a lender's operating expenses—including office overhead, marketing costs, etc.—for making the reverse mortgage. Under the HECM program, the origination fee is equal to the greater of $2,000 or 2 percent of the maximum claim amount (i.e., county FHA loan limit).

Appraisal Fee

An appraiser is responsible for assigning a current market value to each home that's used as collateral for a reverse mortgage. Appraisal fees generally range from $300 to $400. In addition to placing a value on the home, an appraiser must also make sure there are no major structural defects, such as a bad foundation, a leaky roof, or termite damage. Federal regulations mandate that a senior's home be structurally sound and comply with all home safety codes in order for the reverse mortgage to be made. If the appraiser uncovers property defects that require repair, the borrower must hire a contractor to complete the repairs. Once the repairs are done, the same appraiser is paid for a second visit to make sure the repairs have been completed. The cost of the repairs may be financed in the loan and completed after the reverse mortgage is made. Appraisers generally charge $50 to $75 dollars for the follow-up examination.

Other Closing Costs

Other closing costs that are commonly charged to a reverse mortgage borrower, include:

Credit report fee.   Verifies any federal tax liens or other judgments handed down against the borrower. Cost: Generally under $20.

Flood certification fee.   Determines whether the property is located on a federally designated floodplain. Cost: Generally under $20.

Escrow, settlement, or closing fee.   Generally includes a title search and various other required closing services. Cost: $150 to $450.

Document preparation fee.   Fee charged to prepare the final closing documents, including the mortgage note and other recordable items. Cost: $75 to $150.

Recording fee.   Fee charged to record the mortgage lien with the county recorder's office. Cost: $50 to $100.

Courier fee.   Covers the cost of any overnight mailing of documents between the lender and the title company or loan investor. Cost: Generally under $50.

Title insurance.   Insurance that protects the lender (lender's policy) or the buyer (owner's policy) against any loss arising from disputes over ownership of a property. Varies by size of the loan, though in general the larger the loan amount, the higher the cost of the title insurance.

Pest inspection.   Determines whether the home is infested with any wood-destroying organisms, such as termites. Cost: Generally under $100.

Survey.   Determines the official boundaries of the property. It's typically ordered to make sure that any adjoining property has not inadvertently encroached on the reverse mortgage borrower's property. Cost: Generally under $250.

Servicing Set-Aside

The servicing set-aside is an amount of money deducted from the available loan limit at closing to cover the projected costs of servicing the borrower's reverse mortgage account. The servicing set-aside is a calculation, not a charge. The only amount added to the loan balance is the monthly servicing fee, which ranges from $30 to $35. Federal regulations allow the loan servicer, which may or may not be the same company as the originating lender, to charge the $30 to $35 monthly fee.

Pass the TALC

Much like the annual percentage rate (APR) charged on traditional loans, lenders are required to provide consumers considering a reverse mortgage with a total annual loan cost (TALC) statement. This is a single rate that would include all costs and generate the total amount projected to be owed on the loan at a future time when it is applied to all the cash advances the borrower will receive (not including any advances used to finance loan costs). Because this total annual average rate will vary with future changes in the home's value over time, the statute specified that TALC rates should be disclosed for "not less than three projected appreciation rates and not less than three credit transaction periods."

In the following example, and in other program forms found in the appendix, you will see that a reverse mortgage is very expensive if the homeowner moves out during the early years of the loan. (See Figure 2.3.)

Figure 2.3 Federal Housing Administration Home Equity Conversion Mortgage (HECM) Program Total Annual Loan Cost Rate

Borrower Name/Case Number: Fred Fairway   Line of Credit   Refinance: No

Loan Terms		Monthly Loan Charges		
Age of youngest borrower:	63	Mo. Servicing Fee:		$30.00
Appraised Property Value:	$150,000	Mortgage Insurance:	0.5%	annually
Initial interest rate:	3.570%			
Monthly advance:	$0.00	Other Charges		
Initial	$0.00	Shared Appreciation:		None
Line of Credit:	$69,059.04			
Length of Term:	Tenure			

Initial Loan Charges		Repayment Limits
Closing Cost:	$4,800.00	Net proceeds estimated at 93%
Mortgage Insurance Premium:	$3,000.00	of projected home sale
Annuity Cost:	None	

Total Annual Loan Cost Rate

Appreciation Rate	Disclosure Period (Yrs.)			
	2	11	21	29
0%	16.15%	6.71%	5.65%	4.93%
4%	16.15%	6.71%	5.65%	5.29%
8%	16.15%	6.71%	5.65%	5.29%

The cost of any reverse mortgage loan depends on how long you keep the loan and how much your house appreciates in value. Generally, the longer you keep a reverse mortgage, the lower the total annual loan cost rate will be.

This table shows the estimated cost of your reverse mortgage loan, expressed as an annual rate. It illustrates the cost for your age, that life expectancy, and 1.4 times that life expectancy. The table also shows the cost of the loan, assuming the value of your home appreciates at three different rates: 0%, 4%, and 8%.

The total annual cost rates in this table are based on the total charges associated with this loan. These charges typically include principal, interest, closing costs, mortgage insurance premiums, annuity costs, and servicing costs (but not disposition costs—costs when you sell the home).

The rates in this table are estimates. Your actual cost may differ if, for example, the amount of your loan advances varies or the interest rate on your mortgage changes. You may receive projections of loan balances from counselors or lenders that are based on an expected average mortgage rate that differs from the initial interest rate.

Source: Seattle Mortgage

In the next chapter, we will define and explain the variety of reverse mortgage programs. Some offer the ability to tap a greater percentage of the home's equity, others focus on the purchase of another home, while still others target homes with values greater than $400,000. Let's see if we can find one that makes sense for you in Chapter 3.

Good advice is never as helpful as an interest-free loan.
—MASON COOLEY

What's on the Menu?

Picking the Right Reverse Mortgage Program

We often are caught by oxymorons, redundancies, and contradictions in terms in our casual conversations with friends and family. Youngsters have been known to describe themselves as being "totally dead" when their parents discover they have broken a weekend curfew. The lending industry has its curious monikers, too, and reverse mortgages would make a list of the top ten terms needing a better name.

"It's not really a reverse mortgage, is it, if it helps me buy my next home?" inquired an elderly woman to a radio talk show program. "Wouldn't you think it would be more correctly named if it were a full-circle loan."

In this chapter, we will consider the three major reverse mortgage programs and their curious names and options: the Home Equity Conversion Mortgage (HECM), the Fannie Mae Home Keeper Loan, and Financial Freedom's Cash Account, a proprietary jumbo reverse mortgage product. The type of loan chosen also affects the size of a reverse mortgage. The Home Keeper (an interesting label for a loan who's best feature is buying, not keeping) and the Cash Account (not really an account at all) work best for more expensive homes. Each program has its own target market, and more programs will probably surface as lenders discover the dizzying number of potential customers and their reasons for wanting to tap tax-free home equity.

"It really is a conversion mortgage," said Mike Broderick, veteran reverse mortgage specialist for Seattle Mortgage. "The name fits. Sometimes when you say 'reverse' the eyes start to wander."

Reverse mortgages are called so because instead of making mortgage payments, the borrower actually receives money from the lender. The source of funds for the money received is the equity you have stored in your home. Unlike the loan balance of a conventional mortgage, which becomes smaller with each monthly payment, the loan balance of a reverse mortgage grows larger over time. The loan principal increases with each payment that you receive, and interest and other charges accrue each month on the total funds advanced to you to date. (See Figure 3.1.)

All reverse mortgages allow you to retain ownership of your home, and many do not require repayment for as long as you live in your home, pay your property taxes and hazard insurance charges, and maintain the property. When you leave your home permanently—upon your death or when you move away—your loan balance becomes due and payable.

Figure 3.1 The Process of Getting a Reverse Mortgage

1. AWARENESS

Borrower learns about reverse mortgages from a news article, ad, direct mail, word-of mouth, etc.

2. ACTION

If necessary, borrower seeks additional information by contacting a lender.

3. COUNSELING

Borrower seeks counseling from a HUD-approved counseling agency.

Counseling is mandatory regardless of which reverse mortgage product a borrower chooses to get. The counseling is usually conducted face-to-face, although telephone counseling is becoming more prevalent. The counselor provides supplemental information on reverse mortgages, determines whether the borrower is eligible to get a reverse mortgage, and discusses other options that may be available to the borrower to assist them with their daily living.

4. APPLICATION/DISCLOSURE

Consumer fills out application for reverse mortgage and selects payment option: fixed monthly payments, lump sum payment, line of credit, or a combination of these.

Lender discloses to consumer the estimated total cost of the loan, as required by the federal Truth in Lending Act. Lender collects money for home appraisal. Consumer provides lender with required information, including photo ID, verification of Social Security number, copy of deed to home, information on any existing mortgage(s) on property, and counseling certificate.

5. PROCESSING

Lender orders appraisal, title work, lien payoffs, etc. An appraiser comes to your home. The appraiser is responsible for assigning a value to the home and determining the physical condition of the property. If the appraiser uncovers structural defects that require repair, the borrower must hire a contractor to complete the repairs after the reverse mortgage closes.

Source: National Reverse Mortgage Lenders Association (www.reversemortgage.org)

Your legal obligation to repay the loan can be no more than the market value of your home at the time you leave the property. This means that your lender cannot require repayment from your heirs or from any asset other than your home. This is what is known as a non recourse loan. And, before we get into specific plans, let's consider the basics. Here are some of the aspects common to all reverse mortgages:

Borrowers.　Borrowers must be homeowners 62 years of age or older with significant equity in the home. Borrowers will retain title to the property throughout the term of the reverse mortgage. Borrowers must have lived in the home a period greater than six months in the past year. If a coborrower is younger than 62, that borrower must be removed from the title of the home for the property to qualify (see below). There is no credit requirement, yet bankruptcies, with the possible exception of Chapter 13, should be dismissed before closing. Medical history is not considered.

Outstanding debt.　Reverse mortgages must be in a first lien position. All outstanding mortgages on the home, plus any tax liens, judgments, or student loans, need to be paid before or at closing.

Use of funds.　Reverse mortgage money comes to the homeowner tax free and can be used for any purpose: health care, insurance, home modification, travel, gifts.

Eligible properties.　Single-family homes, one-to-four-unit residences where the owner lives in one unit, manufactured homes built after June 1976 (except Cash Account), condominiums, farms on five acres or fewer, and townhomes are eligible for reverse mortgages. It's best if the home is owned free and clear of any debt, yet some debt is usually possible. Some in-city co-ops will be considered. The entire amount of a duplex, triplex, or fourplex is used for the basis of the reverse mortgage loan. Second homes and investment properties do not qualify. An appraisal will be required and mandatory repairs may be possible before the reverse mortgage is granted.

Repayment.   All reverse mortgages become due and payable when the last surviving borrower dies, sells the home, or permanently moves out of the home. A permanent move means a borrower has not lived in the home for one continuous year. Lenders can also require repayment if the borrower fails to pay property taxes, fails to maintain or repair the home, or fails to keep the home insured. These are standard conditions of default on any mortgage. Reverse mortgage lenders usually have the option to pay for these expenses by reducing the loan advances and using the difference to pay the outstanding obligations. Other default conditions could include bankruptcy, donation, or abandonment of the home; perpetration of fraud or misrepresentation; or eminent domain or condemnation proceedings involving the home. Other actions that might spark repayment are renting out the entire home, adding a new owner to the home's title, changing the home's zoning classification, or taking out new debt against the home. Most of the time, reverse mortgages must be repaid in one payment—either from the proceeds of the sale of the home or in cash from other assets. Rather than sell the home, heirs might choose to use other funds to pay off the reverse mortgage or take out a conventional mortgage refinance and keep the home for themselves.

Right of refusal.   After closing a reverse mortgage, you have three business days to reconsider your decision. If for any reason you decide you do not want the loan, you can walk away from the deal. Business days include Saturdays but not Sundays or legal public holidays. The recision must be in writing and on the form provided by the lender at closing. It must be hand delivered, mailed, faxed, or filed with a telegraph company before midnight of the third business day.

Adjustable interest rates.   While new products are constantly being offered, virtually all lenders charge adjustable interest rates on reverse mortgages. This means that the rate can increase or decrease over time. Lenders don't have any control over what the rate will be when the loan closes or how it will change over time.

One spouse younger than 62.   In some cases, a spouse who is younger than 62 has quitclaimed his or her interest in the home to the older spouse in order to conform with reverse mortgage guidelines. A quitclaim deed is a form used to convey an interest in real property. In order to be properly exercised, it must have a granter (person conveying the property) and a grantee (person receiving the property). The quitclaim must be in writing, be signed by the granter, and be delivered to and accepted by the grantee.

"We've had seniors who had their spouses quitclaim if they were younger than 62," said Sarah Hulbert, national reverse mortgage director for Seattle Mortgage. "However, we don't recommend the practice."

Hulbert said she once had a couple execute a quitclaim, but one spouse died unexpectedly not long after the reverse mortgage was finalized. Because the surviving spouse was not on the title, the loan became due and payable.

"This created a tremendous hardship for the surviving spouse," Hulbert said. "She did not qualify for enough money to refinance the original HECM to a new HECM under her name. The house had to be sold. Unless there's a true hardship, it's usually best to wait until both spouses are at least 62."

Special circumstances. In many cases, properties held in living trusts are eligible for reverse mortgages. Each beneficiary must be an eligible reverse mortgage borrower. The trust must be valid and enforceable and provide the lender assurance that notification will be given if occupancy changes. The trust itself cannot be a party to the loan agreement. Properties held in life estates also are eligible but must be approved by the lender.

Impacting Medicare, Medicaid. Reverse mortgage funds that consumers receive will not affect Social Security or Medicare eligibility or benefits because those programs are not based on need. However, Supplemental Security Income (SSI) or Medicaid benefits are different subjects. Both are based on need and could be affected by HECM payments. To determine if reverse mortgage payments would influence a particular situation, consult the local offices for SSI, Medicaid, and other benefit providers. A specialist at a local senior center could also be helpful.

By the time you reach this point, more basics will probably have been added. But let's now consider the major reverse mortgage programs.

What the Heck Is an HECM?

The Home Equity Conversion Mortgage is the oldest and most popular reverse mortgage product. They have accounted for 90 percent to 95 percent of all reverse mortgages made into 2004 and generally provide the largest loan advances of any available reverse mortgage. Often HECMs provide substantially more cash than any other program. They also provide the most flexibility in how the cash can be paid to you. Available since

1989 to homeowners 62 or older, HECMs are insured by the federal government through the Federal Housing Administration (FHA), a part of the U.S. Department of Housing and Urban Development (HUD). Each year Congress approves an appropriation for HUD that includes money used to endorse single-family mortgages insured under the General Insurance Fund and the Special Risk Insurance Fund. All HECMs fall under the General Insurance Fund umbrella.

With an HECM, you receive your loan proceeds according to your choice from among five possible HECM payment plans:

1. *Tenure period: Equal payments for as long as the home is occupied as the primary residence.* With the tenure payment plan, the borrower receives equal monthly payments for as long as the home is the borrower's principal residence. Payments do not increase or decrease, and they continue until the borrower's death or until the home is sold, the title is conveyed, or the borrower permanently moves out. Although monthly payments with a tenure payment plan are smaller than with a term plan, the payments continue for as long as the borrower lives in the home.

2. *Line of credit: A maximum amount of cash reserves that can be used periodically and in varied amounts.* This payment plan option allows the borrower to establish a line of credit equal to the principal limit. Borrowers can then request a loan advance of any amount up to the principal limit whenever needed, as long as the home remains the principal residence. Interest is not charged on the line of credit until drawn and then only against the amount that has been drawn. The unused portion of the line of credit will grow over time. It will increase each month by $\frac{1}{12}$ of the sum of the mortgage interest rate and the 0.5 percent annual mortgage insurance premium.

3. *Modified tenure: A line of cash reserves combined with equal monthly payments.* Portions of the principal limit are set aside as a line of credit while the borrower receives the rest of the loan proceeds in equal monthly payments as long as the borrower occupies the home as a principal residence. This option provides the ability to meet irregular or unexpected expenses if they arise.

4. *Term: Equal payments for a fixed period of time.* A term plan may be a good choice if extra monthly income is needed for a fixed time period—for example, to pay for temporary or extended home health care until the borrower is ready to sell the home and move into group housing or relocate to another community. With a term payment plan, monthly payments are generally higher than with the HECM tenure plan, which provides monthly advances for as long as the borrower lives in the home. The shorter the term, the higher the monthly payments. Under the term payment plan, monthly payments stop when the specified term ends. Borrowers need to plan ahead to determine what to do at the end of that term. Although monthly payments end, borrowers will not have to repay the HECM until they no longer live in the home. However, as long as borrowers remain in the home, they are responsible for maintaining the property and paying all taxes and insurance.

5. *Modified term: A line of cash reserves combined with equal monthly payments for a fixed time period.* The modified term option combines the features of an HECM term payment plan with a line of credit. A portion of the principal limit is set aside to establish a line of credit that can be drawn on at any time. The remainder comes in equal monthly payments over a fixed term. If a borrower has already decided when to move out of the home, the modified or standard HECM term payment plan option may be the best choice.

Moving from One Plan to Another

An HECM is unique in the amount of flexibility in payment plans it offers borrowers. In addition to having five options to choose from, consumers may change payment plans at any time after taking out an HECM and as many times as they decide. They may also receive a lump sum at closing to repay the remainder of an old mortgage, to repair or improve the home, or for other needs at closing.

This flexibility allows the reshaping of payment plans as circumstances change. Examples include adding a line of credit or lengthening a term payment plan. If you decide to change payment plans, you do not have to pay any new loan origination fees or closing costs. There is a modest administrative charge when a change is requested.

How the HECM Rates

The interest rate charged on an HECM adjusts either monthly or annually, depending on which option the borrower chooses. However, these adjustments don't alter the monthly payments that borrowers can receive (if they have chosen the monthly payment option). Instead, the adjustment affects the total interest that is charged on the loan, which is added to the loan balance while the loan is outstanding and is paid when the loan becomes due.

The applied interest rate, or initial rate, is the rate at which interest is charged to your loan balance. Once the interest rate adjustment period has been established at closing, it cannot be changed. Rates for the

HECM are tied to the 1-year and 10-year U.S. Treasury Security Rate (See Appendix A, Figures A.10 and A.11), which are published weekly in many major newspapers and are available from Bankrate.com. Adjustable interest rates, also called variable rates, can be adjusted within a specified range and time and vary according to changes in a specified price index. Adjustable rates on mortgages are usually tied to a published market rate of interest.

With an HECM loan, the *annual* rate cannot increase more than 5 percent over the life of the loan and cannot increase by more than 2 percent in any year. The *monthly* adjusting rate cannot increase by more than 10 percent over the life of the loan, but there is no limit to the amount the rate can change at each monthly adjustment as long as it does not exceed the 10 percent lifetime cap. Remember, the applied interest rate is different from the expected average interest rate. The applied interest rate is the rate that is charged to the borrower's loan balance throughout the life of the loan. The expected average interest rate, computed by using the 10-year Treasury Index, is used solely to determine the principal limit. (This differs on some of the proprietary jumbo loans mentioned later.)

For example, on July 15, 2004, the one-year Treasury Index was 2.04. The margin (amount added to the index for profit) was 1.50 for the monthly program to reach the applied rate of 3.54 percent on the loan. The expected rate included the 10-year Treasury Index at 4.49 percent. Add the margin of 1.50, and the expected rate worked out to be 5.99 percent.

The margin added to the annual program leaped to 3.1 percent from 2.1 percent on July 1, 2004. That move made the annual program not as desirable for borrowers. More changes are expected as the additional options arrive on the market.

A new rule was introduced in 2004 that allows lenders to set the expected interest rate on the most popular reverse mortgage program at the time of the loan application or at closing, whichever date brings the lower interest rate. Similar to interest rate lock-in provisions on conventional mortgages, HECM borrowers will now have the comfort of knowing that the interest rate cannot increase during the period between application and closing. In the past, borrowers ran the risk of rates rising during that time, potentially reducing the amount of proceeds available to them. In addition, mortgage lenders offering HECMs will no longer need to recalculate the principal limit on the day of settlement. Lenders are not allowed to charge a fee for the 60-day lock.

Partial payback   A borrower may prepay all or part of the outstanding balance at any time without penalty. However, no prepayment of an amount in excess of the outstanding balance is allowed. Repayment in full will terminate the loan agreement. A borrower may choose to make a partial prepayment to preserve more of the equity in the property or to increase monthly payments if a payment plan with monthly payments was selected. By reducing the outstanding balance, the borrower increases the net principal limit available.

Refinancing an HECM   A rule installed in 2004 curtailed the costs of the mortgage insurance premium on federally insured reverse mortgages. The new rule states that the mortgage insurance premium (MIP) will be paid on the difference between the home value at the time the original HECM was made and the newly appraised home value at the time of refinancing. For example, if the original home value is $250,000 and the newly appraised home value is $300,000, then the 2 percent MIP will be paid on $50,000 instead of $300,000. Previously, seniors who refinanced their reverse mortgage were charged an MIP equal to 2 percent of the appraised home value, plus an annual premium thereafter equal to 0.5 percent of the loan balance.

Getting some counsel   Counseling is required as part of the HECM program. The one-day session is free and can be helpful in determining if a reverse mortgage fits a borrower's needs. So, using this service can be a good idea even if you are thinking about applying for some other type of mortgage.

"One key fundamental feature to the reverse mortgage process is the information session," said Wells Fargo's Jeff Taylor. "That's what makes it different from every other mortgage we are used to. It requires the senior, and any adult children if they choose, to attend the session and hear all of the other options that might be available in a particular state or local community. That session may help them to justify getting or not getting a reverse mortgage at the time.

"If someone is just trying to defer tax payments or find another way to make homeowner insurances payments, there might be a better program for them. The information session allows the senior to make the choice independently. Once that's done and they have certification, then—and only then—can a reverse mortgage lender begin the process."

Financial planners and state agencies were concerned that reverse mortgage lenders were putting the cart before the horse in the process. Many officials pushed to have counseling offered and completed before any reverse mortgage applications were taken. They got that wish in 2004 when Dr. John Weichert, FHA commissioner, issued a letter regarding timing and content of counseling sessions. In a capsule, those guidelines are as follows:

- A lender cannot order an appraisal, title search, or FHA case number, or in any other way begin the process of originating an HECM, before the borrower completes the required counseling.

- A lender cannot steer, direct, recommend, or otherwise encourage a senior client to seek the services of any one particular counselor, but must provide an entire list of agencies within the state approved by HUD, AARP and/or Fannie Mae.

- Until a lender receives a copy of the counseling certificate, it cannot charge the borrower an application fee, appraisal fee, or charge for any other HECM-related services.

- Counselors are not permitted to promote, represent, recommend, or speak for any specific lender. Senior clients who are seeking assistance in locating a lender must be referred to HUD's listing of approved HECM lenders. (To find the HUD-approved counseling agency, telephone 888-466-3487 or visit www.hud.gov and click on the section for seniors.)

Borrowers will receive a Certificate of HECM Counseling, which is valid for 180 days, after completing the session. If more than one homeowner is applying for the loan, the lender will consider the counseling certificate valid for all borrowers as long as the certificate is signed by at least one borrower within the 180-day expiration period. Lenders could waive the expiration deadline if borrowers did receive the counseling and believe a second session is not warranted. (See Figure 3.2.)

Figure 3.2 Certificate of HECM Counseling

U.S. Department of Housing and Urban Development
Certificate of HECM Counseling

Homeowner(s)Name(s)_____
Property Address City/State/Zip_____

The U. S. Department of Housing and Urban Development (HUD) requires that homeowner(s) interested in pursuing a Home Equity Conversion Mortgage (HECM) receive information about the implications of and alternatives to a reverse mortgage. The HECM counselor must adhere to all of FHA's guidelines regarding information that must be provided to the potential HECM mortgagor and must tailor the session to address the unique financial circumstances of the household being counseled.

COUNSELOR CERTIFICATION:
In accordance with Section 255 of the National Housing Act and 24CFR 206.41, I have discussed in detail the following items with the above referenced homeowner(s):

1. Options other than a Home Equity Conversion Mortgage that are available to the homeowner(s), including other housing, social service, health and financial options.
2. Other home equity conversion options that are or may become available to the homeowner(s), such as other reverse mortgages, sale-leaseback financing, deferred payment loans, and property tax deferral.
3. The financial implications of entering into a Home Equity Conversion Mortgage.
4. A disclosure that a Home Equity Conversion Mortgage may have tax consequences, affect eligibility for assistance under Federal and State programs, and have an impact on the estate and heirs of the homeowner(s).
5. Whether the homeowner has signed a contract or agreement with an estate planning service firm that requires, or purports to require, the mortgagor to pay a fee on or after closing that may exceed amounts permitted by the Secretary or in Part 206 of the HUD regulations at 24 CFR.
6. If such a contract has been signed, the extent to which services under the contract may not be needed or may be available at nominal or no cost from other sources, including the mortgagee.

I hereby certify that the homeowner(s) listed above have received counseling according to the requirements of this certificate and the standards of the U.S. Department of Housing and Urban Development, as described in mortgagee letters, handbooks, regulations, and statute. This interview was held: [ ] Face-to-Face [ ] Telephone and the amount of time required to cover the above items was as follows: _____.

_____   _____
Counselor Name (Printed and Signature)   Date

_____
HUD-Approved Counseling Agency Name and Address (City/State/Zip) and telephone number

_____
HUD-Approved Counseling Agency Employer Identification Number

HOMEOWNER CERTIFICATION:
I/we hereby certify that I/we have discussed the financial implications of and alternatives to a HECM with the above Counselor. I/we understand the advantages and disadvantages of a HECM and each type of payment plan, as well as the costs of a HECM. This information will enable me/us to make more informed decisions about whether I/we want to proceed with obtaining a HECM.

_____   _____
Homeowner Signature   Date

_____   _____
Homeowner Signature   Date
(All homeowners shown on the deed must sign the mortgage and this counseling certificate.)
Date Counseling Completed: _____ Certificate Expiration Date:
_____   (180 days from date HECM counseling completed.)

Fannie Mae Provides a Keeper...
Home Keeper for Purchase

The problem had been the inability to move.

True, some folks simply want to stay in the family home where they raised kids, cut lawns, and pruned roses. Others, who wanted to move on to perhaps something more manageable, had been strapped by finances or stringent reverse mortgage rules that required seniors to stay in the home that had the reverse mortgage. Fannie Mae, once known officially as the Federal National Mortgage Association, officially adopted its nickname as its corporate name about the same time it came up with a reverse mortgage program to complement FHA's HECM. While the Fannie reverse does add the wrinkle of helping seniors buy a new home, the basic program usually does not render the cash, and has higher interest rates, than its government companion. Many analysts believe it's only a matter of time before FHA refines its HECM for purchase transactions.

In a nutshell, Fannie Mae, the nation's largest provider of mortgage money, was first to the table with an acceptable reverse mortgage that allows elderly homeowners to move to another home, receive a large chunk of cash, and have no monthly mortgage payment. Under the program, known as the Home Keeper for Home Purchase Loan, the buyer would use some of the proceeds from the sale of his or her previous home for a large down payment. The rest of the proceeds could go into savings or be used to pay off bills. (For more information, telephone 800-732-6643 or visit www.fanniemae.com.)

The Home Keeper loan is an adjustable-rate mortgage, and standard origination and closing fees are applicable (most can be included in the loan balance). The interest rate on the Home Keeper mortgage is based on the most current weekly average of the one-month secondary market certificate of deposit (CD) index and a margin determined by Fannie Mae. This means that the interest rate on the loan can change monthly as the index changes on one-month CD ARMs. The interest rate cannot increase by more than 12 percent over the life of the loan. This limit on the maximum interest rate increase is known as the rate cap. There is no limit to how much the interest rate may increase per monthly adjustment, as long as the change does not exceed the 12 percent lifetime rate cap. For example, if the original interest rate on the loan was 7 percent, the interest rate could never exceed 19 percent.

The amount of funds available to the borrower is determined by a formula and varies with: (1) the age and number of borrowers at the time of application; (2) the adjusted value of the home; and (3) current interest rates. Home Keeper loans can be larger than HECMs because Fannie Mae's maximum mortgage is larger than the FHA maximum mortgage limit. Similar to the HECM, the consumer may choose to receive the funds from a Home Keeper mortgage as: (1) fixed monthly payments for life (i.e., for as long as the borrower occupies the home as his or her principal residence; (2) a line of credit; or (3) a combination of monthly payments and line of credit. (See Figure 3.3.)

Home Keeper borrowers are charged an origination fee that may not exceed 2 percent of the loan amount or 2 percent of the adjusted value of the home, (whichever is greater), a monthly servicing fee ($15 to $30), and other closing costs. Unlike the HECM, however, there is no mortgage insurance premium. Like the HECM, many of the closing costs can be financed and included in the mortgage.

The Home Keeper's secret sauce is that it enables seniors to obtain a new home and a reverse mortgage in a single deal: Home Keeper mortgage in

Figure 3.3 Fannie Mae's Home Keeper Mortgage and FHA's HECM Capsule Comparison

Features	Home Keeper Mortgage	HECM
Payment plans (plans vary in Texas)	▪ Line of credit ▪ Tenure ▪ Modified tenure ▪ Term ▪ Modified term	▪ Line of credit ▪ Tenure ▪ Modified tenure ▪ Term ▪ Modified term
Loan limits	Current Fannie Mae limit*	Varies based on area*
Eligible properties	Single-family homes, manufactured housing, units in PUDs, some condos	1-to-4 unit homes, condos, manufactured housing, units in PUDs
Factors used to determine loan amount rate	▪ Number of borrowers ▪ Age(s) of borrowers ▪ Adjusted property value (the lesser of the property value or the maximum loan amount set by Fannie Mae limit*)	▪ Age of youngest borrower ▪ Expected average interest ▪ Maximum claim amount (the lesser of the property value or the FHA loan limit based on your current geographic area.*)
Borrower protection	Should lender fail, Fannie Mae will guarantee payment to borrowers	Should lender fail, FHA will make direct payments to borrower
Counseling	Session required	Session required. Must be provided by HUD-approved agency before loan application
Upfront cost	▪ Origination fee—no more than $2,000 or 2% of adjusted property value ▪ Property appraisal ▪ Property inspection ▪ Other closing costs ▪ Credit history	▪ Origination fee—no more than $2,000 or 2% of maximum claim ▪ Mortgage Insurance Premium 2% of maximum claim amount ▪ Property appraisal ▪ Other closing costs

*Loan limits usually change annually

connection with the purchase of a new home—in a single transaction. The transaction reduces the out-of-pocket cash needed by the consumer to buy a new home, eliminates any new monthly mortgage payment, and helps the consumer to keep more of the sales proceeds from his or her old house—or a larger amount of savings—to use for other purposes.

For example, a senior sells her home for an $85,000 profit and wants to buy a new home costing $125,000. To avoid a mortgage payment on the new house, she would need to pay $125,000 in cash. This means she would have to use the entire $85,000 from the sale of her first home, plus another $40,000 from her savings. If she doesn't have the $40,000, she can't buy the new house unless she qualifies for a new home mortgage, which might be difficult and which, in any event, would require making monthly mortgage payments again.

Under the Home Keeper for Purchase, the woman could buy the new home for $125,000 in cash using $60,000 from a new reverse mortgage and $65,000 of the $85,000 in sales proceeds from her old house. This method would allow her to keep the remaining $20,000 in savings from the sales proceeds from her old house and make no monthly mortgage payments. The loan would be an attractive vehicle for retirees who wish to move to be closer to adult children or others who want to leave the crime and congestion of expensive cities. People often tend to move back to the environment of their childhood.

Financial Freedom's Cash Account...
An Option for Expensive Homes

What happens when a senior is sitting on a ton of equity resulting from years of a torrid housing market? The bread-and-butter programs—

FHA's HECM and Fannie Mae's Home Keeper—are curtailed by loan ceilings that are of little use to some of the more expensive neighborhoods in the country. Visit www.financialfreedom.com for more info.

Arriving on the scene in 1996 with the first acceptable jumbo reverse mortgage was Irvine, California–based Financial Freedom, the reverse mortgage arm of Lehman Brothers Bank, FSB, until the nation's biggest purveyor of reverse loans was purchased by IndyMac Bank in 2004. Financial Freedom places virtually no limit on the value of a home it will consider for a reverse mortgage. The company now offers reverse mortgages in all 50 states and has substantially expanded its business and office network through its acquisition in 2000 of the reverse mortgage business of Unity Mortgage Corp., one of the East Coast's leading reverse mortgage originators and servicers and in 2001 of the correspondent business of Senior Homeowners, another reverse mortgage originator.

Financial Freedom offers its Cash Account reverse mortgage in three forms. While all programs could change at any time, these options typically will consider one-to-four-unit dwellings where one of the units is owner-occupied, condominiums, townhomes, planned unit developments, and co-ops in New York City. Here's a quick summary of the packages available:

Basic Cash Account.   Lump sum, line of credit, and tenure advances. Origination fees are 2 percent of the first $500,000 of value, 1.5 percent of the next $500,000 of value, and 1 percent on any amounts greater than $1 million in value. For example, a home valued at $1.5 million would have an origination fee of $22,500. Other closing costs on that same home include a $500 application fee, $2,500 for title insurance, $350 for processing, and $1,000 for closing. There is no mortgage insurance premium even though the loan is non recourse. An appraisal is required for properties in excess of $2 million. The interest rate is the six-month LIBOR Index plus a margin of five percentage points. The program has a lifetime cap of six percentage points greater than the initial interest rate. For example, for the week of July 19, 2004, the six-month LIBOR Index stood at 1.84. Adding the margin of five percentage points, the initial interest rate on the Cash Account would be 6.84 percent. The loan could go no higher than 12.84 during its term.

Cash Account, Zero Point Option. Financial Freedom announced a no-origination fee portfolio product labeled the Zero Point Option in September 2003. The package is an attempt to counter the high-cost reputation that has surrounded reverse mortgages while offering consumers the chance to tap into amounts greater than the FHA-insured product. While there is no origination fee, there are third party closing costs (appraisal, title, credit, etc.) that are capped at $3,500. The Zero Point Option is also tied to the six-month LIBOR Index. In order to balance the no-fee structure, consumers who choose the Zero Point Option must take out at least 75 percent of the maximum funds available at closing. For example, if $100,000 is available, borrowers must take out (and begin paying interest on) $75,000. In some other reverse packages, the cash can be put in a line of credit and used as the consumer needs the funds. However, the Zero Point Option would allow only 25 percent of the funds to be placed in a line of credit.

"We thought it was a logical combination because borrowers looking for a loan like this already have a plan for the money," said Jim Mahoney, Financial Freedom's chief executive officer.

Cash Account, Simply Zero Option. Nine months after Financial Freedom rolled out the Zero Point Option, the company introduced Simply Zero, the philosophy being if Simply Zero could increase loan volumes by 200 percent, perhaps an absolutely no-cash-out-of-pocket program would also be big dividends. Simply Zero features no origination fee and no closing costs.

"Now, with Simply Zero, we have even eliminated origination fees and third party costs to provide borrowers with a loan that answers their needs and which removes a key barrier—the perception that these loans are expensive," Mahoney said.

Simply Zero is also tied to the six-month LIBOR Index. The only significant difference from the Zero Point Option is that the borrower is required to withdraw all available funds (and begin accruing interest) when the Simply Zero reverse mortgage closes. Borrowers have used the funds for a variety of options, including the purchase of single premium immediate annuities and other potential revenue producers.

"We tell our customers to be very careful when they are investing their reverse mortgage funds," said Seattle Mortgage's Broderick. "If they can't get at least as much in return as the rate they are paying on their reverse mortgage, there's really no reason to spend the time and effort."

What, exactly, is LIBOR?

The London InterBank Offered Rate is an average of what international banks charge each other for large-volume loans. (See Appendix A, Figure A.9.) The index responds very quickly to market conditions and is calculated for a variety of loan adjustments. It has become a common gauge used by U.S. banks to calculate adjustable rate mortgages: one-month, three-month, six-month, one-year, etc.

In Chapter 4, we'll read how some seniors used their reverse mortgage funds. For some, the loan was the only option for paying monthly bills or emergency care. For others, it provided an extra cushion for a more comfortable life.

I am a kind of paranoid in reverse.
I suspect people of plotting to make me happy.
—J.D. SALINGER

The Many Uses of Reverse Mortgage Funds

Solving the Needs and Wants of Real People in Real Situations

There's a grandmother in Georgetown, DC, who took out a reverse mortgage on her million-dollar home and gave her two daughters $200,000 apiece so that they could use the money now, when they needed it for their own children, instead of getting the cash later in her estate when the grandkids had grown and moved on.

How about the senior living near Boston, Massachusetts, widowed at a young age, who got a reverse mortgage to put her daughter through nursing school?

An Oregon man, still working at age 68, used the cash from a reverse mortgage to buy a flatbed truck that would carry the long sticks of PVC pipe needed for his sprinkler business.

In this chapter, we will present some of the endless ways persons over age 62 have utilized reverse mortgages to solve critical needs, acquire a lifelong dream, or set up a reserve account that brings flexibility and peace of mind. Funds from a reverse mortgage can be used for any purpose: supplemental income, medical expenses, travel, college tuition, home improvements, extinguishing credit-card debt or buying a new car or boat. Here are a few stories.

Sister Maria Lends a Hand in St. Louis

Mention the Dogtown neighborhood to a St. Louis, Missouri, resident, and you'll get a variety of impressions. Old homes—some of them eclipsing the century bracket and inhabited by older folks, single professionals, and younger couples trying to make a start as first-time homebuyers—highlight this old village within a big city. Some of the homes are being renovated with stylish appointments, while others are being torn down for greater-density, in-city living units. One home on Tamm Avenue was built in 1860 and could even be older, according to the Dogtown Historical Society.

The neighborhood is rich in Irish tradition, although some Poles and other groups have been around just as long. Oldtimers say the place got its name when so many visitors for the 1904 World's Fair noticed the number of dogs in the area. The neighborhood also has a reputation for helping and taking care of its own. Sister Maria, a nurse and member of the Religious Order of the Sacred Heart, recently came to the aid of Dorothy, 79, a friend in St. James the Greater parish.

"I had met her at the hospital and she began putting all of her medical expenses on her credit card," Sister Maria said of Dorothy. "There were certain things that just weren't covered and that was the only way of getting the medication."

Sister Maria also found that Dorothy's home needed a new furnace, siding, windows, and air conditioning. Dorothy lived alone and did not want to leave the house.

"I saw an advertisement for a reverse mortgage, but I really learned about it when a person from one of the social service agencies came to talk about it at a parish meeting," Sister Maria said. "When I heard about the program, I thought something like that could help Dorothy stay in her home."

Gail Hawkins, a Wells Fargo reverse mortgage loan officer in St. Louis, helped to put Dorothy's package together. Not only was there a large credit card bill for medical expenses, but there was also an outstanding balance of more than $6,000 on a department store account that Dorothy's late husband had started more than a decade earlier. The home appraised for approximately $67,000, yet Dorothy was able to pay off all her debt and make all her necessary repairs—including the new furnace, windows, siding, and air conditioning—with the reverse mortgage funds. She will make no payments until the home no longer serves as her primary residence.

"She was paying the minimum on the Sears account every month," Sister Maria said. "I don't think she would have ever paid it off."

Paying for the Results of a Waterfront Landslide

Dave and Liz Merrill awoke one spring day to a huge canyon in their front yard. Not only had a landslide come dangerously close to destroying the retired couple's oceanfront home just north of Santa Barbara, California, but they also had no clue how to fund the enormous repairs.

The slide affected six homes, and three of them had to be evacuated. A new retaining wall would have to be built, plus the challenge of dealing with a new well water system, road easements, roof certifications, and pest inspections.

"We had heard that a reverse mortgage might help, but when we looked around, there was so much that had to be done," Liz Merrill said. "I just didn't know if you would be able to get enough money to do all of that."

Just about everything in Santa Barbara is expensive, especially the housing market. The average price of a single-family home in the city is now greater than $1 million. Even though Dave is a retired physician, the cost of raising nine children had cut into their savings to the point where the new wall seemed huge—in more ways than one.

The couple applied for a jumbo reverse mortgage from Financial Freedom Funding. They were able to borrow $400,000 on their 1,800 square-foot, three-bedroom, two-bathroom home that was built in 1951. The home appraised at $1.2 million, and the Merrill's closing costs were capped at $3,500 on the Zero Point Option Program.

"It was very unfortunate because the county was making a lot of demands but not assisting the families in any way," said Rachel Brichan, Financial Freedom reverse mortgage specialist. "I think the permits cost as much as the actual construction. You can still see some of the cracks in the exterior decks. One of the homes had a lap pool in front of the property that was completely lost."

The couple eliminated their small underlying mortgage, paid for the new retaining wall and all the accessory work, set up an annual contract to handle future deferred maintenance, and have a $100,000 line of credit to supplement their retirement needs.

"Other people whose homes are more expensive than ours have asked about our reverse mortgage," Liz said. "Many of them are not terribly wealthy, they just happened to be living in an area where the homes have really shot up in price. They are saying to themselves 'why not take advantage of that value. We don't want to sell.'

"We didn't really have a choice. We didn't want to walk away from this place, although some of the owners considered it. We found a way to make this work and we didn't even know about the reverse mortgage a year ago."

Former Aircraft Mechanic Flying High in New Plane

Tom Hardington's never been far from air—or water. As an aircraft mechanic during World War II, he made stops in Daytona Beach, San Diego, and Wailuku, on the Hawaiian Island of Maui, specializing in propeller repair and maintenance.

The lifelong pilot, 84, has lived in Munhall, Pennsylvania, hard by the Monongahela River just east of Pittsburgh for more than 60 years with his late wife, Wilda. In fact, he even flew weekend floatplane excursions on the river during the summer. But the years in the air that bring the most excitement to his voice were from 1947 to 1948 when he would fly floatplanes from dawn to dusk on Lake Conneaut, a resort community in northwest Pennsylvania not far from the Ohio border.

"It was just after the war and I had a buddy with a place up there," Hardington said. "You talk about a great summer job. . . . We'd just give people airplane rides all day long. Picked up them at the dock near the resort, flew around the area for about 20 minutes and took them back down to the lake near the hotel. At night, we'd tether the planes to a dock on the other side of the lake, gas 'em up and get ready for the next day."

Since then, Tom has met numerous airplane partners through his 30 years at Kemper Insurance in downtown Pittsburgh, at flying clubs, and by loafing at a variety of airports where he would swap old stories with veteran pilots and mechanics. However, he never owned a plane of his own until he was 83.

Hardington's granddaughter, Wendy Fitzgerald, a reverse mortgage consultant with Wells Fargo, suggested he take some cash out of his home and purchase the plane he'd always wanted. That conversation came on the heels of a friend's announcement that a medical condition would force him to sell his beloved plane.

"I bought the plane and part ownership of the hangar," Hardington said. "You never know how much time you have left in the air, especially at my age, and I really knew the plane. Been up in it lots of times. But I've got a couple of new knees I have to figure out before I do a lot more flyin'."

Hardington took out an $83,000 reverse mortgage, receiving $25,000 as a lump sum and the remainder as an available line of credit. He said he was living comfortably off a modest pension and Social Security benefits but never really had the cash to plop down on a plane.

"We raised our children and there were always so many things to pay for right in front of you," Hardington said. "The money to actually own a plane then wasn't really in the picture. I had always thought that I'd leave what I could to the kids, but they told me 'we already have a house.' They told me to do what I wanted to do with my home."

So he bought the plane he'd always wanted and has been flying—in more ways than one—ever since.

In the Nick of Time: Reverse Funds Halt Foreclosure

Marjorie Bristow had heard about a reverse mortgage years ago, but the Sequim, Washington, resident, 76, had no idea the financing option for older homeowners would be the answer to her property problems.

"It's a long, hairy story but this thing really bailed me out," said Bristow of the reverse mortgage that allowed her to stay on the curious, two-acre parcel four miles west of the popular banana-belt town. "Just how much time do you have to listen?"

There are no income or medical requirements to qualify for a reverse loan. Consumers may be eligible for a reverse mortgage, even if they still owe money on a first or second mortgage. In fact, many seniors get a reverse mortgage to pay off a first mortgage, and Bristow landed one just in the nick of time. Like most homeowners who get behind in payments, Bristow's road to default and subsequently the brink of foreclosure was unexpected. In fact, lenders will tell you that the major reasons for default—divorce, loss of job, death—rarely are in anybody's plans.

For Bristow, the problems started when three Social Security checks, usually showing up like clockwork in her checking account via direct deposit, failed to appear.

"I had $2,200 in my checking account so I went out and bought a '73 Jeep Commando rather impulsively," Bristow said. "I had some money left over so I started buying just about everything that wasn't nailed down. Well, that didn't last long. When the Social Security checks didn't show up, my checks began bouncing all over town. I think I owed just about everybody."

In addition, Bristow's son had moved to Seattle and his contribution to the monthly mortgage payment went with him. A couple of part-time renters also didn't keep their word, so Bristow's monthly mortgage payment of $764 was a figure far from her income.

"I didn't know what to do," Bristow said. "I didn't want to sell the place because I didn't know where I would go if I did sell it. But all of a sudden that didn't make any difference because the auction (foreclosure sale) was staring me right in the face."

Bristow contacted Wells Fargo's Theresa Korpela about the possibility of securing a reverse mortgage on the property. The parcel appraised at $135,000, and the reverse loan of $92,500 paid off the underlying liens, thereby halting the foreclosure proceedings. In addition, Bristow will have to make no mortgage payments until she moves out or dies. Then, her estate either refinances the loan or sells the property.

"I don't think I'll be going anywhere," Bristow said. "I've got 103 cedar trees on this place, a nice area to garden, a hurricane fence. . . . It works for me. . . . Unless it's to visit my sister in upstate New York. She's 90 and got a cattle ranch I've been dying to see."

In Search of a Dream . . . and Swimming with Dolphins

Mary Galo, 66, has always wanted to swim with dolphins.

"It's just something I've always wanted to do," said Galo, a retired nurse, part-time poetry writer, and longtime resident of Fairview Heights, Illinois, about a nine iron across the Mississippi River from St. Louis, Missouri. "They seem to be very special creatures and I've dreamed about being around them in the water."

Swimming with dolphins, and the lure of other travel adventures, was not the primary reason Galo began investigating the possibility of a reverse mortgage on her $98,000 residence. The place needed a new roof, and Galo also wanted to wipe her credit card slate clean. She says she's always been conservative and down to earth, working as a nurse in U.S. Air Force hospitals across the country as she followed the many relocations of her first husband, an Air Force commander. When the kids came along, she worked in flower shops, J.C. Penney department stores, newspaper classified departments, and even published a book of poems during one stint in Florida. She considered the reverse mortgage as logical even though she was at the tail end of the pay-it-off Silent Generation. Her first husband died 20 years ago, and she married another Air Force man, John, seven years her junior.

"A friend of mine was 80 years old and his house was a lot older than he was," Galo said. "He started telling me about this thing called a reverse mortgage. He knew that my home was paid off and just sitting here. We really started to think about it, but then we had to figure out how to handle my husband's age."

Galo's husband, John, happened to be 59, three years too young to qualify for a reverse mortgage. However, the couple decided to place the house only in Mary's name, only in order to meet the requirements for the reverse mortgage (see Chapter 1). All reverse mortgage borrowers must be at least 62 years of age.

The couple decided to use a quitclaim deed to transfer John's interest to Mary. The couple said it turned out to be a rather painless process, yet John was required to participate in the usual Home Equity Conversion Mortgage (HECM) counseling coordinated by AARP.

"The only thing that really surprised me was the closing," Mary said. "And of course, the value of the house. Shocked the hell out of me. . . . I thought it was worth around $80,000 and the appraisal came back at $98,000. I wonder if other people really know what their homes are worth. . . . Anyway, I couldn't believe the number of pages I had to sign. They must have torn down two forests just to make the paper needed in this deal. I just signed and signed. . . . I guess the same thing happened a few years ago when we took out a home equity loan."

After paying for the roof and knocking off her credit card balances, Mary said she does not plan to touch her reverse mortgage line of credit—unless it's for an extraordinary vacation. Her pension from 12 years of nursing, John's Air Force retirement, and Social Security checks more than wash the monthly bills.

"I'm going to be conservative," Mary said. "I'm going to leave it right where it is . . . until I can find that great place where you can swim with the dolphins. I've heard there's one down in Florida, but there's got to be another one more exotic . . .

"And, did I tell you what I'm going to do after that? There's this train trip across the Old West where you get to see all of the old places the West is famous for. Doesn't that sound interesting? All on one train. Now, I'd need some money for that . . ."

It's All About Travel . . . and Bike Trips

"You get used to living a certain way," said Luther Sitton, 79. "And the dollars simply haven't been there for me lately to live that way."

Sitton, who likes to spend his summers on bicycle trips with riders half his age, is pondering ways to produce more income now that some of his stocks have turned sour and his certificates of deposit are hard-pressed to earn 4 percent.

"I've got people coming back now who made initial inquiries two years ago," said Lee McCutcheon, reverse mortgage specialist for Seattle Mortgage, a national reverse lender. "Some of their revenue streams have completely dried up and they need help. Seniors who were looking pretty good—and I don't mean they had a huge excess of cash every month—are hurting because of the market dive. Many of them are far from comfortable now."

Sitton, a wheat farmer, is a good example of a senior wondering where to turn for retirement income in a down economic time. He owns his lakefront home free and clear, has some decent performing stocks remaining, yet lost a significant amount of money on popular technology issues and is leery of another setback.

"We are seeing a lot more inquiries now than ever before," said Peter Bell, president of the Washington, DC–based National Reverse Mortgage Lenders Association, a national nonprofit trade association for financial services companies that originate, service, and invest in reverse mortgages. "Some seniors have recognized that their portfolios have not performed as they anticipated. They are exploring other options and reverse mortgages certainly are an option."

In Sitton's case, it's all about travel.

"I guess I've spoiled myself a little bit since my wife passed away," Sitton said. "But I like to go just about everywhere and ride. Stay in nice hotels, too. I give money to the kids and my charity friends. If I cut back, it will be on the trips—and I really don't want to do that.

"I've never thought about a reverse mortgage before, but this might be the time," Sitton said. "It would be a way of seeing a few more bucks a month. Besides, I'm in no hurry to move. In fact, I have no idea where I would move."

Area Limitations Don't Stop Some Folks in Need

Sometimes, one of the key ingredients of a reverse mortgage—property location, age of the borrower, or interest rate—just doesn't mix. A potential borrower can be stymied by the inability to qualify for enough money to make a reverse mortgage become a realistic option.

Other times, depending upon need and other circumstances, older homeowners simply will take what they can get. For example, when Peggy Stuckey of Hansville, Washington, applied for a reverse mortgage on her Puget Sound waterfront home near Seattle, she was limited to the rural loan limit of approximately $100,000 less than borrowers in Seattle. Even though her home was worth at least three times the FHA loan ceiling, she went ahead with the HECM reverse mortgage program anyway.

"I understood that other places had other rules, but that's just the way it is," Stuckey said. "I wanted to stay in my home, here, not someplace else."

In 2004, the House Subcommittee on Housing and Community Opportunity held a hearing on a bill that would boost lending limits in high-cost areas for all FHA single-family programs, including HECM. It sought to eliminate the current FHA loan limit ceiling, equal to 87 percent of the Fannie Mae/Freddie Mac conforming loan limit ($290,319 in 2004) in high-cost areas, and allow FHA limits equal to 100 percent of the median home price in each locality. HECM loans, insured by the FHA, a part of the U.S. Department of Housing and Urban Development (HUD), are pegged to increases in the Fannie Mae/ Freddie Mac loan limit and vary by geographic area.

"I'll be 80 years old and I wanted to stay right here in Driftwood Key," Stuckey said. "The reverse mortgage gives me some money every month, plus I have some left in case I need to repair my dock or bulkhead."

Stuckey was looking to supplement her monthly income, which took a turn to the south with her Enron stock. Many seniors face the same challenges.

"The industry as a whole has seen an increase in the number of reverse mortgage borrowers who are opting to use a reverse mortgage to help fund their retirement, specifically as a result of the downturn of the financial markets," said Sarah Hulbert, the national director for Seattle Mortgage's reverse mortgage division. "Many portfolios that previously were generating an income level sufficient to fund a person's retirement are no longer doing so."

Hulbert is part of an industry group pushing Congress to adopt a single national limit for reverse mortgages that would serve all areas of the country.

"If seniors really want access to the money they have built up in their homes, we should do what we can to help them," Hulbert said. "After all, it's their money, and a lot of them really need it just to keep going."

Underestimated Lift: Elevator Created Option to Moving

Graham Coffee, 85, didn't need a big, comfortable, luxury automobile. Many of his friends have them, but he'd earmarked his reverse mortgage money for something else.

"I've already been through that stage in my life," said the former aerospace engineer now living near Laguna Beach, California. "I'd really rather have this elevator instead—and it costs about the same amount of money."

Or less. According to Kevin Lew of Ability Development, Inc., the basic residential elevator package starts at about $20,000 and can be installed in a 4 square foot space previously designated as a closet. Lew represents about seven elevator manufacturers—all of whom have extended their target audience far beyond retired seniors.

"My typical clients are actually Baby Boomers who are getting older and want to plan for the future," Lew said. "Some of them want the flexibility of accommodating a parent who might be coming to live with their family. They also see the definite need for themselves. So, the elevator is really serving two families, two generations."

Coffee's story is also extremely common. He retired from McDonnell Douglas Corporation in 1987 and found the perfect retirement home in the climate he and his wife dearly enjoyed. The couple was fairly certain their children had left the nest for good and decided their larger family home was no longer a requirement. They scaled down to a modest, two-story home on a hill with a partial view of the Pacific Ocean.

"At the time, my wife and I were in relatively good physical condition and never dreamed our body parts would need or demand maintenance," Coffee said. "However, in retrospect—and with hindsight always being 20/20—we now realize we should have opted for a one-story house instead of the two-story model we bought."

The Coffees eventually realized that climbing the stairs to their second-floor bedroom had become more than exercise. Not only had the trek grown to be a constant effort, but lugging up heavy pieces of furniture was also out of the question.

"An accident waiting to happen," Coffee said. "No doubt about it. With my bad leg, it was just a matter of time."

The couple first considered purchasing a one-story home in the neighborhood. However, they were not attracted to the design of local homes in their price range and did not want to leave their friends.

"It was also debilitating for us to think of packing and moving at our age," Coffee said. "We realized we would be leaving our peekaboo view of the blue Pacific Ocean, giving up our nearby shopping centers and hospital along with some of the best doctors in Southern California. It became apparent that starting all over at our age might be a huge mistake. If we had won the Lotto, it might warrant a second thought."

The solution was a residential elevator that now serves as a people mover, freight elevator, and dumbwaiter. Coffee did most of his research on the Internet and decided on a Canadian firm that would accept his own design. Unlike many residential units, the Coffee elevator is away from visitor traffic patterns yet not tucked away in a back closet.

"I don't like walking into a home and immediately see a chair lift or elevator," Coffee said. "I know some people like to display them, but I'm not one of them. Ours is open, not claustrophobic, but you have to be looking for it to see it."

Elevator supplies say there is no typical unit. All offer several preengineered configurations plus the ability to customize endless combinations of configuration, fixtures, and finishes. Most companies also supply detailed drawings to help architects and builders include plans for a home remodel or custom new construction. Some residential units can travel up to 50 feet (providing ample basement-to-top-story access) and service six different landings. All units usually have safety devices and electronic controls that monitor cab position, door latches, and automatic lighting.

"A lot of people seem to think it's a good idea to move closer to your kids when you get older," Coffee said. "Well, your kids move too. Once you get to a new area, get settled and meet some people, your son or daughter could be transferred. We thought about all of the moving possibilities. We decided it was best to stay here—make it comfortable for us and for the children when they come to visit. The elevator and the reverse mortgage have made all of that possible."

A Giant Leap to a Second Home

The reverse mortgage, which must be on a primary residence, can also be used to help acquire a second home. (In Chapter 3, we discussed how the Fannie Mae Home Keeper mortgage can be used to actually acquire a primary residence).

Joan and Mike Chevalier of St. Louis, Missouri, have a home valued at $235,000. Mike is 72 years old, and Joan is 68. They executed a reverse mortgage on their residence based on her age and an expected interest rate of 7 percent. They netted a lump sum of approximately $106,000 on closing of the reverse mortgage. Shortly thereafter, they purchased a vacation condo in New Mexico where Joan had longed to become a part of the arts scene. They put the $106,000 into the New Mexico condo and added $19,000 from Mike's retirement funds. They now own the New Mexico condo free and clear.

After a decade of no loan payments on their Minneapolis family home, they chose to downsize. They sold their primary residence, paid off the underlying debt, and moved to the New Mexico condo. Using an average appreciation rate of 4 percent on the primary residence and a 7 percent interest rate on the loan, the balance on the loan would have increased to $253,198, and the value of the home to $347,857. If the home netted that amount upon sale, Joan and Mike would put $95,659 in their pocket. Also, remember, they have made no mortgage payments for the past 10 years.

Refinancing the Reverse . . . for Cars, Business

Carol Upmeyer, 69, is a baseball fan.

In fact, she works part-time as a ticket-taker for the Seattle Mariners and relishes her position at the home-plate entry gate. However, like many seniors, she simply could not make ends meet on her monthly income, especially when it came time for a major purchase.

"I needed a car," Upmeyer said. "I mean, I *really* needed a car. I had to have something reliable to get to work."

Upmeyer, a former small business owner and pottery specialist, used most of the money from her first reverse mortgage to settle her business affairs. She was stunned to hear that she could refinance her reverse mortgage and pull out an additional $30,000 from her home. She bought a car and also paid bills. About $11,000 remains in a line of credit that grows at a moderate interest rate.

The best candidates for refinancing of HECMs are existing borrowers living in high-cost major metropolitan areas whose homes have appreciated in value significantly and where the FHA loan limit has increased significantly in recent years.

"It's absolutely amazing to me the number of people who have never heard of reverse mortgages," Upmeyer said. "Of those who have heard of them, I bet you there are very few who know you can refinance them. Most people think a reverse mortgage is final."

A drop in interest rates, appreciating home values, and an increase in age have put Upmeyer, and many of the others who have reverse mortgages, in a prime position to pull more money out of their homes. The older you are, the more you can draw.

Another woman who knows reverse mortgages are not final is Dr. Elizabeth Duncan, 82. In fact, she doesn't plan to keep her second reverse mortgage very long. As soon as she builds up her professional psychotherapy practice east of Seattle, she intends to refinance to a conventional mortgage.

"A lot of people think these mortgages are so final," said Duncan, who used a reverse mortgage to buy a new home in a retirement community. "But they aren't final. You can end it when you feel like ending it. You still own your home, and you can still do what you want."

Both cases show the flexibility of the reverse mortgage and how far the instrument has evolved. Once perceived only as a last-ditch effort to keep the family home, they are now used to buy homes, purchase cars, make needed repairs and improvements, finance education, pay for in-home care, or provide supplemental income.

"Reverse mortgages are not for everybody," said Duncan, who utilized a Fannie Mae product (Home Keeper) then refinanced into HUD's Home Equity Conversion Mortgage (HECM). "In fact, you probably shouldn't take one out unless you really need it. But I'll tell you what . . . a lot of seniors would not lose their homes if they knew about reverse mortgages."

Sarah Hulbert, national director of reverse mortgages for Seattle Mortgage, says it's sometimes difficult getting seniors to understand things have changed.

"People have had this misunderstanding that reverse mortgages can do one thing and that they are very rigid," Hulbert said. "Getting the word out that these programs are very flexible has been a challenge. Some seniors have heard from friends about one option, yet there are many ways they can go."

In Chapter 5, we will study the agency that has been responsible for most of the reverse mortgages used in the United States today. While often maligned and seldom honored, HUD took the lead while others waited to see how rough the road would be.

A historian is a prophet in reverse.
—FRIEDRICH VON SCHLEGEL

Paving the Main Reverse Road

HUD Has Provided Terrific Testing Grounds

Every time the U.S. Department of Housing and Urban Development (HUD) stubs its toe, you hear howls about its function in housing. Should the government really be involved in homes and loans? Some members of Congress would like to see the Federal Housing Administration (FHA) taken out of HUD and put into the private sector. For years, government housing options—specifically FHA loans—were perceived as being heavily wrapped in red tape.

In this chapter, we look at the history and philosophy of the agency that introduced and stood by the country's most popular reverse mortgage product and also a couple of its first cousins—low down payment first mortgages and the purchase-rehabilitation package known as the FHA

203K loan. Many private lenders have fostered their own forms of those plans, which consumers can find in today's market (some are mentioned in Chapter 6). While the periodic dark side of the agency has surfaced over time—investigations of former secretaries and allegations that some programs were labeled "inept, detrimental, and costly" by the Office of Inspector General—HUD and other government agencies are a critical part of the public housing landscape, despite the calls by some critics to take the agency private. (HUD believes if FHA went private, borrowers would be charged higher fees and interest rates than those currently charged by FHA, resulting in fewer home ownership options. In addition, the department points to a task force conclusion that the sale of FHA to private owners would not attract any buyers offering a reasonable price.)

Gordon Schlicke, who retired in 1998 as vice president of training and development for Mellon Bancorp after serving in a variety of management positions, has been known to do a stand-up comedy routine for escrow, title, lending, appraisal, legal, and real estate sales conferences with experiences from 42 years in the lending business. One of his favorite targets is HUD.

"Of course your FHA loan is screwed up. . . . Can you spell HUD backward . . . ?"

"New FHA rules effective July 1 have not been released. But, officials said they will be effective July 1 anyway, regardless of when they are released."

"The latest FHA changes are never in the Latest FHA Mortgagee Letter. All Mortgagee Letters should be entitled: Information-Which-Has-Already-Gotten-Out Letter."

"By now, I thought FHA was convinced that every American knows that lead paint is dangerous. I think the lead paint notice will be required up to the moment that lead disappears from our planet and is taken off our table of elements. To encourage people to read the form, you could title it: 'According to the Secretary of Housing and Urban Development— Housing Can Kill.' "[1]

But the undeniable truth is that HUD (800-767-7468 or www.hud.gov) has provided a variety of vital avenues toward homeownership that many conventional lenders historically had been too nervous to test.

FHA insures loans so that if the borrower defaults, the lender is guaranteed to receive the outstanding mortgage amount. For the past 70 years, an FHA loan has been the primary low down payment option for homebuyers. The popularity of FHA loans has dwindled in the past decade as the private market has grown more sophisticated and efficient at creating and providing mortgage money. However, the FHA process burden was unraveled more than a decade ago when the agency gave direct endorsement authorization to private lenders so they could process loans without waiting for FHA approval. And, like all conventional loans made in this country, FHA could not avoid increasingly fatter files due to a variety of new disclosure forms and regulations.

A prime FHA target, first-time homebuyers—many of whom will be relatively new to the United States—are pushing the housing ladder. Analysts believe that the immigrants hold the keys not only to the residential building industry but also to critical segments of the economy. That's because many newcomers pay cash, reducing the concerns of

---

[1] Gordon Schlicke, *The Lighter Side of Lending,* Mortgage Originator, 1999.

escalating consumer debt except in big-ticket purchases like homes. Therefore, HUD is the critical player at both ends of the housing finance ladder—first-time loans and reverse mortgages.

FHA Housing Commissioner Saw Reverse Mortgages Come Full Circle

What goes around comes around. Just ask John Weicher about reverse mortgages.

Weicher, appointed as HUD's assistant secretary for housing in 2001, oversees all FHA programs in his role as Federal Housing Commissioner. The person in his political position (which comes with the potential to be ousted/appointed by a new administration) clearly is the prime mover of reverse mortgages in this country. That's because HUD insures the nation's most popular reverse mortgage product—the Home Equity Conversion Mortgage (HECM). Weicher has served HUD four times under four different presidents. From 1989 to 1993, Weicher was assistant secretary for policy development and research for HUD Secretary Jack Kemp in the Bush administration. Weicher was HUD's chief economist from 1975 to 1977 under Secretary Carla Hills in President Gerald Ford's administration. From 1973 to 1974, he spent one year as a HUD division director in the Nixon administration.

Reverse mortgages have been around almost as long as Weicher. An expensive, awkward idea first tried 30 years ago by independent bankers, reverse mortgages evolved into a demonstration program sponsored by HUD in 1993 and now to a permanent, refined economic vehicle that generated more than 16,000 loans in fiscal year 2003 and was closing in on 40,000 in 2004.

"Not only has there been tremendous growth in reverse mortgages the past two years, but they are also responding to the same forces that move conventional, or forward, mortgages," Weicher said in 2003. "That has been the main milestone in the program."

Weicher has had his share of public relations problems as well. In 2001, his appointment to his current job was questioned by the real estate industry, which felt another person might be friendlier to the housing community. No specific concerns were made public.

"The position [of FHA Commissioner], which manages and operates FHA mortgage insurance programs for both single and multifamily housing, is the most critical policy position within HUD," said Jerry Howard of the National Association of Home Builders (NAHB) at the time of the nomination. "Dr. Weicher's past track record and statements regarding the future of FHA and FHA's multifamily mortgage insurance programs have raised some red flags for multifamily builders and other leaders of our association. We look forward to having an opportunity to meet with Dr. Weicher to discuss a range of housing policy issues prior to our taking a formal position on his nomination."

A month later, after reviewing the public record and comments made during the Senate's confirmation hearing, the NAHB decided it would accept Weicher as Federal Housing Commissioner for HUD.

Weicher experienced the early problems with reverses and eventually became convinced they were a viable product for consumers.

However, that did not mean he supported reverses in all situations—especially when they made it easier to tap the equity in expensive homes. In June 2004, the House Subcommittee on Housing and Community Opportunity held a hearing on a bill that would have boosted lending limits in high-cost areas for all FHA single-family programs, including HECM. Weicher testified that HUD did not support the bill. He contended most Americans would not benefit from this legislation. His statements did really come as a surprise. After all, he was speaking as the top officer of the FHA, the agency established by the National Housing Act of 1934 to stabilize a depressed housing market and provide insurance on loans to homebuyers who otherwise could not find loans. High-cost areas did not fit the profile.

Because of his testimony, it was unlikely that the George W. Bush administration would push for its passage. Organizations that testified in support of the bill included Fannie Mae, Freddie Mac, National Association of Mortgage Brokers, Mortgage Bankers Association, and the National Council of State Housing Agencies.

Home Improvement—with No Strings Attached

While HUD is mostly known for its reverse mortgages and low down payment home loans, FHA has a home improvement loan program, too. This program comes in handy for folks who need cash and can't get a home equity loan due to already high loan amounts or slumping home values. Title 1 loans of up to $25,000 are available to owner-occupants and investors who want to repair or improve their property. Up to $15,000 can be obtained regardless of home value. And if you need

$5,000 or less, no security is necessary. To obtain the loan, you need to own the property or hold a long-term lease to it. Borrowers have to execute a note agreeing to repay the loan and meet very lenient qualifying guidelines. Total debt (including present home loans) may not exceed 45 percent of monthly income. The loan is great for people who can't borrow any more money in the conventional market. It works well for investors who purchased a run-down home that they want to fix up and resell in a hurry. With this loan, they don't have to spend all of their money to do the work.

The Title 1 loan fills a need, but the loan does not come cheap. Fees vary from lender to lender but can be 10 percent of the loan amount for loans up to $20,000 ($1,000 for a $10,000 loan; $2,000 for $20,000) and interest rates start at about 12 percent. Obviously, these loans are significantly more expensive than home equity loans. In fact, the interest rate is nearly double what can be obtained in the conventional market. But some people don't have the luxury of qualifying for the best loans available and need unconventional financing just to get along with their lives. Banks and other qualified lenders make these loans from their own funds; HUD then insures the lender against a possible loss. Title 1 of the National Housing Act, thus the loan name, authorizes the loan insurance program.

For example, a couple near Boise, Idaho, purchased a home three years ago for $120,000 and received a recent appraisal for $105,000. They desperately needed to borrow some money to make repairs, but they owed as much on the home as the appraised value. The Title I loan turned out to be a real benefit to them. Because Title 1 guidelines do not require borrowers to have equity established in the property for amounts less than $15,000, new homeowners or individuals who have recently refinanced have a chance to make improvements on their home right after they purchase—something virtually impossible under conventional guidelines.

Title 1 loans may be used for any improvements that "will make your home basically more livable and useful." Therefore, you can use Title 1 cash for built-in dishwashers, refrigerators, freezers, and ovens. However, the loans cannot be used for certain luxury-type items such as swimming pools or outdoor fireplaces. Title 1 money cannot pay for work that has already been done.

Improvements can be made by the homeowner or through a contractor or dealer. The loan can be used to pay for materials and labor. In addition, the cash from the loan can pay for architectural and engineering costs and building permit fees. The federal government requires an inspection for loans greater than $7,500. When the work is finished, the borrower must furnish the lender with a completion certificate.

The FHA Title 1 Loan may not be the perfect way to finance a home improvement project, but it could be the only way for some folks. To find a lender offering the program in your area, call (202) 708-1112, or visit www.hud.gov.

Throwing Your Mortgage in Reverse

The FHA insures the most popular reverse mortgage program, the HECM. Similar to interest rate lock-in provisions on conventional mortgages, HECM borrowers now will have the comfort of knowing that the interest rate cannot increase during the period between application and closing. In the past, borrowers ran the risk of rates rising during that time, potentially reducing the amount of proceeds available to them. In addition, mortgage lenders offering HECMs will no longer need to recalculate the principal limit on the day of settlement. Lenders are not allowed to charge a fee for the 60-day lock.

Reverse borrowers make no monthly payments on a mortgage during its term. The loan comes due when the borrower permanently moves out of his or her home. However, seniors can outlive the value of their home without being forced to move. The homeowner cannot be displaced and forced to sell the home to pay off the mortgage, even if the principal balance grows to exceed the value of the property. If the value of the house exceeds what is owed at the time of homeowner's death, the rest goes to the estate. The home does not have to be paid off entirely, but the greater the equity, the greater the reverse loan amount. Age, location, and loan type also factor in the reverse mortgage amount.

Buy and Repair—with the Same Loan

When buying a house that is in need of repair or modernization, homebuyers usually have to follow a complicated and costly process, first obtaining financing to purchase the property, then getting additional financing for the rehabilitation work, and finally finding a permanent mortgage after rehabilitation is completed to pay off the interim loans. The FHA 203K program was designed to roll all financing into one package. The borrower can take out one mortgage loan, at a long-term fixed or adjustable rate, to finance both the acquisition and the rehabilitation of the property. The mortgage amount is based on the as-will-be, or projected, value of the property and takes into account the cost of the work.

The loan covers the purchase or refinancing and rehabilitation of a home that is at least a year old. A portion of the loan proceeds is used to pay the seller or, if a refinance, to pay off the existing mortgage, and the remaining funds are placed in an escrow account and released as rehabilitation is completed. The cost of the rehabilitation must be at least $5,000, but the total value of the property must still fall within the FHA loan limit in the region. The value of the property is determined by either the value of the property before rehabilitation plus the cost of rehabilitation or 110 percent of the appraised value of the property after rehabilitation, whichever is less. Under 203K, owners can do their own refurbishing, but all 203K loans require a contractor bid for the job. That way, if the owner is injured or becomes ill, the lender knows there will be enough funds to finish the work. The huge benefit is that FHA loans are assumable. That means that the homeowner (or sometimes a nonprofit corporation) can take out the initial mortgage, then have the loan assumed by the next owner or qualified family when the rehabilitation is complete.

Where We've Been with the Federal Government in Housing

Historically, when the government accepted responsibility for providing low-income housing, it was at the local level, particularly by county government. Veterans' homes, orphanages, and poor farms were occasionally supported by the state, but most often they were financed, owned, and operated strictly by county government. The limited government services were also provided almost exclusively to white citizens, with minorities denied access to even the most meager of facilities. With the collapse of the banking system in 1929, the federal government was forced to produce solutions to what quickly became a national housing crisis. Most home loans then were short-term, nonamortizing deals financed by local investors or local banks. Most of these loans forced homebuyers to refinance their homes every few years at the prevailing interest rate. The collapse of the banking system, and the resulting loss of available capital to refinance these short-term home mortgages, put millions of Americans in jeopardy of losing their homes.

The Roosevelt administration began a number of initiatives directed at stabilizing the nation's housing stock, encouraging home construction, and promoting home ownership. The first of these programs was the Federal Home Loan Bank System that established a complex system of government support for home mortgages. The Housing Act of 1934 created the Federal Housing Administration (FHA), which served as a review committee for banks and other loan institutions to make loans to low-income families. (In 1948, the role of the FHA changed to providing mortgage insurance; the Veteran's Administration was also created that year to provide long-term mortgages with low down payments to veterans.) The act was modified and expanded as the Housing Act of 1937 and provided for the establishment, through state law, of local Public Housing Authorities (PHAs) to build, own, and operate the housing.

The next major low-income housing initiative came about through President Lyndon Johnson's Great Society Initiatives. The Housing

Acts of 1965 and 1968 sought to privatize low-income housing by providing direct subsidy to developers who would build multifamily housing for low-income families. The federal government provided low-interest loans to developers and guaranteed the payment of rents to property managers. By the early 1970s both the public and the public-private programs had become highly controversial at the local level. Critics cited examples of deterioration and lack of maintenance that were attributed to profiteering and slumlord practices. Local officials also opposed the construction of housing projects in their communities because of the introduction of low-income and minority families into previously stable working-class neighborhoods. As a result of the criticism and concerns, President Richard Nixon put a moratorium on the production of new public housing. However, to help counter a recession in the early 1970s, Nixon authorized pumping even more federal funds into housing production.

In 1974, President Nixon introduced another approach to the provision of low-income housing: the Section 8 Rental Assistance Program, which provided low-income families with a rent certificate. This certificate would pay for a portion of the rent in any privately owned rental housing unit where the landlord was willing to accept the certificate. The family paid 30 percent of their income toward the rent and utilities, while the federal government paid the balance up to a HUD-designated maximum level. The number of Section 8 certificates has grown incrementally larger each year and now includes rent vouchers to subsidize tenants in a slightly different manner.

President Nixon also began a process of turning authority over to local and state government for federal housing and community development through the consolidation of a number of categorical housing, urban renewal, and other programs into a Community Development Block Grant. Jimmy Carter later pushed for tenant ownership of the privately owned subsidized low-income multifamily housing projects by helping tenants to purchase the property as cooperatives. However, many of the tenant cooperatives failed to make even the small portion of the mortgage payments for which they were responsible, and HUD was forced to foreclose. The projects were eventually sold back to private investors at HUD auctions.

In 1987, Congress and President Ronald Reagan established the Low Income Housing Tax Credit as an investor subsidy to spur production of low-income housing developments by private investors. These credits are awarded to investors by state housing agencies through a competitive process based on rules adopted by each state. At the time President Nixon was inventing the Section 8 program (1971) and block granting authority for community development programs (1973), local states had begun to issue tax-exempt bonds for the purposes of providing below-market-rate loans to homebuyers and apartment developers. The freewheeling issuance of these bonds, and subsequent state abuses of this program, resulted in a revenue drain. In response, the federal government passed a series of restrictions on state powers to issue tax-exempt bonds for housing finance. Restrictions included a limit on the income of borrowers under the program, a maximum house price, and a limit on the amount of bonds a state could issue each year.

The reverse mortgage program, changes to Title 1 loans and FHA 203K loans, and other federal mortgage wrinkles now serve a variety of homeowners in all age groups and backgrounds. In our next chapter, we will study some alternate routes other than the reverse road.

CHAPTER 6

The reverse side also has a reverse side.
—JAPANESE PROVERB

Taking an Alternate Route

Homeowners Who Can't... or Simply Don't Want To

Sometimes, the family home is just too big, and it just makes sense to sell and move on with the next chapter of life. Sometimes, the home might be perfect, yet the memories too tender to take.

Not everyone gains from staying put, even if they wanted to and had the funds to do so.

Folks who probably should not even consider a reverse mortgage are those who live in a consistently flat housing market, have all their health care costs solved, or want to leave every dollar of their home's value to their estate. Others who are stunned by the fees and feel they can get a better a return by working their money elsewhere may never be comfortable living under a roof that will be tied up until they move out. (Wise people have been known to say, "If you won't sleep at night, don't do it.") Still others will absolutely never borrow against the roof over their head once it's paid off, period.

In this section, we will explore some of the alternatives to getting a reverse mortgage. Some of them are clearly obvious, while others will be different and unexpected. There will be practical decisions and suggestions for emotional experiences. We'll begin with a mother of seven who had recently lost her spouse and was certain how she wanted to handle her near future . . .

Simply Selling and Moving On . . .

How do you deal with 46 years of memories and possessions? Jane Fitzpatrick, at least on the surface, chose to take the matter-of-fact road: put the for sale sign in the yard of the family home, a two-story stucco structure in West Los Angeles that became more than an anchor of stability for family and friends; call the seven kids, have them come and get what they want, give the rest to charity; then close the door and keep moving.

Don't look back.

The decision was very un-Fitz-like. Certainly there would be an appropriate prayer of thanks and gratitude, perhaps supplied by the parish priest or the popular Jesuit from the local high school where five Fitzpatrick boys left their marks—a few even academic. Clearly there would be another backyard barbeque, a fitting send-off to the home that was headquarters for so many celebrations, tears, reunions, broken bones, and broken hearts. The boys left blood and sweat on its basketball court and hid cigars in the garage as teenagers, and more than a quarter century ago, one of them stood shaking nervously in an upstairs bedroom over the thought of actually losing his bachelorhood as wedding rehearsal dinner guests arrived at sunset in the festive garden below.

Mrs. Fitz could not, and would not, host "another session" without her beloved husband—especially one down this memory lane. That sentimental journey would have to wait—perhaps until even after the final stages of Parkinson's had taken her gentle partner of 55 years. He would be with her only in spirit at that time, which may be the only way she could digest moving from this special place.

Jane had made up her mind that there was simply too much physical work to do to deal with feelings and emotions. This had always been her way, and now she, then at age 78, needed again to lean on *her way* despite the expectations. Mr. Fitz, then 83, never wanted to leave the house. While several of his buddies headed to the safer beach cities to be closer to their grown kids, there was no doubt Big Fitz was staying put. "Really," he always said, "what could be better than this?"

It was fewer than three blocks to church—and he made an appearance virtually every day. It was about a driver and a nine iron to the country club where he enjoyed the food ("best chow around") and people ("Bud Russo said to say 'hello' ") more than the golf ("I'm still lousy").

The subject of moving never surfaced when the kids lived at home. However, it had been nearly 20 years since there had been more than two full-time residents. Rick had followed older brothers Mike and Bill to the Pacific Northwest 27 years ago, while Pat, Kate, and Maureen had called the San Francisco Bay Area home for nearly as long. The youngest, John, is the only sibling who stayed. Had he known the number of family members that would be seeking sun and relaxation at his Manhattan Beach home, he probably would have relocated elsewhere.

The most less-than-subtle hint at moving the Fitzes out of the family home occurred nine years ago. Some of the siblings suggested the folks get an electric gate and floodlights to guard the yard and driveway. The house had been burglarized a few times in the later years, including one ugly night when the car was stolen. But as much as the kids would have liked to see the folks move, it did not surprise them that they stayed. You could see it in Big Fitz's face—the place was crammed with too many memories for him to pack off to an unknown place. And probably most important, it was still the perfect ballyard for the grandkids who arrived for vacations and holidays, just as it was for his own kids a generation ago.

When it became clear that Big Fitz would not be coming home from a local nursing home, the size, maintenance, and emptiness of the family house became too overwhelming for Jane. After two of the kids took their families home a few days after a Christmas visit, Jane said it was time to move on.

The kids were relieved and pleased their mom had made the choice. The home was absolutely too big, the garden too ornery, the unused rooms too cold for Jane to stay. They said it was far easier to leave the family home when both spouses were still alive. That way, all involved could at least begin to grieve the loss of the home before the overwhelming loss of a partner or parent.

The last of the heavy furniture had been moved to Mrs. Fitz's new address—a nearby condominium. Rick pulled the silverware tray from its familiar place in the kitchen drawer and placed it on the floor of the rental car. He had time for one more shuttle trip to the new condo before visiting his dad in the nursing home. Then, it was off to the airport.

Rick walked out the front door, turned around on the lawn that had served as host to so many football games, and stared up at the house one last time. He thought of the countless number, and variety, of people who said goodbye on that exact spot in the past 46 years. He also thought of his dad, and how he never really left there. Big Fitz did not sell and move to the beach. And Rick knew, very clearly, why his dad never wanted to say goodbye.

Keys to Choosing the Next Place to Live

Had Big Fitz lived, he probably would have jumped eventually at a reverse mortgage. However, he was gone. Mrs. Fitzpatrick had chosen a nearby condo, nicely appointed by many of the familiar pieces of furniture from the old family home. Her children had been given, or assigned, the beds and desks that took up most of the space in the bedrooms of the old house. She chose to have a two-bedroom unit so the kids—and grandkids—could continue to visit. The second bedroom also afforded the possibility of live-in care down the road. She remained in close proximity to her friends, church, golf, physicians, and favorite stores.

However, not all seniors want, or are able, to remain in the same area, especially after the loss of a spouse. While some do choose to stay and age in place alone, others head to a community near an adult child.

Many seniors want to remain independent and choose a small, single-family home while others choose to try out an apartment—at least for the short term. Seniors often have specific issues and needs—the same issues and needs Boomers will face in a short few years. One of the better books on moving was written by Portland, Oregon–based researcher Bert Sperling and his partner Peter Sander. *Cities Ranked and Rated* (Frommers, 2004) includes a thorough section on health and health care in addition to in-depth analysis of crime, climate, local economy and jobs, cost of living, education, transportation, leisure, arts and culture, and quality of life. The book also features an assortment of public and private sources widely used in demographic and market research.

For parents, partners, friends, family—especially adult children: Before relocating to any new community, here are some seemingly older questions to consider that might be as far away as tomorrow. The first, of course, is can you find something that will replace what you already have at the same price?

Housing

How much cash could you net by selling your home? What types of housing are available in the areas you are considering? What are costs for small, detached, single-family homes? Are views attainable? What type of maintenance is required for quality rental homes? Do apartments and condominiums restrict young people? Does the condominium association permit subletting a bedroom? Are there special security provisions for owners who choose to live elsewhere part of the year? How are most homes in the area heated? What is the representative heating cost per year for an average home or apartment? Are electric rates favorable and predictable? How do they compare with major urban cities? Are there special programs for seniors?

Health Care

What level of emergency service is already in place? What is planned for the future? Are competent doctors, nurses, and clinic specialists available and accessible? If not, how close are they in terms of miles and time? Where is the nearest full service hospital, and what are its latest technologies and specializations? Is there a long-term care facility with high standards in the community? Are pharmacies and emergency clinics available at all times? Are local hospitals full or underutilized? Would projected growth cause an overload that might jeopardize other citizens' health services? Is special care for the handicapped available? Are visiting nurses or in-home services easy to arrange?

Climate

What is the truthful definition of local climate? What are the average temperatures in summer and winter? What are the wind conditions (how will it affect golf shots?) and how much rain falls in specific months? When does the snow arrive, how long does it stay, and is it a limiting factor on the movement of persons and vehicles? What is the humidity? Is the area affected by dust, pollens, or industrial discharges?

Public Safety

Is the community adequately policed? Does it boast a low crime rate? What is the response time for police or fire calls? Are there specific records of house break-ins, assaults, purse snatchings, and car theft? Does the community have a 911 or similar response in place for police, fire, or medical services now? What is the future probability of such a service online?

Government and Tax

What local taxes exist in addition to federal and state taxes? Are there any special tax exemptions for seniors? What are property tax valuations? Are city and county offices staffed by helpful representatives to provide quick answers? Are special taxes or levies likely? What has been the history of such taxes?

Utilities and Services

What is the quality of local land and mobile telephone services? Do they offer any special benefits or pricing for senior citizens? What is the quality of the television reception? How many channels? What are the costs of cable services? Is there sufficient programming information? Are Meals on Wheels or similar food services available for the elderly?

Water/Sewage

Does the community provide clean and safe water? What is the cost per year for a typical household, couple, or single person? Is there a bottled water delivery service? How is sewage and solid waste handled? Is there a nearby sewage treatment plant? What percentage of the homes in the community have individual septic fields? Have costs been stable? When are future assessments expected? Will they cover any specific problems?

Recreation

What recreation opportunities exist for mature people? What sports—besides golf and tennis—are emphasized? What kinds of opportunities are available for fishing and hunting, and what does licensing cost? Are there nice parks, walks, and scenic views that are safe at all times of the day? Are there distinctive geological features in the area? How many months a year is it possible to play golf? Are the greens fees expensive or affordable? Is membership in a club available? Does the club restrict the number of rounds a guest can play? Does the club membership offer other benefits, such as social events? Are organized events, such as ballroom or square dancing, available? Do clubs, hobby groups, and church organizations welcome newcomers and visitors?

Business

Are new people made to feel welcome in the community? How does the community accept new business and new business ideas? Is there a local chamber of commerce or small business development center? What has been the history of consultants, antique shops, and small bookstores? Are there a variety of restaurants and food services that cater to seniors or offer senior discounts? Does the community offer shopping at retail services that are complete enough to save long trips?

Cultural Amenities

Are there a local symphony and nearby theaters with live stage productions? Is it easy for newcomers to participate in historical or art museums, bridge clubs, churches, lodges, and special interest clubs? What is the predominant entertainment outside the home? What types of films do the movie theaters present? Is there a special time for seniors? What types of newspapers serve the area? Can they be delivered to a part-time residence out of the area? At what cost?

Transportation

Are there local bus, train, taxi, and van services available? How long is the drive, and how many miles to a major airport? Are flights reasonably priced? Are private aircraft able to land and obtain hanger or tie-down space? Is the local airfield open at night, and does it offer services to private fliers? What are the conditions of local roads and highways? Are there freeways or limited access roads linking the community to any major urban centers?

Affording a New Place—at Your Child's Place

Many older people may be eligible for help in adapting their home so that it continues to meet their needs as their health or mobility declines. These alterations to the home can help to maintain older people's independence, privacy, confidence, and dignity as they age in place. The local senior center, the home improvement agency, the social services department, and the local authority housing department should all be able to advise elders on how to obtain help with installing aids and adaptations in their home. Most older people live in ordinary mainstream housing, and they usually want to stay in their own homes as they get older. Aging-in-place programs offer older people help with the routine maintenance, repair, and improvement of their homes in order to help them to continue to live an independent life in their own home. The process is geared to the assessment and improvement of people's own homes to suit their requirements, specifically in organizing the process by which the repairs are carried out and by ensuring that these repairs are made to a sufficiently high standard to represent value for the money they spend.

When a parent loses a spouse, the surviving spouse will often look to move near, or with, an adult child. Knowing and accepting that a parent or older (perhaps disabled) family member is coming to live with you is one thing; finding a way to finance that accommodation is a totally different matter. The cost of adding a room or wider hallways can be expensive, especially when other hard-earned available dollars have already been spent on another project or emergency. Typically, homeowners dip back into the value of their residence via a home equity loan to perform the remodel. However, some low- and moderate-income borrowers are not able to come up with the required cash or eke out any more equity for still another expenditure. Others don't have the income to qualify for a home equity loan. Now companies like Fannie Mae, the same company backing the Home Keeper Reverse Mortgage, are helping families with aging parents and others with disabilities not only to finance the remodel, but also to help individuals qualify for a home purchase of their own. The HomeChoice program provides both options— two wrinkles that could make a difference and solve stressful situations.

"Older persons, or those with disabilities, do often have some income, and there are finally some programs that help tailor those incomes into owning a place to live," said Paul Johnson, who has developed a special niche for the loans at Washington Mutual Bank. "This is an area that we can really develop and I think the HomeChoice program has begun to take that step."

On the remodel side, the retrofitting mortgage helps individuals stay in their homes—or shift to a family member's home—rather than move to an institutional setting. This option combines a conventional first mortgage loan with a specialized second mortgage, often at a lower-than-market interest rate.

Pilot Homesharing Programs Supplement Income

They are not your average landlords. They take in all sorts of renters, usually only one at a time. But don't expect them all to be sitting around kitchen table waiting to serve you lemonade.

Marcie Whatley, 88, is one of the oldest and one of the most independent members of a Senior Services Homesharing program sponsored by United Way in several pilot regions of the country. Like many retirees, she participates primarily for extra help with monthly expenses, plus the occasional ride to the store or help in the yard. It usually takes several weeks to solidify a compatible match, but sometimes the process is very fast. It also has been a lifesaver for older people who really want to stay in their home—or retain a feel of home in another's residence. In Marcie's case, for example, it took only one interview to determine some very clear preferences: She enjoys intellectually stimulating conversations, free thinkers, and people who spend little time in her kitchen. Her first tenant lasted only six months.

Homesharing is an intergenerational program. In the pilot programs now being tested, one person in the match must be 55 years of age or older. All parties must undergo a background check, and home seekers must provide three long-term references. The Seattle program was started 20 years ago and currently has 65 matches in place with a variety of combinations.

"You know, I don't even ask for references anymore," Marcie said. "Nobody is going to say that they cheat or steal. Besides, I like to solve the world's problems."

The amount of rent charged is up to the homeowner, but the average renter usually pays about $350 to $375 per month. The tenant can reduce that amount by doing household chores, yard work, or running errands for $10 an hour. Not all of the landlords are seniors; some are first-time homebuyers providing shelter for folks 55 and older.

While retirees often need additional monthly income, young owners also need cash. With quality, affordable housing options continuing to be in high demand and short supply in many areas of the country, Homesharing makes a lot of sense.

Borrowing from Peter to Pay Paul

Home equity often is the primary asset for consumers. Sometimes, especially after the loss of a spouse, older folks are forced to sell and seek less expensive housing. Others who would rather gamble on the possibility of qualifying for a home equity loan are sometimes able to actually secure a low-rate home equity loan and bypass the fees of a reverse mortgage. It can happen when competition is fierce and lenders are especially eager to do business in specific neighborhoods with consumers who have a ton of equity in their homes. The low-documentation or no-documentation loans are typically reserved for consumers with obvious monthly incomes. But lenders are more focused on assets than income, and when the asset being leveraged is a single-family home or condominium, the risk of any lender losing money quickly becomes remote. Toss in the pent-up demand for homes in many areas, coupled with consistent (if not runaway) appreciation, and lenders chuckle over the possibility of taking a loss.

A reverse mortgage really can be viewed as a home equity loan without a payment. Both programs tap the built-up cash present in a primary residence. The conventional home equity loans will usually carry no origination fee and often the lender pays for the appraisal, if one is even required. Similar to a reverse mortgage line of credit, no interest is charged on the home equity loan until it is actually used. Most home equity loans do not grow over time as reverse mortgage lines of credit do; yet the up-front fees on the reverse mortgage are far greater.

A borrowing method that has been utilized in the past, and accelerated during the tech wreck stock market bomb at the turn of the century, is obtaining a loan before the flow of income dramatically declines. For example, some high techsters would refinance their homes, or take out huge lines of credit, knowing full well that they were going to have a job 60 days down the road. They qualified during the time they were gainfully employed, knowing that if times really got tough, they could make monthly payments on their mortgage from their home equity line. In essence, they were borrowing from Peter to pay Paul. It is not a genuine way of doing business, but it is done. Ironically, some lenders don't really care about job status as long as they receive their payments every month.

The dilemma quickly surfaces when a borrower is close to maxing out his or her line of credit and bills continue to be greater than income. Adding to the credit line is possible, yet the borrower would simply be digging a bigger hole. By the time the line of credit's ceiling has been reached, it's usually too late to do anything else but sell the home. There would be no hope for a reverse mortgage at this point because the borrower had spent too much of the equity.

If you are a senior and considering a conventional line of credit yet do not have enough income to make the monthly payment on the loan and live comfortably at the same time, line of credit may not be for you. If you do decide to proceed, make sure you have some sort of exit strategy—perhaps selling the home in five years and buying down. You could find yourself with no money, no place to go, and a fat mortgage payment.

Another Way to Approach Property Taxes

If you are considering a reverse mortgage mainly as a way to pay property taxes, check with the county or local senior center about property tax reductions and deferrals. Most states have done a decent job of providing the individual county assessors the ability to reduce or defer property taxes for senior citizens and disabled persons. The amount reduced or deferred is made up when the senior eventually sells the house. These programs usually exempt eligible taxpayers from all excess levies and may exempt a portion of regular levies on a primary residence or a parcel of land up to a designated size. Common excess levies are approved by the voters and typically include school construction bonds and maintenance of operation levies.

Income limits and age minimums vary, but let's consider a typical situation in some states. Typically, for a reduced tax, you must be 61 years of age on December 31 of the year of application or unable to work due to a physical disability. In addition, your household income must be $28,000 or less in the year before application. For a deferral of property taxes, you must be 60 years of age with a gross household income of less than $34,000. All sources of income must be reported for yourself, your spouse, and all cotenants.

Hundreds of counties now have their own Internet home page, and most now have a common-form address to ascertain assessed values, maps, ordinances, covenants, and countless consumer tips. In some counties, consumers only need a street address to access a variety of information about the property, including information collected by the county assessor's office, a history of sales, and how-to information about tax deferrals and reductions.

Local Reverse Mortgages from the Community

Many jurisdictions have their version of Senior Home Services, a home repair and remodeling service that allows seniors to use funds only on their primary residence. These funds do not require payment until the senior moves out of the home. Some of these loans have a low fee or no fee at all. The homeowner typically receives the cash in a lump-sum payment, and interest accrues on the amount until it is repaid. Local senior centers, libraries, and housing agencies are often a good place to start a search for these loans, sometimes referred to as deferred payment loans. There usually are income and age guidelines, and some loans are only available in urban areas. Loans sometimes can be forgiven if a home-owner remains in the house for a specific amount of time. If you need extra cash only for a home repair, it's a good idea to ask around for deferred payment loans at the senior center.

What about Supplemental Security Income?

According to AARP, many citizens ages 65 and older who are eligible for monthly cash benefits from Supplemental Security Income (SSI) are not getting them. Again, income ceilings change regularly, but let's try an example. To qualify for Supplemental Security Income in 2003, your liquid resources (cash and savings) had to be less than $2,000 ($3,000 for a couple). Certain resources, such as a home, a small burial fund, or one car, usually do not count. Income ceilings were capped at a monthly amount of $572 ($849 for a couple). If you have a job, those incomes can vary.

Taking the Stock Pledge

If you still owe money on your mortgage and your goal is to halt monthly payments and funnel the cash elsewhere, stock brokerages and other financial firms offer borrowers the chance to pledge stock as col-lateral, thereby borrowing up to 100 percent of the purchase price or current value of the home without cashing the stock. Typically, the bor-rower must pledge in stock or other securities at least 30 percent of the mortgage amount into a separate account. Since all securities fluctuate, the securities pledged also must have cushioned market value of 130 percent of the pledged amount.

This program looks great—as long as the stock holds its value. (It's not unlike trading securities on margin, although few consumers clearly understand the margin process). If, for instance, you pledge Microsoft stock and the software company's share value plummets, you will need to add to the pledge account. And if you default on your loan, the securities in the pledge account could be cashed to cure the debt. You would then also be liable for capital gains tax ramifications on the sale of the stock.

If you choose any alternative mortgage program that you don't fully understand, seek clarity from the loan officer or outside source (attorney, escrow officer, title officer) before signing any binding agreement.

In the next two chapters, we will explore the unexpected, momentous role reverse mortgages will play for older homeowners. Millions wish to stay in their homes as long as possible, and health care, coupled with home modification, are critical to granting those wishes.

CHAPTER 7

If one considered life as a simple loan, one would perhaps be less exacting.
We possess actually nothing; everything goes through us.
—EUGÈNE DELACROIX

Aging in Place . . . and Funding Health Care

The Prime Target for Reverse Mortgage Money

The familiar theme, "you can pay me now, or you can pay me later," introduced earlier in this book certainly is present in the financial and physical aspects of aging in place.

This chapter will address the underestimated primary need of reverse mortgages—the health care component of aging in place—especially critical for the reverse mortgage–age qualified GI Generation. Most members of this group did not have any form of long-term care insurance and are paying later to balance those costs along with groceries, transportation, and property taxes. For many of them, these costs are a threat to their retirement years. Reverse mortgages are often the only solution. And if younger generations pay now and save for retirement and/or invest in long-term care insurance, part of the huge burden of health care costs would be lifted down the road and the options for their reverse mortgage money would increase. (A sampling of the variety of uses can be found in Chapter 4.) In the next chapter, we'll discuss the physical component of aging in place and how reverse mortgages can fund the home modifications needed to stay in the home. We'll also examine the amenities younger generations deem important for their eventual retirement home.

Now, repeat after me: "Seniors do not care for nursing homes." In fact, they'll do just about everything they can to stay out of them as long as possible. An AARP bulletin noted that the state of Indiana once had 15,000 empty nursing home beds, yet older Hoosiers preferred to be on a 30,000-person waiting list for home and community care services.[1] The example returns the phrase "don't go there" to its original meaning. In a nutshell, long-term care threatens to bankrupt Medicaid and the states that pay for it. The best hope for a cure lies in cutting down on the need for institutional care. The least expensive, most acceptable alternative is simply keeping seniors in their homes as long as possible—commonly known as aging in place.

My father, who died several years ago from Parkinson's Disease, would have much preferred watching Notre Dame battle Southern California from the comfort of his own den on a football Saturday where he could shuffle to his favorite bathroom in his favorite bathrobe and slippers without having to worry about how he looked in the hallway. He certainly would have taken my mother's famous chicken and a cold beer from the kitchen refrigerator over a chance to eat institutional food in a cheerless

---

[1] Barbara Basler, "Suing to Get Out in the World," *AARP Bulletin,* June 2004.

cafeteria at an hour that interrupted college football. We simply did not work fast enough to get the house, and my mom, ready for dad's needs.

Perhaps the first major event to focus on reverse mortgages as the prime funding source for aging in place was mentioned in the Introduction of this book—the Use Your Home to Stay at Home program initiated by the National Council on the Aging (NCOA) and commissioned by the Centers for Medicare and Medicaid Services (CMS) and the Robert Wood Johnson Foundation. The CMS grant totaled $295,000; The Robert Wood Johnson Foundation grant totaled $99,900. Dr. Barbara Stucki, PhD, a Bend, Oregon, researcher and consultant, was the project manager and lead author of the program's primary study, the *National Blueprint for Increasing the Use of Reverse Mortgages for Long-Term Care.* The goal was to begin work toward a public-private partnership to increase the use of reverse mortgages to help pay for long-term care. The project combined discussions with analysts, research, and consumer surveys to identify cost-effective government interventions and other incentives that can facilitate the use of reverse mortgages. Stucki, a former senior policy analyst for the American Council of Life Insurance and an AARP employee, found that approximately 13.2 million of the nearly 28 million households with owners age 62 and older in the United States are good candidates for reverse mortgages.

"I really didn't know if I would find a pony until I started digging," Stucki said. "I found a pony, and it was a lot bigger than I thought. These good candidates could get on average $72,128 on a reverse mortgage. That was the key for me. It showed there was a significant chunk of change for millions of households. While some homeowners have pulled equity out of their homes to make improvements as they've aged, the concept of home equity to pay for health care is relatively new.

Using reverse mortgages for many can mean the difference between staying at home or going to a nursing home."

Of the 13.2 million, about 5.2 million are either already receiving Medicaid or are at financial risk of needing Medicaid if they were faced with paying the high cost of long-term care at home, Stucki reported. This group would be able to get $309 billion from reverse mortgages that could help pay for long-term care. In 2000, the nation spent $123 billion a year on long-term care for those age 65 and older, with the amount likely to double in the next 30 years, according to NCOA. Nearly half of those expenses are paid out of pocket by individuals, and only 3 percent are paid by private insurance. Government health programs pay the remainder.

Even in 2000, the number of Americans over 55—comprised mostly of the GIs and Silents—constituted more than a quarter of the population. By 2020, when the Baby Boomers reach 65, that percentage reaches nearly one-third. By 2050, it's over 40 percent. (See Figure 7.1.) This is a major and growing market for reverse mortgages, not only in the future, but also now. If the recent numbers are any indication, the number of reverse

Figure 7.1 U.S. Population by Age, 2000–2020					
Age	**2000**	**2005**	**2010**	**2015**	**2020**
Total Population	275,306	287,716	299,862	312,268	324,927
55 and over	58,836	66,060	75,!45	85,878	95,841
65 and over	34,835	36,370	39,715	45,959	53,733
85 and over	4,312	4,968	5,786	6,396	6,763

Source: U.S. Bureau of the Census, Middle Series Projections

mortgages made each year should continue to double the previous year's volume for the foreseeable future. It's simply a matter of numbers. For example, during the partial federal fiscal year of October 1, 2003, to May 31, 2004, the U.S. Department of Housing and Urban Development (HUD) had insured a record 23,682 Home Equity Conversion Mortgages (HECMs), the country's most popular reverse mortgage loan. In the 2002 to 2003 period, HUD had insured 10,455 HECMs, an increase of 127 percent year-over-year. Since the HECM program began in 1990, HUD has insured approximately 104,990 HECMs. Nearly two-thirds of those loans—62,619—have been originated since 2000.

Like all projections, reverse mortgages to age in place depend on a lot of ifs. While the U.S. Bureau of the Census numbers appear to be reasonable and reliable, the market projection will be affected not only by demographics, but also by interest rates, prices, and alternative choices. The reliability of any projection over time will be subject to prevailing conditions. That said, the underlying base of demand for a reverse mortgage product simply to age in place—established by the structure of the population—is very strong. (See Figure 7.2.)

Figure 7.2 Benefits and Challenges of Linking Reverse Mortgages with Long-Term Care

- **Huge, unmet need for help to age in place that only reverse mortgages can finance**
- **Demand-driven approach**
- **Huge market potential**
- **Education and collaboration required**

Source: National Council on Aging
Kenning Group

"The reverse mortgage may not be the silver bullet everyone is looking for but it certainly is part of the pie," said Don Redfoot, AARP senior policy advisor. "They will be very useful to people who are 'self-insuring,' using the funds to supplement the services they already will be receiving with other quality care. They also will be used to make the home modifications that will be needed for people to be more comfortable at home for a longer period of time. And that's important. . . . For an older person, a home represents their life story."

AARP, formerly known as the American Association of Retired Persons, is a nonprofit membership organization that addresses the needs and interests of persons 50 and older. (See Figure 7.3.) The group was founded in 1958 by a retired California educator, Dr. Ethel Percy Andrus, and represents more than 35 million members. About half of its members are working, either full- or part-time. Nearly a third of its members are under the age of 60. Those ages 60 to 74 comprise 46 percent of membership, while 21 percent are age 75 and older. The organization, which estimates about half of all U.S. homeowners 65 or

---

Figure 7.3 Problem—Mismatch between What Seniors Want and What They Can Get

- Over 90 percent of elders want to continue to live at home for as long as possible.
- The typical 75-year-old has three chronic conditions and takes on average 4.5 medications.
- Only one-third of government spending on long-term care for seniors funds home care.

Source: National Council on Aging
Kenning Group

older have lived in their houses for 25 years or more, has long been opposed to seniors taking out reverse mortgages solely to purchase long-term care insurance policies—especially if all of the reverse proceeds were used for insurance premiums. Obviously, the older the person, the more expensive the policy, as you will see in the section to follow.

"People who purchase long-term care insurance and those that take out a reverse mortgage are very different segments of the population," Redfoot said. "Reverse mortgages can be a very expensive proposition for people using the funds only for insurance products. Most of the time, they would be better served by borrowing on other terms."

Stucki contends that reverse mortgages could play an important role in helping more seniors—affluent, modest, poor—to pay for services and improvements in their homes, such as adding bathroom grab bars, which would help to keep them accident-free and healthy.

"Ultimately, it's really got nothing to do with money," Stucki said. "It's keeping individuals from working themselves into an early grave trying to take care of dad. People can look at their homes as an insurance policy. Let's turn to it to get the help we need. And that help can mean everything . . . whether it's part-time aid to come for a few hours a day just to be around so mom isn't so dependent on the kids. That is the message. Look at what's possible with this home."

A U.S. Bureau of the Census report estimated that caregivers of older family members or friends can spend approximately $20,000 out of their own pockets over a four-year period to help offset an elder's care costs. Most of the time, these adult children (nieces, nephews, grandchildren) have children of their own and lose income for taking time away from their primary jobs. An AARP study found that most 45- to 55-year-old Americans are not overly stressed during their actual caregiving time and received satisfaction in providing care for loved ones. However, care helpers, especially those with lower incomes, eventually tended to struggle, and the continual juggling of caregiving, children, and employment began to raise stress levels.[2]

A 2004 survey funded by the MetLife Foundation estimated there were 44.4 million caregivers who provide unpaid care to another adult. Almost six in ten of these caregivers (59 percent) either work or have worked while providing care. Approximately 62 percent had to make some adjustments to their work life, from reporting late to work to giving up work entirely—surprising not only their employers but also the federal government.[3]

The number of men caregivers was surprisingly high, the study revealed. Nearly four in ten caregivers (39 percent) were men, and 60 percent of them were working full-time. Caregivers are defined as people age 18 and older that help another person age 18 and older with at least one of 13 tasks that caregivers commonly do on an unpaid basis. Nearly eight in ten people who need care are age 50 or older (79 percent). Caregivers say that older care recipients' (ages 50+) main problems are aging (15 percent), and their main health problems are heart disease, cancer, diabetes, Alzheimer's Disease, or other mental confusion. Caregivers say that younger recipients' (ages 18 to 49) main problems are mental illness and depression (23 percent).

[2] *In the Middle: A Report on Multicultural Boomers Coping With Family and Aging Issues,* AARP.
[3] *Care-giving in the U.S,* AARP, The National Alliance for Care-giving, MetLife Foundation.

Some key highlights of the MetLife Foundation report follow:

- The value of family caregiving to society is estimated at $257 billion annually.

- A typical caregiver is female, 46 years old, married, has some college experience, and provides care to a woman age 50 or older.

- More than eight in ten caregivers (83 percent) say they assist relatives.

- A typical care recipient is female, widowed.

- The average age of care recipients ages 50+ is 75 years.

- Among caregivers who are caring for someone other than a spouse, the most burdened caregivers say they make an average monthly financial contribution of $437.

- Almost one in five caregivers (17 percent) say they provide 40 or more hours of care per week.

Medicaid, the federal and state health care program for low-income Americans, covers almost half of the nation's nursing home costs. To qualify for Medicaid benefits, an individual's income and assets cannot be above a certain level (the financial criteria differ in each state). Many people who receive Medicaid assistance were in a low-income bracket when they entered a nursing home. Other people qualify for Medicaid long-term benefits once they have spent down their savings—that is, they pay for expenses out-of-pocket until their savings are depleted. In a nutshell, most health industry observers believe long-term care threatens to bankrupt Medicaid and the states that pay for it. The best hope for a cure lies in cutting down on the need for institutional care. Nursing home costs can reach $350 a day per person—about $130,000 a year. In a 2003 report, the U.S. Justice Department's Civil Rights Division estimated that for the price of two beds in a San Francisco nursing home for one year, five persons could be served in a local apartment complex with full support.[4]

The majority of people who cannot perform everyday tasks want to stay in their own homes as long as possible with necessary services supplied by family members or in-home agencies. Activities of daily living (ADLs) are the everyday activities involved in personal care, such as feeding, dressing, bathing, moving from a bed to a chair (also called transferring), toileting, and walking. Physical or mental disabilities can restrict a person's ability to perform personal ADLs. These ADLs are commonly used in the health care and professional caregiving world to describe a person's ability to care for himself or herself. Often the ability or inability to perform specific ADLs is used as qualifying criteria for special services or programs.

A key consideration for people who are choosing a long-term care insurance policy is how reduced physical functioning is measured according to the policy. In many cases long-term policies will provide assistance when the consumer needs help with at least two ADLs. According to the Citizens for Long Term Care, the amount of money available to families for in-home care has actually decreased in recent years, despite Medicaid waivers in some states. In an attempt to remedy the in-home funding, HUD and private funders are working on an experimental program in a few states in which Medicare cash payments are given to qualified disabled citizens who may use the money to pay for in-home caregiving services.

[4] Barbara Basler, "Suing to Get Out in the World," *AARP Bulletin,* June 2004.

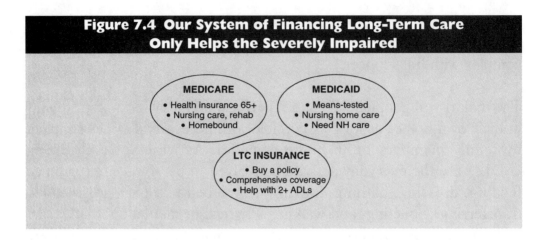

Figure 7.4 Our System of Financing Long-Term Care Only Helps the Severely Impaired

Seniors who don't have long-term insurance or can't afford to pay costs out-of-pocket often qualify for Medicaid, which foots the bill for certain long-term care expenses. But Medicaid generally only covers care at nursing home facilities. Reverse mortgages offer an opportunity to keep elders in their home longer and thereby reduce Medicaid's responsibility for long-term care costs, which are expected to double in the next 30 years. (See Figure 7.4 and Figure 7.5.)

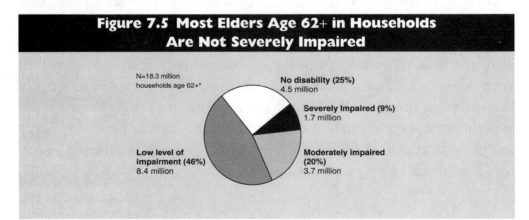

Figure 7.5 Most Elders Age 62+ in Households Are Not Severely Impaired

"A great number of Baby Boomers think that Medicare pays for long-term care, but it doesn't," said William D. Novelli, AARP's chief executive officer. "They're in for a bit of a surprise there. A lot of them think, 'well, I'll just spend down what money I have and Medicare will put me in a nursing home.' Well, that's hardly a good idea. They can look at long-term care insurance and they can take better care of their health. They can stay independent longer by engaging in physical activity, by quitting smoking, by watching their diets. So there are a whole number of things that Boomers can do and even older people . . ."

The home is an exempt asset for purposes of calculating Medicaid eligibility, which means a person who needs nursing home services and who has no other significant source of revenue is likely to qualify for Medicaid services without the need to reduce the value of that asset. On the other hand, because many home and community services are not covered by Medicaid, a low-income older person who is trying to remain at home for some period of time prior to a nursing home admission could use cash generated from a reverse mortgage to buy that time. There are a variety of other complex issues related to the interplay of Medicaid eligibility and reverse mortgages.

Steven A. Moses, president of the Seattle-based Center for Long-Term Care Financing, is obviously of proponent of long-term care insurance policies. He believes, however, that the average family waits too long to discover how inadequate nursing home care can be. Once an insurable health care event takes place, it's too late to buy long-term care insurance that would cover extra professional assistance and care in the nursing home.

"You can't buy fire insurance when the house is up in flames," Moses said.

What usually happens to Mom and Dad is the least preferred option, according to Moses. Most of the time the family depends upon Social Security and Medicare, only to discover any benefits are short-term. Finally, they end up considering Medicaid, a government program that does pay for custodial nursing home care for as long as needed.

"Medicaid is a means-tested, public assisted program," Moses said. "It is welfare. It has a dismal reputation for problems associated with access, quality, low reimbursement, discrimination, and institutional bias. Nevertheless, because of its generous and elastic eligibility rules, Medicaid has become the primary third-party payer for long-term care in the United States.

"It's the path of least resistence for people who did not save or insure for long-term care. But if you end up on Medicaid, you'll most certainly end up in an underfinanced nursing home that is struggling to provide low-cost care of uncertain quality."

For years, Moses has floated the controversial idea of eliminating home value from the Medicaid component. That way, consumers would either have to buy long-term care insurance policies or spend home equity (via a reverse mortgage) before qualifying for Medicaid.

"It would go a long way to solving the health care mess in this country," Moses said. "It would improve the quality of care, reduce the enormous amount of money the government pays to health care while retaining Medicaid for the poor."

A Brief Look at Long-Term Care Insurance

The debate over long-term care insurance and how to pay of it will continue for decades. As mentioned earlier, AARP is not eager to see seniors take out a reverse mortgage for the sole purpose of purchasing a long-term care policy. But a reverse mortgage borrower who would use at least a portion of those funds to offset the cost of a long-term care policy could be well served. In the classic "You can pay me now or you can pay me later," children have the option of helping to pay for the folks' expensive insurance premiums now (and perhaps guarding their inheritance) or waiting to liquidate their inheritance, if any, to help subsidize nursing home care. The same goes for Baby Boomers. Pay for long-term care now via insurance polices or gamble down the road? If care is needed when they are old and gray and no private insurance is in place, it's time to pay out of your pocket.

So, who actually needs long-term care insurance? The main reason people buy private insurance is to avoid being financially wiped out by long-term care costs. So, long-term care insurance is really a gamble on your health. (Why do you think they call it insurance?) The bet can pay off, and there is also a chance that you'll pay premiums year after year and never need the coverage. Agencies differ on the chances of consumers ending up in a nursing home or needing in-home care. It's a big, fat catch-22. If you don't have coverage, you could blow your life savings on two years in a nursing home. If you do have it, you could stretch your budget to make the payments on the premiums and then never need the coverage. However, if you purchase long-term insurance and you eventually require the coverage, you will have better, quality care and a greater chance of leaving your assets to your estate, while easing the burden on Medicare and Medicaid. (See Figure 7.6.)

Figure 7.6

Long-Term Care Insurance Opportunities:

Long-term care insurance gives you financial protection against the cost of long-term care services.

It helps give you more control and choices over your long-term care coverage. You are able to choose the type of services and customize your care based upon your financial and social needs.

You won't have to use your savings or life insurance to pay for your health care needs. This will allow you to leave money or other items to your heirs (family and friends).

The Federal Long-Term Care Insurance Program offers long-term care insurance at a group rate for Federal and U.S. Postal Service employees and annuitants, members and retired members of the Uniformed Services.

Your family or friends won't have to worry about how you will get or pay for your long-term care.

Long-Term Care Insurance Requirements/Limits:

If you don't buy a long-term care insurance policy from a reliable insurance company, you might not get the coverage you need in the future.

Make sure you buy the right long-term care insurance policy that is right for you. Some policies offer more coverage than other polices. You may have to pay additional long-term care costs. Read the policy carefully to see what is and what isn't covered.

Some people might not be able to get a long-term care insurance policy because they have a pre-existing condition. A pre-existing condition is a health problem you have before getting a new insurance policy.

Long-term care insurance policies can be expensive. You might not be able to continue to pay the monthly premium. Remember, it is better to buy a long-term care insurance policy at a younger age when premiums are lower. If this is done, a periodic review is advised to make sure your policy covers your current and future long-term care needs.

Generally, if you buy a long-term care insurance policy without a nonforfeiture benefit and don't use it, you won't get your money back for the policy.

Source: Centers for Medicare & Medicaid Services

According to the United Seniors Health Cooperative, a nonprofit organization based in Washington DC, people should consider long-term care insurance only when they have at least $75,000 in assets (excluding home and car), an annual retirement income of at least $35,000 (depending on costs in the state where you live), the ability to pay premiums without making any lifestyle changes, and the ability to afford the policy even if premiums increase during your lifetime. These are only general rules of thumb. However, if you don't fall within these guidelines (AARP would argue that today's reverse mortgage borrowers do not), you would be better off letting your money earn interest, paying for care as the need arises, and relying on Medicaid if long-term care becomes necessary. However, remember if you do plan to rely on Medicaid, care will be minimal and probably not what you anticipated. Private long-term care would be a welcome supplement. Even if you do fit the above profile, be sure to consult a financial adviser, life or health insurance counselor, or an attorney about all your options.

Each long-term care policy has its own eligibility requirements, benefits, costs, and restrictions. Policies are not standardized, so the services covered by different companies vary greatly. Services generally covered include nursing home care (skilled, intermediate, and custodial); care in your own home and in adult day care centers, assisted living facilities, personal care homes, and hospices; and care for people with cognitive disorders like Alzheimer's Disease. Services generally excluded include psychological disorders, such as anxiety or depression; alcohol or drug addiction; illness or injury caused by war; attempted suicide; or intentional, self-inflicted injuries.

Annual premiums for long-term care plans vary depending upon company, the comprehensiveness of the coverage, and the date the plan was purchased. Here are the approximate annual costs for long-term care insurance followed by some helpful hints.

Age at time of purchase	Cost Range Nursing home only	Cost Range Nursing Home and Home Care
55	$250 to $1,100	$300 to $1,500
65	$450 to $2,000	$600 to $2,600
75	$1,100 to $3,000	$1,170 to $5,000

Seek definition.   Make sure you understand exactly what kind of facilities the policy will cover before you buy it. There are no national standards on what counts as a long-term care facility. For example, an adult day care center or assisted living facility can vary widely from state to state and company to company. So if you buy a policy in one state and then retire to another state, there might not be facilities in your new state that match the definition in your policy.

Basing your benefits.   Even with private coverage, your health care needs will not be completely met because most policies do not pay for everything you require. However, it's best to gauge your choice of daily benefits on how much nursing homes in specific areas charge. Home care benefits are usually 50 percent of nursing home care benefits.

Along for the rider.   Life insurance companies also offer policies with long-term care riders on many whole life or universal life products. Some customers choose riders because they gain the security of knowing they have coverage for long-term care. However, check on how the rider handles the rising cost of care. Consumers may best be served with a separate and independent long-term care policy.

What about my bride? Most companies give a spousal discount only if you and your spouse purchase identical policies. But purchasing identical policies might not be a good idea, as women tend to live longer than men and are more likely to live alone in their later years, resulting in different long-term care needs.

Raising the ante. Often, insurance agents promise that there will be no rate hikes. However, make certain your policy clearly states your premiums will not be raised. Brochures might say the insurer won't raise your rates unless it raised them for your entire class, yet what constitutes your class?

U.S. citizens are living longer and, for the most part, healthier lives. The risk of needing nursing home care before age 75 is relatively low, and most people will not need nursing home care for longer than a year. Reverse mortgage funds would continue until the homeowner permanently—not temporarily—moves out of the house.

Aging in the Community Also Has Its Place

Patrick H. Hare, a Washington DC, author and land use and transportation planner specializing in accessory apartments, has referred to tradition suburban single-family homes as "Peter Pan" housing, designed for people who will never grow old. To be able to age in place in comfort in an older, single-family home, a person typically has to be able to go up and down stairs, do simple home maintenance, contract for major home maintenance, drive a car, and enjoy living alone. Most of us will lose one or more of those physical abilities before we die, and probably few of us ever really like living alone. Disabilities typically mean home modifications.[5]

[5] Patrick Hare, *Frail Elders and the Suburbs,* 1992.

A 2003 AARP study revealed that while seniors and Baby Boomers say they are very optimistic about their future living conditions, a substantial number may have unrealistic expectations and also don't know if their community offers the services they deem important. The purpose of the study was to examine people's expectations regarding their home, the community in which they live, and the services that are now available within their community that could help them remain independent, comfortable, and safe as they grow older. While it is encouraging that people 50+ have an optimistic view of the future, there may yet be cause for concern.

"The probability of being poor at some point in old age remains very high, and many people underestimate the costs associated with aging," said Tony Copeland, AARP counselor. "Respondents' views may also reflect unrealistic expectations about their physical abilities as they grow older."

Copeland's comments reflect the fact that while almost all respondents in the AARP report[6] want to stay in their home for the rest of their lives, many do not envision making changes to their home unless a specific need arises. Curiously, a previous AARP housing survey showed that nearly 25 percent of Americans age 45+ say they or someone they live with will have trouble maneuvering around their home in the coming years.

"Some of the questions mean different things to different people," Copeland said. "For example, 'in their home' may be taken to mean the home they are presently in or the home they see themselves living in at some future date. The difference can be subtle but very significant."

[6] *These Four Walls . . . Americans 45+ Talk About Home and Community*, AARP.

The majority of respondents considered themselves to be planners and respected the importance of planning for the future. Significantly fewer, however, had given a great deal of thought to the home features or community characteristics they will need in their later years, the study revealed.

"There's a real need to educate the 50+ population about the availability of services in their community—and the home features now available— that can help them remain independent as they age," Copeland said. "That way, when the need arises, they'll know where to turn."

Most respondents acknowledge and value home features that can help to ensure they have a safe and comfortable home environment. However, while they recognize the value of these features, many lack them in their current homes. Gopal Ahluwalia, the research specialist from the National Association of Home Builder's (NAHB) economics department, noted that the amenity gaps (features seniors say they want that developers are not providing) common to both the NAHB and AARP studies are grocery stores and drug stores within a planned community. Other wants and needs that are not being met include sidewalks, better transportation, and home meal service.

"Builders have done a good job in some areas in providing what the 50-plus market wants—including wider roads, grab bars in hallways and bathrooms and a master suite on the main floor," Ahluwalia said. "But we need to continually take into consideration more services in our planning. It's not feasible to have drug stores, grocery stores, hospitals in every neighborhood but better public and private transportation would go a long way to solving this."

One More Move Before the Reverse House

While the reverse mortgage business today typically is centered on GI Generation homeowners living in the same family home they've occupied for years, the Silent Generation and Baby Boomers could easily have one more house move in them before settling into their eventual retirement home. Some of the later two groups still have children at home and college tuitions, but they are definitely open to discussing the possibilities of one more jump. However, the huge Boomer group—and many Silents—has again confounded analysts with its actions. Instead of coming into their final home heavily leveraged, the majority of them, more than 60 percent, would prefer to pay cash—a huge step toward reverse mortgage potential. And, they are not buying down. More than half of buyers in age-qualified, age-targeted, and independent living communities are spending the same or more on homes approximately the same size as the ones they now own.[7]

"Probably the most striking aspect of the initial results of this study is that many home buyers aged 50 and older are not simply cashing out the equity they built up in the home they raised their children in and downsizing into a less expensive house or apartment," said Jack L. Haynes, executive vice president of the National Builder Division at Countrywide Home Loans, based in Plano, Texas. "Baby boomers continue to rewrite the rules of consumer behavior at every stage of life, and home builders and mortgage lenders need to be prepared to meet their changing demands."

An even higher number are paying with cash or with high down payments of 30 percent or more. Builders noted that the majority of

---

[7] *2003 Builder Survey,* National Association of Home Builders, Countrywide Home Loans.

buyers use equity in their current home and are willing to pay extra for high-tech options and upgrades in their homes. In addition to examining the amenities, features, and services that builders are planning and incorporating into communities designed for the 50+ demographic, the study examines where seniors are relocating, how much they are spending on homes, what type of financing they are using, builders' perceptions about buyers' motivations for moving, and regional trends.

"This is absolutely something we've never seen before," Haynes said. "It's not about grab bars and raised toilet seats. It's about luxury and longevity factors after 50 that are totally new."

It's about the new senior Boomer homes—and the appliances and accessories that come with them. There will be overstuffed chairs that lift and recline, pedestal washers and dryers that feature angled baskets and enlarged doors, refrigerators with large, pull-out bottom freezers, and stovetop ranges that feature front controls for shorter folks and others in wheelchairs.

"Successful builders are offering yard service, high-speed Internet access, universal design features, and social activities to attract 50 and older customers," said Kent Conine, a home and apartment builder from Dallas. "This study will help builders targeting this burgeoning market understand what older Americans want in their dream home and how they can afford it."

Two of the other surprises found in the survey were the number of senior Boomers who indicated wired homes ranked very important on their want list, as well as the desire for a single-story home with a large master bedroom. According to the NAHB, the demand by 50+ buyers for one-story, single-family homes has risen from 17 percent in 1970 to 75 percent in 2003.

"We knew that technology in the home was important to the 45- to 50-year old buyer, but we did not anticipate how many people over 55 really wanted it enough to pay for it," Ahluwalia, said. "Previously reports indicated some of this group did not want to deal with technology but now we see a majority of them are as comfortable around a computer as a 15-year-old."

"The move to a one-story home was very clear, but there was absolutely no demand for homes to become smaller," Ahluwalia said. "In each of our past five surveys, the size of the home requested by these buyers continued to be about the size of their previous home. Depending upon where these buyers were from, we heard they wanted us to continue building homes between 1,600 square feet and 2,400 square feet. There was no 'smaller, smaller, smaller.' We didn't think this was possible."

Mark Goldstein, co-founder of the San Ramon, California–based Impact Presentations Group, is a specialist in the demographic, lifestyle, and psychographic trends of the senior housing market. He continues to remind professionals in the mortgage and housing industry who serve the 50+ markets that the huge Boomer group has revamped every life stage it has entered—and retirement is next.

"Not only will this group re-invent retirement," Goldstein said, "but it also will not stand for hype. The style of marketing must be educational or they won't be buying.

Building Beyond Boomers

Among the top motivating factors for moving to an independent living, age-restricted, or age-targeted community are the following:

■ Builders reported that nearly half of buyers indicated a desire to be closer to children, grandchildren, and family.

■ More than half of the builders in the 50+ market were building single-family, detached homes in 2002. Seventy-five percent of single-family homes for seniors started by builders during 2002 were one story.

■ About half of builders built 50+ senior communities in close-in suburbs in 2002. One-fourth built in outer suburbs, 15 percent in central cities, and 11 percent in rural areas.

■ Builders noted that customers prefer homes that promote safety and a sense of security. Strategically placed streetlights and home security systems were included in more than half of the homes built.

■ Builders have responded to the fact that today's seniors are increasingly technologically savvy. Nearly 70 percent of them built communities with high-speed Internet service, while many included structured wiring and intercom or entrance phones.

■ Convenience is a major plus for senior buyers. More than three-quarters of the builders surveyed built 50+ communities in close proximity to shopping centers, while many built homes close to churches or medical facilities.

"Most reinventions have begun too late," Goldstein said. "I think the health care industry has found this out. Health care saw the demographic coming but it didn't get what actually drove the people in the demographic. It is the psychographics, or the mental and emotional connections. The strategy for change must come before an industry finds out that things are not going right. It must come when business couldn't be better."

In the next chapter, we will consider some of the basic home construction projects that reverse mortgage dollars would fund. These projects, when completed with universal design concepts in mind, would enable all generations—present and future—to age in place.

CHAPTER 8

I don't do glitz. I do reverse chic.
—EILEEN KRUTCHIK

Reverse Mortgage Cash for Modification

The Changes That Will Allow All Ages to Stay at Home

Finding the perfect house is a dream we all share. Having that house remain perfect—or even functional—for our specific needs during the later part of our lives is a totally new ballgame. Many older Americans are now finding their once perfect house that sheltered their babies no longer is perfect for them after the kids are gone or when they reach retirement. Imperfect yet mostly paid off, perhaps owned free and clear of any major debt. . . . This is, and will continue to be, the name of the housing challenge for senior homeowners.

Do you sell, pay the closing costs on the house and the real estate commission, and move to a different neighborhood, church, grocery store, and senior center? Or, do you stay in the home and remain in the familiar environment you've enjoyed for years? If you decided to stay—and an overwhelming number of elders would prefer to stay put—what will you do to make it work? Or more pragmatically for GI Generation make-doers, what changes offer the best potential for making it comfortable for you? While many elders couldn't care less about their return on their investment to age in place, others are more than curious. They would like to see any cash spent now returned later in an increased value for the home. That way, their children would stand a better chance of recovering the reverse mortgage funds spent for the repairs and improvements.

In the previous chapter, we discussed why a reverse mortgage provided one of the only financial keys to the health care component, enabling elderly homeowners to stay in their homes as long as possible. In this chapter, we will explore how reverse mortgages would support the needed funding for the physical part of the puzzle—home modification. We will begin by defining some of the basics behind home modification and how those alterations can serve all generations over time if done with stylish, attractive, universal design concepts in mind. We'll consider some fairly significant remodeling projects—beyond the basic home modifications—with planning and renovation ideas followed by cost estimates of the more popular and necessary aging-in-place jobs, as well as tips that could make your renovation as easy as possible, from professionals in the field. And in an attempt to help you get the best bang for your buck, we'll take a look at average returns nationally for typical improvements, as well as cost and return figures for specific projects in different areas of the country. That way, you'll get an idea what sort of return you could receive on your reverse mortgage money down the road should you choose to spend those dollars to be more comfortable in your home today. Again, a growing number of elders will simply have no other funds to tap.

As we've mentioned several times in this book, national surveys consistently reveal a strong preference of persons older than 65 to remain in their homes—to age in place. In nearly 10 years of studies before 2000, greater than 80 percent of respondents expressed this preference. Since then, AARP reports the number has reached 90 percent—but accommodating that preference and those numbers have been another matter. Nearly a quarter of Americans ages 45 or older say they or someone they live with will have trouble maneuvering around their home in the coming years. In addition, fewer than 10 percent of the nation's 100 million housing units have features to make them universally accessible.[1]

Households of all ages have roots in their communities and strong emotional ties to their homes. Few people want to move solely because their house no longer fits their needs. The problems faced by older individuals are compounded by the fact that they live in the oldest housing stock. These homes may have deferred maintenance, with roof or plumbing leaks, heating deficiencies, or dangerous electrical problems in addition to a lack of adequate lighting, railings, storage, and other accessibility concerns. Modification needs may get lost among many other pressing maintenance items, prolonging dangerous arrangements that may lead to falls and malnutrition or isolation within the home or the community.

Falls are a constant nightmare. According to the National Center for Injury Prevention and Control, falls are the leading cause of injury

---

[1] *In the Middle: A Report on Multicultural Boomers Coping With Family and Aging Issues,* AARP.

deaths among older adults and the most common cause of nonfatal injuries and hospital admissions for trauma. The Center for Disease Control and Prevention reported that in 2001 more than 1.6 million seniors were treated in emergency departments for fall-related injuries, 373,000 were hospitalized, and over 11,600 deaths were reported in people ages 65 and older. Several things can be done to reduce the risk of falls in the home. Experts report that one-half to two-thirds of all falls occur in or around the home. Common environmental fall hazards include lack of stair railings or grab bars, slippery surfaces and rugs, unstable furniture, and poor lighting. Other older homeowners, with neither the means to modify nor the money to move, will live constrained and unsafe lives because of their homes. Backers of home modifications, or home mods, believe that significant health care cost reductions are possible if home modifications become more common. These changes can help consumers to avoid injuries and reduce their use of medical services or institutional care. Susan Duncan, a housing consultant whose Bellevue, Washington–based company, Adaptations, helps families with accessibility and design questions, was instrumental in organizing the 2003 National Aging in Place Week. She said the keys to having all age groups grasp universal design is to highlight the latest features and remove some of the outdated terms in building and remodeling.

"The two most important terms we need to keep explaining and repeating are 'universal design' and 'visitability,' " Duncan said. "The terms we absolutely no longer want to use are the cutesy phrases like 'physically challenged.' And, if you are going to use 'disabled,' you always need to attach people to the term—such as a 'person with a disability' or the 'disabled population.' The language landscape has really changed with civil rights laws."

Representatives from regional departments on Aging and Disability Services have led the movement to eliminate the word "handicapped" from directional signs and even casual conversation. "Accessible" is now the acceptable term for easier access (a building is accessible; not handicapped parking).

"People who are older grew up with the word 'handicapped' and it became part of their culture," Duncan said. "But the Americans with Disabilities Act of 1990 started to change the landscape and how we identify people and places."

Duncan and other independent counselors are campaigning to make all homes—not just those hosting a party, meeting, or reunion—visitable. According to Concrete Change, a nonprofit, Decatur, Georgia–based company, the essentials for visiting—and for surviving in your house with a temporary disability—are simply to get in and out of the house and be able to use the bathroom. Steps at most entrances of a home stymie people who use wheelchairs or walkers or are impaired by stiffness, weakness, or balance problems. Wheelchair users often are stopped—by inches—from fitting through the bathroom door in a friend's or relative's home.

Recent trends have individuals returning home from the hospital with more acute conditions. Accessible, safer homes make it possible for some to leave rehabilitation or nursing settings sooner to homes that support their recovery and lessen additional injuries or secondary disabilities.

"When did we start making bathroom doors so tiny?" asked Susan Mack, the California-based occupational therapist and president of

Homes for Easy Living Universal Design Consultants in Murrieta, California. "I know friends in wheelchairs who simply will not attend holiday parties because they don't want to be lifted into the home. It's simply embarrassing for them. And, if they do attend, there's a 99.9 percent chance they won't drink anything because they know they'll never be able to get into the bathroom."

Home modifications (See Figure 8.1.) refer to adaptations to homes that can make it easier for someone to carry out daily activities, such as preparing meals, climbing stairs, bathing, as well as changes to the

Figure 8.1 Helping at Home: Basic Home Modifications

Activity	Common Home Modification
Using the bathroom	■ Install grab bars, shower seats or transfer benches ■ Place non-skid strips or decals in the tub or shower
Turning faucets or doorknobs	■ Install faucet or doorknob adapters
Getting in and out of the home and narrow doorways	■ Install permanent or portable ramps ■ Widen doorways or install swing-clear hinges
Climbing stairs	■ Install handrails on both sides for support ■ Install a stair glide ■ Increase lighting at the top and bottom of stairway

Source: National Resource Center for Supportive Housing and Home Modification

physical structure of a home to improve its overall safety and condition. These project designs have come a long way. They are custom, attractive amenities that no longer sing out "an old person lives here" and can also enhance the resale value of the home once the present homeowner must move to another place. These improvements and alternations can serve all ages, hence the name universal design.

Universal Design: More Than Equipment for Special Cases

Universal design, or UD, is not one amenity or concept. It is a building/remodeling philosophy that is being implemented in all regions of the country. The ideas are being tried and tested in many of today's new homes in an effort to capture and retain the huge Baby Boomer group as it seeks to move out of the traditional family home and into its next versatile, flexible shelter.

"I have heard someone refer to universal design as design features that are good for the least able of us and are also good for the best and rest of us," said Tracy Lux of Trace Marketing, a Sarasota, Florida–based company specializing in the mature market. "Consumers need to be educated so they don't see the features as handicap equipment but rather as an opportunity to age in place."

According to North Carolina State University's Center for Universal Design, UD is defined as "the design of products and environments to be usable by all people, to the greatest extent possible, without the need for adaptation or specialized design. The intent of universal design is to simplify life for everyone by making products, communications, and the built environment more usable by as many people as possible at little or no extra cost. Universal design benefits people of all ages and abilities."

Lux said many universal design features have become known as designs for easy living. Special-task lighting, well-placed ovens and microwaves, and elevated washers, dryers and dishwashers are among the changes being refined. Christine Price, aging specialist with Ohio State University and assistant professor of human development and family science in the College of Human Ecology, agrees with Lux. The true value of universal design is that it applies to everyone—not just consumers with physical limitations. According to Price, universal design is a movement that advocates all environments be not only accessible to people regardless of age, size, or physical ability but also that these features be attractive and appear seamless in the design of the home. For example, UD features include installing lever-style doorknobs and faucet handles, providing kitchen counters with different heights, placing electric outlets higher and light switches lower on walls, and creating at least one no-step entry into the home.

Why now? Why all the bother with a one-design-fits-all theory for living? First, GI Generation members not only need these changes now, but they are also expected to stay in a universal-design home longer plus save on medical costs. An AARP study compared seniors living in a UD house with seniors in traditional settings. The study found significant cost differences for health care—those in UD settings paid less than half the amount paid by those living in regular designs. The study pointed to savings by "undergoing less physical decline." For example, by providing at least one no-step entry to homes, the likelihood of falls and injuries is reduced and the possibility for safer exits during a fire or other emergency is increased. Other products, like the elevated dishwasher, can be therapeutic in helping to use muscles and maintain wellness. In addition, the Boomer group is the largest, healthiest, and wealthiest group ever seen on the American landscape. Their passage into their retirement years will have an equally profound effect on the types of housing in demand. Boomer homes will be houses—not apartments or condominiums—typically one-story with three bedrooms.

"Seniors and boomers are so active now that some of the activities are clearly putting stress on their bodies," Mack said. "I've got people who are getting hip and knee replacements in their 60s and people in their 40s getting their knees scoped. This did not happen with previous generations because they didn't live as long nor put this stress on their bones so soon."

"If you've got a sports injury, do you want to come home to a house that is fraught with hazards and barriers? These are not just designs and ideas for the frail elderly. We are also providing solutions for people who never thought they were going to get old—and least this quickly."

More importantly, U.S. builders and remodelers have anticipated the huge need—and financial rewards resulting from it—and jumped on board. The National Association of Home Builders (NAHB), a Washington, DC–based trade association representing more than 205,000 members involved in home building, remodeling, property management, and other services, now offers a certified aging in place (CAPS) designation. CAPS, created by the NAHB Remodelors Council in collaboration with the organization's Seniors Housing Council, research center, and AARP, is a three-day program that provides information about aging-in-place home modifications, including background on the older adult population, common aging-in-place remodeling projects, marketing to the aging-in-place market, codes and standards, common barriers and solutions, product ideas resources, and communication techniques.

Projects for the aging-in-place remodeling segment range from installation of bath and shower grab bars and adjustment of countertop heights to the creation of multifunctional first-floor master suites and the installation of private elevators. CAPS training participants learn the mechanics and nuances of effectively assessing clients' needs and integrating myriad considerations into unified, aesthetically pleasing, functional solutions.

In addition, no one can deny that we live in a very dangerous world. The desire to find safety, or experience the mere perception of safety, has kept U.S. residents closer to home since September 11, 2001—spending more time in the home itself. Retirees are not the only segment of the population looking and the possibilities of cocooning. In fact, Americans are moving at some of the lowest rates in more than 50 years.[2] The 40 million people who moved between 2002 and 2003 comprised 14 percent of the population, down sharply from a rate of 20 percent in 1948 when the Bureau of the Census first began collecting information on movers.

Some seniors are just now beginning to think about ways to tastefully modify their homes to enable them to remain living independently—and more safely and comfortably. Solutions often exist, but people are not always aware of the products. For example, Lifease, Inc., based in New Brighton, Minnesota, charges a modest fee for its online questionnaire,

---

[2] U.S. Census, *Geographical Mobility: 2002 to 2003.*

LivAbility, that allows homeowners to assess their needs and abilities and then obtain personalized suggestions to improve their living environment. After the questionnaire is completed, the Lifease engine selects solutions based on the input. The resulting report includes ideas and products for safety, convenience, comfort, and independence in the home. Low and no cost solutions are listed. If the solution is a product, web sites are given for the suppliers with a range of prices. If appropriate, the rationale for listing the product is included. Another company, SAFE Aging, Inc., based in Tarpon Springs, Florida, has developed a paper questionnaire for older adults that identifies potential risks or hazards that can threaten health, safety, or function in the home. The Safety Appraisal For Elders can be completed privately at home, with or without assistance, at any pace, and is also modestly priced.

Planning the Work

This section provides you with a capsule guide for deciding upon and executing the typical major renovations—roof, bathroom, and kitchen—often needed to age in place. Any renovation will cause you to spend resources, and all dollars, including your reverse mortgage funds, are precious. As with any expenditure, you should work through a decision process before the project starts. No matter what it is that you will be doing to the house, ask yourself the following questions:

1. *How long do I realistically intend to stay in this house?* While the answer is often impossible, give some thought to a best guesstimate. While minor home modifications are fine for the short term, it's usually not advisable to go through the anxiety of a major room

remodel if you definitely will move out in a few months. Roofs are a different story because they often are mandatory.

2. *Who will do the work?* When you employ construction help, it's important to find efficient and honest workers. If you have used contractors in the past, you probably have a roster of dependable helpers.

3. *How will I find contractor referrals?* Your primary sources are friends who may have used contractors in the past. The local senior center can also help. Also, ask the local homebuilders association about its CAPS specialists.

4. *How will I pay for the remodel?* If you are using a reverse mortgage for all or part of the remodel, consider a program that features a line of credit. That way, you will only pay interest on the funds you actually use, and the remaining balance can increase over time. For example, you could pay one lump sum for a roof replacement, then wait until other remodeling bills or maintenance receipts are sent to you before drawing on your credit line.

Before viewing the statistical results for the return on home improvements, understand that elders don't really care if they recoup their investment to age in place. Others simply want the peace of mind of knowing that their children might recover a portion of the remodeling costs if or when the house is eventually sold. Table 8.1 shows the national averages for the rate of return for kitchens, bathrooms and master suites. Two levels of expenditure, mid-range and upscale, are identified. A value of 100 percent means that the investment is fully recouped in the sales price. However, the table is merely a gauge and does not reflect only aging projects. The same project done in two different areas may cost different amounts. The impact of any home improvement on the ultimate sales price is not the same in all cases and

Table 8.1 Percentage of Cost Recouped from Various Improvements (National averages, 2002)	
Improvement	**Percentage Recouped**
Bathroom Addition, mid-range	94%
Bathroom Addition, upscale	81%
Bathroom Remodel, mid-range	88%
Bathroom Remodel, upscale	81%
Major Kitchen Remodel, mid-range	67%
Major Kitchen Remodel, upscale	80%
Master Bedroom Remodel, mid-range	75%
Master Bedroom Remodel, upscale	77%
Basement Remodel	79%
Siding Replacement	79%
Window Replacement, mid-range	74%
Window Replacement, upscale	77%
Roof Replacement	67%

Source: Remodeling Online, op.cit.

usually depends on the location and condition of the overall house and the market demand at the time the home is marketed for sale. The numbers presented in the following tables are reference numbers only and are intended for comparison purposes. They do not represent any amounts that must actually be spent.

Specific Changes

We now take a peek at bathroom additions and remodels, master suite additions, kitchen remodels, and roof replacement in a variety of U.S.

cities and regions. In each case, two figures are presented. The first number represents a mid-range bathroom addition; the second an upscale project. The cities chosen represent a mid-range for the region. The estimates are not meant to be definitive but are presented to give you an idea of what you can expect generally in the way of cost and return from any renovation project and, in most cases, your reverse mortgage dollar.

Roof Replacement

One of the first places seniors plop down reverse mortgage money is for a new roof over their heads. (See Table 8.2.) When asked how they are going to spend their funds, they often say: "After I get a new roof, I'm flying to Florida" or "I need a new roof before I do anything else." A bad roof will make even the best of houses unlivable. So it is a necessary evil that the owner cannot do without.

Table 8.2 Roof Replacement Project Costs and Costs Recouped Selected Metropolitan Areas, 2002		
Metro Area	**Project Cost**	**Percentage Recouped**
Atlanta	$8,955	62%
Cleveland	$13,008	62%
Philadelphia	$14,832	66%
San Diego	$12,576	84%
National Average	$11,399	67%
Source: Remodeling Online, op.cit.		

Bathrooms: Additions and Remodeling

There has been a tendency in new construction to build the bathroom bigger and include more fixtures as well as more space. Older bathrooms suffer in comparison to newer houses because of the limited space dedicated to this room years ago by builders and homeowners. Bathroom additions tend to be the most profitable of all discretionary house projects. Table 8.3 sets out the costs and rates of return for the addition of a bathroom at two levels. The first is a full 6 ft. by 8 ft. bath added to a home with one and a half baths. This is a mid-range bathroom. The second number represents the addition of a full bath to a master bedroom, which includes separate shower and whirlpool tub.

Table 8.3 Bathroom Addition Project Cost and Cost Recouped Selected Metropolitan Areas, 2002		
Metro Area	**Project Cost**	**Percentage Recouped**
Atlanta	$13,615 (mid-range)	94%
	$36,329 (upscale)	96%
Cleveland	$16,098 (mid-range)	81%
	$38,562 (upscale)	74%
Philadelphia	$16,178 (mid-range)	103%
	$38,756 (upscale)	93%
San Diego	$16,216 (mid-range)	100%
	$38,726 (upscale)	94%
National Average	$15,058 (mid-range)	94%
	$37,639 (upscale)	81%

Source: Remodeling Online, op.cit.

Returns tend to be higher in larger metropolitan areas, even though costs are seemingly unrelated to city size. In part, this is a result of higher prices in larger metro markets where small percentage changes in value can result in large dollar returns. This reinforces the need to look closely at local conditions when considering a renovation project.

The returns to bathroom remodeling tend to be lower, as a national average, than those for adding a new bathroom. This is understandable considering the fact that a remodel, even if it expands the existing bathroom, adds less capacity than a new room addition. Table 8.4 displays the results of *Remodeling Online*'s 2002 survey of selected cities. The top figure, the mid-range remodel, updates and replaces the fixtures in

Table 8.4 Bathroom Remodeling Project Cost and Cost Recouped Selected Metropolitan Areas, 2002		
Metro Area	**Project Cost**	**Percentage Recouped**
Atlanta	$8,980 (mid-range)	99%
	$21,394 (upscale)	119%
Cleveland	$7,984 (mid-range)	76%
	$23,649 (upscale)	62%
Philadelphia	$10,486 (mid-range)	118%
	$23,941 (upscale)	104%
San Diego	$10,314 (mid-range)	80%
	$23,730 (upscale)	105%
National Average	$9,720 (mid-range)	88%
	$22,639 (upscale)	91%

Source: Remodeling Online, op.cit.

an existing bathroom at least 25 years old. The upscale version expands a 5 ft. by 7 ft. bathroom to 9 ft. by 9 ft. and also includes new fixtures.

Here, the age of the housing stock is an issue. In areas dominated by older stock, newly remodeled bathrooms can stand out, while in other areas, where new construction is the norm, even a remodeled older bathroom carries little appeal in terms of house value.

Kitchen Remodel

Kitchens have become more than just for cooking and eating. They are gathering places where entertainment accompanied by food takes place. The numbers presented in Table 8.5 represent averages for a particular pair of remodels. The first number is a mid-range remodel of an out-of-date 200 square foot kitchen, bringing design, cabinetry, appliances and fixtures. The second is an upscale remodel in which the quality of all the components is higher. The two specifications are used to give a basis for comparison across areas of the country, but they also show the range that is possible in the remodeling of a kitchen. Various quality levels are far more available in kitchen appliances and fixtures than in bathroom fixtures. You can thus choose to move along a design and construction spectrum and do more or less than is indicated in the reference remodels.

Population density appears to be related to return in kitchens, as it was for bathrooms. In each of the four regions of the United States, the highest returns tend to be in the most populous metro areas and the lowest in smaller areas.

Remember, the process of altering a home to age in place is often complicated by the limited dollars you have. While reverse mortgages can be

Table 8.5 Kitchen Remodel Projects Costs and Costs Recouped Selected Metropolitan Areas, 2002		
Metro Area	**Project Costs**	**Percentage Recouped**
Atlanta	$41,201 (mid-range)	88%
	$68,181 (upscale)	98%
Cleveland	$44,546 (mid-range)	68%
	$71,715 (upscale)	64%
Philadelphia	$45,111 (mid-range)	91%
	$72,272 (upscale)	96%
San Diego	$44,971 (mid-range)	69%
	$72,333 (upscale)	84%
National Average	$43,213 (mid-range)	67%
	$70,368 (upscale)	80%

Source: Remodeling Online, op.cit.

critical to these renovations, it's always important to plan before you remodel. Renovating your house is not an all-or-nothing process. Every area offers a lot of possibilities to spend more or less. However, if you are spending money to be more comfortable and safer as you age, do your best to get what you pay for.

CHAPTER 9

Constant success shows us but one side of the world.
Adversity brings out the reverse of the picture.
—CHARLES CALEB COLTON

Early Black Eyes: Scanning the History of the Reverse

Like Adjustable Rate Mortgages, Industry Took Its Lumps

Remember payment shock?

That was the term used when homeowners received their new loan payment coupons after their adjustable rate mortgage (ARM) underwent its first adjustment period. Heavily discounted, one-year ARMs gave the new mortgages a bad reputation. When borrowers finished the first year of seemingly easy payments, the discounted rate ended and consumers were forced into surprisingly higher, second-year payments—which resulted in the chilling reality of a monthly cash outlay commonly referred to as payment shock.

A similar shock surfaced with some of the first reverse mortgages. In this chapter, we will take a look at the evolution of reverse mortgages and how their early years often mirrored those of the maverick ARMs. Some early programs were flawed and contained huge appreciation shares for the lender coupled with big-time up-front fees. Now with the federal government insuring a majority of the reverse mortgages in this country, the perception toward reverse loans has changed and the programs are becoming more acceptable and recognized by consumers. However a few of the early loans are still in circulation, giving the entire reverse industry a black eye every time an equity share program hits the pages of a major metropolitan newspaper. Consumers typically complain more often than they praise—and rightfully so. If they pay for a service, they should expect a service in return. But some of the seniors who signed up for the first reverse mortgages did not know exactly what they were signing, leading to frustration, anxiety, and financial loss. Some of the negativity of the early reverses simply was a result of the risk-averse GI Generation, still the prime target for the next several years before the early Boomers or Silent Generation come around the senior corner.

"I don't think the few cases where reverse mortgages got bad press had any permanent effect—it was a hard sell long before that," said Jack Guttentag, known internationally as the revered Mortgage Professor and professor of finance emeritus at the Wharton School of the University of Pennsylvania. "My experience with reverse mortgages goes back to the 60s, I was involved with the HELP program in Buffalo and the American Homestead program in NJ. It was then, and still is, a hard sell because it is complicated and the people involved are placing their most important asset at risk, at a time of life when their capacity to absorb risk is at its lowest. There isn't time to start again."

First authorized by the federal government in 1981 but almost unused before 1983, ARMs supplanted a system of fixed-rate loans and stimulated a drowsy home market. These loans caught on quickly, simply because the market needed them. As an inducement to borrowers, some lenders offered rates that were ridiculously low, qualifying borrowers for the first year of the loan but setting up potential bombshells shortly down the road—especially in a rising-rate market. However, lenders continued to refine and develop ARMs, and most now contain monthly, annual, and life-of-the-loan caps that limit adjustments. The original, bold ARMs suffered an initial setback yet were a healthy learning experience for the industry in the long run. They paved the way for a useable, practical option to what banks traditionally required.

Reverse mortgages traveled the same road. The industry established interest rate caps, pre-application counseling, interest-rate lock ins, streamline refinances, and other consumer protections that made the new reverse mortgages a viable option to needed cash and retirement preparation.

"I think the wheel began to turn with the development of the FHA's HECM," Guttentag said. "The 'imprimatur' of the federal government has been a big help and the number of deals keeps rising. This will continue for the indefinite future."

The reverse mortgage road clearly has contained huge chuckholes on the road to acceptance. A few years ago, a syndicated column addressed the case of a woman who signed up for a reverse mortgage and ended up owing the lender $765,000 after the home had sold. The example sent a shock wave through the reverse mortgage community, which had taken significant steps to create viable programs for house-rich-cash-poor persons 62 years of age and older.

Basically, the story chronicled the situation of a borrower, a 69-year-old woman in an unnamed location, who took out a reverse mortgage in April 1998 on a home that was then valued at $980,000. The loan she had chosen had an equity appreciation-sharing feature that entitled the lender, Transamerica Homefirst, to 50 percent of the increase in value over the life of the loan. According to the story, the loan's terms also required her to purchase an annuity that wouldn't start paying her until 2012. Assuming she was still alive, the annuity would then begin paying $1,816 per month in place of payments from the lender. It was a dramatic case due to the extraordinary run-up in the home value and the percentage of the appreciation share targeted for the lender.

In fact, Fannie Mae, which purchases all FHA Home Equity Conversion Mortgage (HECM) loans in addition to the company's own Home Keeper mortgages, once funded appreciation-share reverse mortgages but stopped when confronted with the prospect of high payoffs harmful to elders and their heirs.

To its credit, the National Reverse Mortgage Lenders Association (NRMLA), a national trade association for financial services companies that originate, service, and invest in reverse mortgages, decided to increase its educational efforts regarding the various reverse mortgage products. It rolled out a code of conduct. In effect, it told its members, "Don't get mad, get even. Get out there and make sure the correct information is getting out to seniors." By presenting an ongoing educational forum for lenders, informing consumers about the benefits of reverse mortgages, and working with federal, state, and local policymakers on issues affecting reverse mortgage lending, NRMLA said it plans to ensure that this contemporary personal financial management tool effectively serves the needs of the audience for whom it has been created. NRMLA members now originate and service more than 90 percent of all reverse mortgages in the United States. One association member firm originates and services reverse mortgages in Canada. In 1998, the association created a set of best practices that it has urged its members to incorporate in their business operations and interactions with consumers.

The syndicated story turned out to be the poster child of all that was bad with reverse mortgages—a uniformed senior borrower, a misleading program, and subsequently, a furious group of family members who had to deal with the ramifications of the awful loan. While similar stories have since surfaced, this piece did the most to force the industry to look at some of its curious previous creations. While the case is highly unrepresentative of most of the market, consumers remember black eyes—even when suffered by a stranger.

According to documents filed in a Westchester County, New York, arbitration proceeding, the borrower's estate claimed that she was misled into applying for a mortgage with "unconscionably high" costs without counseling or legal guidance. The complaint also alleged that she received an "artificially low appraisal," which, when combined with the appreciation-sharing feature, allowed the lender to be "guaranteed a profit of at least $225,500 even if the borrower died the day after making the loan." The appraisal arranged by the lender on the property valued it at $980,000, according to the complaint. Two follow-up appraisals paid for by the borrower's estate put the market value around $1.4 million at the time of the loan. The estate sold the home in May 2001 for $2.2 million, more than double the reverse mortgage appraisal value. A local real estate professional sales person claimed the $980,000 value placed on the home was so low, "there would have been a buyers' stampede" if it had been listed for sale.

The borrower, according to the syndicated story, received $58,000 of benefit over a span of 32 months. After she passed away, her estate was presented with a balance due of $765,112 (now totaling more than $800,000 with penalties). The heirs filed a lawsuit. Shortly after the borrower's death in 1998, her daughter recalled "we knew that she had taken out a reverse mortgage, but we had no idea of the details. When we read the loan documents after her death, we were horrified," according to the syndicated story. Transamerica Homefirst no longer is in business. However, its package of loans—and many of its problems—was purchased by Financial Freedom, the nation's largest reverse mortgage lender.

"The industry has worked hard to install a number of consumer safeguards in all the products that are in the reverse mortgage marketplace," said Jim Mahoney, chief executive officer of Financial Freedom Funding, a subsidiary of Lehman Brothers that was sold to Indy Bank in May 2004. "There are no more shared appreciation or shared equity loans and that has brought us a long way. These consumer safeguards have really allowed seniors to access their home equity in comfort and security. It's also allowed us to grow and the main reason why our business seems to be doubling year over year."

The first reverse mortgages were developed in Great Britain in the early 1930s. The loans were called home equity reversions and continued as a small business until 1970 when a group of investors took control of the company and renamed it Home & Capital Trust Ltd. According to the National Center for Home Equity Conversion, the first known reverse mortgage written in the United States was in 1961. Nelson Haynes, a banker at Deering Savings and Loan in Portland, Maine, constructed a reverse mortgage for Nellie Young, the widow of Haynes' high school football coach. In 1981, Ken Scholen founded the nonprofit National

Center for Home Equity Conversion (NCHEC) in Madison, Wisconsin. The same year, Scholen was the first person to give Congressional testimony on reverse mortgages when he appeared before the U.S. House Select Committee on Aging. While several companies were writing reverse annuity mortgages (RAMs) in the 1980s, the first HECM loan was made under an FHA pilot program in 1989.

"When the federal government came in after the demonstration program and said, 'you are going to be repaid even if you go belly up', that's what made the big difference," said Wells Fargo's Jeff Taylor. "While we have been fighting an image problem because of a few bad players, the acceptance of the HECM program has really accelerated this industry. The mystique is finally starting to get removed. It is finally more than helping the little old lady living on a can of soup. The programs have been stepped up and are very appealing to a different brand of seniors who also want to do some tax shelter strategy."

The United States does not stand as the lone country to pitch a reverse mortgage concept to its people. Here is a quick overview of some of the places that have offered a similar program:

Canada. Canadian Home Income Plan (CHIP) was founded in 1986 to provide Canadian seniors with a program founded mostly on an American model. As Canada's first and only reverse mortgage program, its introduction followed two years of research into similar successful programs in other countries. Reverse mortgages seem to be gaining popularity because they offer a tax-free stream of money usually paid in the form of a monthly annuity.

France. Closely related to the concept of reverse mortgages is the French system of *viager* a Middle Ages practice that has experienced renewed popularity in Europe. The French government promotes the system as an effective way to reduce dependence on social security programs. It is a private contractual arrangement between the buyer and the seller of a property. The buyer pays the seller a down payment and the remaining amount is payable in form of monthly payments *en viager* (i.e., for life).

Singapore. NTUC Income, an insurance company, was the first financial institution to introduce a reverse mortgage product in Singapore. However, unlike the nonrecourse reverse mortgages in the United States, most of the loans in circulation require borrowers to make up the difference if they outlive the value of their homes. Many citizens live in public housing, reducing the possibilities for a mass reverse mortgage market.

Great Britain. The early attempts, begun more than 70 years ago, carried no consumer protections (is this beginning to sound familiar?), became very controversial, and fell by the wayside. Since 2001, there has been renewed interest in reverse mortgages because of borrower protections. In addition, the Royal Commission on Long Term Care has encouraged British citizens to take more responsibility for providing for retirement and paying for long-term care. Local authorities have been authorized to make loans on the value of the house with the loan being paid on the borrower's death or eventual sale of the property.

In the Epilogue, we will take a peek at the future of reverse mortgages and what needs to be done for them to be readily acceptable by more consumers. The biggest, healthiest, and wealthiest group ever seen on the American landscape is right around the corner and, it has not been scared to borrow.

The mortgage market changes virtually from day to day, so you can wait a few weeks and, if you haven't committed suicide in the meantime, try again, even with the same lenders.
—WILLIAM G. CONNOLLY, AUTHOR

Going Forward in Reverse

Awareness, Combining Assets Will Expand the Market

In December 2002, while writing a newspaper story about a Bellingham, Washington, couple who were struggling to remain in their home—thanks to the terms of an outrageous loan refinance they claimed a subsidiary of Illinois-based Household International persuaded them to accept—I got a call from the Washington State Department of Financial Institutions. The department, like similar agencies in most states, regulates mortgage brokers. It had investigated hundreds of cases brought against Household for predatory lending practices the past few years.

Household eventually agreed with the attorneys general in all 50 states and the District of Columbia to settle several pending lawsuits involving alleged predatory lending practices for a reported $484 million. There was other legal action as well. Lawsuits filed by the Association of Community Organizations for Reform Now (ACORN) in California and Illinois and by AARP in New York also accuse Household International and its subsidiaries, Household Finance Corp. and Beneficial, of engaging in fraud by misleading borrowers about the terms of loans.

The caller, Chuck Cross, Washington State's chief investigator and one of the national leaders in the Household case, said he had received an inquiry about reverse mortgages.

"I don't know anything about reverse mortgages," Cross said. "How do they work? This guy told me about the loan fees, and they just look too high to me."

That, in a nutshell, is what the reverse mortgage industry combats every day and will until it can find a way to reduce its fees and better explain its complex system. The challenge clearly is education—if the chief investigator in a state's Department of Financial Institutions doesn't understand reverse mortgages, who would?

"The fees will come down," said Wells Fargo's Jeff Taylor. "I think when more of these loans are made and people begin to understand their flexibility that the secondary market will respond and the fees will come down. Seniors will continue to look to them for long-term care and to eventually buy retirement residences. Bottom line, they'll be less expensive for the consumer to get."

The education challenge will not be easy to overcome, especially in today's environment where seniors are skittish of corporate quarterly statements, some executives who couldn't care less about the shareholders, and the number of Household-type pitches that can dilute an elder's nest egg faster than a Roger Clemens' fastball. The sub prime market is battling a similar impression. Sub prime loans, for borrowers of all ages who do not fit the conforming loan requirements due to income, credit, or job problems, definitely are a viable, needed option for thousands of consumers. These people live on the edge, and nothing is going to change those habits. However, most of these borrowers respect their mortgage payments, yet understandably, the default rate is greater in the sub prime market because the loan risk is greater. The huge difference is that the federal government guarantees a majority of the reverse mortgages written today. That cannot be said of most of the sub prime loans in the United States.

Compounding the educational challenge is that some news operations react the same way—they do not understand reverse mortgages, have read only the disaster stories associated with the loans, and don't have the time to ascertain what they are all about. Some major metropolitan newspapers in this country refuse to consider any stories about reverse mortgages—unless the story chronicles a consumer losing thousands of dollars to a greedy lender.

In 2003, at the annual meeting of the National Reverse Mortgage Lenders annual meeting in Chicago, I stayed late into the night filing stories to newspapers all over the country. There had been real news in mortgage banking: Dr. John Weicher, the FHA Commissioner, said reverse mortgages had finally turned the corner, that lenders would be able to lock the interest rate of loans at application, and that he would consider a streamline refinance whereby consumers would get a break on their mortgage insurance premium if they chose to refinance their reverse.

Some editors welcomed the stories with open arms; others mumbled finally, some good news about reverse mortgages; yet a third group was dead-set against running any item, large or small, in their editions.

"We don't run any stories about reverse mortgages," said Jo Kovach, advertising promotional sections manager for The *Cincinnati Inquirer/ Post*. "The same with predatory lending stories. We stay away from both of them."

"On the surface, the reverse mortgage idea really flies in the face of what mortgages have been in this country," said Richard Garrigan, author and professor of finance emeritus at DePaul University in Chicago. "We had been taught to make mortgage debt as miniscule as possible. The idea that mortgage debt actually grows is outside the spectrum of what they've been in contact with for years. But what has also changed is how wealth is accumulated. We are now over-promised at the government level and under-saved at the household level. You bring all this into the demise of the traditional pension plan and you ask, 'if you have any wealth, where is it?' It's probably in your home, and that has not always been the case."

That wealth is often underestimated in its amount, and its location, especially for the generations that are now snapping up second homes for recreation, investment, and retirement and will soon be reaching the traditional retirement years.

Dr. Sung Won Sohn, executive vice president and chief economic officer for Wells Fargo Bank, said a greater than expected percentage of wealth in the United States is held in homes—both primary and second homes.

"The equity in the typical second home often is greater than the assets people have in securities, like stocks and bonds," said Sohn, who once worked with Federal Reserve Chairman Alan Greenspan and was a senior economist on the President's Council of Economic Advisors. "If you consider a typical Boomer-age homeowner has about $120,000 of equity in the primary home, there is often about $60,000 in a second home."

Sohn believes that when a consumer eventually occupies his or her last home, there's a good chance those equity stakes could be combined—giving the senior greater equity in one place. For example, an elder could move into the investment, recreation, or retirement home he's had for years, making it the primary residence. He then could sell the long-time family home, pocketing up to $500,000 tax-free of gain ($250,000 for a single person), making a significant sum of cash available to pay off any mortgage debt on the place he now calls home. That move would represent a prime reverse mortgage candidate and replace, at least for a time, the expected high-debt perception of retiring Boomers.

"The challenge will be convincing the Boomers to keep their loan balances in a workable range to even consider a reverse," said Financial Freedom's Rachel Brichan. "I can see many of my friends and present customers coming to me down the road and asking for a reverse when their ratios are too high. If they have a $600,000 home and they still owe $400,000 there's not much we're going to be able to do for them."

How will reverse mortgages become a $74 billion industry by 2015 as some analysts project? The reverse mortgage business is poised for a period of unprecedented growth. Individuals over the age of 62—those who obtain reverse mortgages—make up the fastest-growing segment of

America's population. The GI Generation will discover it for health care and daily household bills; the Silent Generation, once it has decided how they will handle long-term care insurance, will find a way to use it as a financial tool; and the Boomers will utilize reverse mortgages because they love to borrow—for anything—and that will not change.

Reverse mortgages are not for everyone. But it is important that congressmen, consumers, financial advisors, and accountants know that they have become a viable option to some seniors, especially those struggling with health care funds and who need cash to remain in the home. The tax-free income also makes sense to consumers who reside in rapidly appreciating home markets or do not wish to the pay capital gains tax by cashing stock or other commodities.

"The typical Congressman in this country knows as much about a reverse mortgage as a donut," Peter Bell, president of the Washington, DC–based National Reverse Mortgage Lenders Association (NRMLA) told more than 350 lenders gathered for the event.

The more options created for senior homeowners, the better. Options are why Dunkin' Donuts goes beyond glazed; why Baskin Robbins created 31 flavors. While the upfront fees can be absolutely stunning if you cash out the loan in its first few years, the main focus for borrowers will be aging in place—for the long haul. But many seniors need extra funds simply to make ends meet, and reverse mortgages are the only way for some of them. The tax-free income also makes sense to consumers who do not wish to cash stock or other assets.

"We think a borrower should have a need or desire for the money with the intent to use it in the near future," said Seattle Mortgage's Mike

Broderick. "If they really don't know what they are going to do with the money, we usually tell them to wait and make sure. It doesn't justify the high closing costs, and accompanying interest and fee costs, to just have it."

The reverse mortgage industry has made positive strides, especially since 2002. The advent of the streamline refinance, ability to lock the expected interest rate at application or closing (whichever is lower), and the consumer protection requirement of a mandatory counseling before application all took place within an 18-month period. What would significantly improve the product is a single national limit, enabling homeowners in rural regions the ability to tap as much equity as those elders in high-cost areas of the country. The ability to borrow should not be curtailed by geographic location.

"We believe our time has come," said Financial Freedom's Jim Mahoney. "If you look at the fact that home values continue to increase in many parts of the country, this is a great liquidity tool for seniors in their retirement planning, estate planning, and just meeting their day-to-day cash needs.

"Folks with million-dollar homes often have the same needs as those with lower home values. They are taking the money and using it in ways they never thought they would because their incomes have been fixed—or perhaps falling with the performance of their stock portfolios. This is a very safe, secure way for seniors to stay in their home, continue to gain in the appreciation, and pass on a nice estate to the heirs with the leftover equity."

AARP. (1995). *Making Your Community Livable: Programs That Work.* Washington, DC.

AARP. (2002). *Home Made Money: A Consumer's Guide to Reverse Mortgages.* Washington, DC.

Ahlstrom, A., Tumlinson, A., and Lambrew, J. (2003). *Linking Reverse Mortgages and Long-Term Care Insurance.* George Washington University, Washington, DC.

Belser, S.H., and Weber, J.A. (1995). "Home Builders' Attitudes and Knowledge of Aging: The Relationship to Design for Independent Living." *Journal of Housing for the Elderly, 11* (2), 123–137.

Fannie Mae. (2003). *Money from Home: A Consumer's Guide to Reverse Mortgage Options.* Washington, DC.

Gaberlavage, G., and Forsythe, P. (1995). *Home Repair and Modification: A Survey of City Programs.* Washington, DC: Public Policy Institute, American Association of Retired Persons.

Internal Revenue Service (2002). Publication 936—Limits on Home Mortgage Interest Deductions, Washington, DC.

Malizia, E., Duncan, R., and Reagan, J. (1993). *Financing Home Accessibility Modifications.* Raleigh, NC: Center for Universal Design.

National Center for Home Equity Conversion. (1997). *A Capsule History of Reverse Mortgages in the United States.* NCHEC Press.

Scholen, Ken. (1995). *Your Retirement Nest Egg: A Consumer Guide to the New Reverse Mortgages.* NCHEC Press.

Struyk, R.J., and Katsura, H.M. (1985). *Aging at Home: How the Elderly Adjust Their Housing Without Moving.* Washington, DC: Urban Institute Project Report 3166-3.

Stucki, Barbara (2004). *Use Your Home to Stay at Home.* The National Council on the Aging. Washington, DC.

Sample Amortization Schedules and Constant Maturity Indexes

Borrower Name/Case Number:	Betty Boop Tenure Payment	Refinance: No
	Variables	**Calculated**
Date of Closing:	9/1/2005	9/1/2005
Borrower's Birth Date:	10/10/1941	Age: 64
Expected Interest Rate:	6.500	6.500%
Property Appraised Value:	$150,000	$150,000
Maximum Claim Amount:	$150,000	$150,000
Prin Lim - Shared Prem Fac:		.554-19
Principal Limit:		$83,100.00
Upfront Premium:	FINANCED	$3,000.00
Other Closing Costs:	$4,800.00	$4,800.00
Initial Draw:	$0.00	$0.00
Monthly Servicing Fee:	$30.00	$4,887.94
Net Principal Limit:		$70,412.06
Line of Credit:	$0.00	$0.00
Monthly Payment:	CALCULATE	$432.16
Length of Term:	TENURE	TENURE

TOTAL ANNUAL LOAN COST RATE

LOAN TERMS		MONTHLY LOAN CHARGES	
Age of youngest borrower:	64	Mo. Servicing Fee:	$30.00
Appraised Property Value: annually	$150,000	Mortgage Insurance:	0.5 %
Initial interest rate:	3.720%		
Monthly advance:	$432.16	OTHER CHARGES	
Initial Draw:	$0.00	Shared Appreciation:	None
Line of Credit:	$0.00		
Length of Term:	TENURE		

INITIAL LOAN CHARGES		REPAYMENT LIMITS
Closing Cost:	$4,800.00	Net proceeds estimated at 93%
Mortgage Insurance Premium:	$3,000.00	of projected home sale
Annuity Cost:	None	

Appreciation Rate	DISCLOSURE PERIOD (Yrs.)			
	2	10	20	28
0%	59.51%	8.30%	2.82%	N/A
4%	59.51%	8.30%	5.65%	5.10%
8%	59.51%	8.30%	5.65%	5.10%

The cost of any reverse mortgage loan depends on how long you keep the loan and how much your house appreciates in value. Generally, the longer you keep a reverse mortgage, the lower the total annual loan cost rate will be.

This table shows the estimated cost of your reverse mortgage loan, expressed as an annual rate. It illustrates the cost for your age, that life expectancy, and 1.4 times that life expectancy. The table also shows the cost of the loan, assuming the value of your home appreciates at three different rates: 0%, 4%, and 8%.

The total annual cost rates in this table are based on the total charges associated with this loan. These charges typically include principal, interest, closing costs, mortgage insurance premiums, annuity costs, and servicing costs (but not disposition costs—costs when you sell the home).

The rates in this table are estimates. Your actual cost may differ if, for example, the amount of your loan advances varies or the interest rate on your mortgage changes. You may receive projections of loan balances from counselors or lenders that are based on an expected average mortgage rate that differs from the initial interest rate.

Source: Seattle Mortgage

Figure A.1 Amortization Schedule—Annual Projections

Borrower Name/Case Number:	Betty Boop -Tenure Payment	Refinance:	No
Age of Youngest Borrower:	64	Initial Property Value:	$150,000
Expected Interest Rate:	6.250%	Beg. Mortgage Balance:	$7,800
Maximum Claim Amount:	$150,000	Expected Appreciation:	4%
Initial Principal Limit:	$83,100	Initial Line of Credit:	$0.00
Initial Draw:	$0.00	Monthly Payment:	$432.16
Financed Closing Costs:	$7,800	Monthly Servicing Fee:	$30.00

NOTE: Actual interest charges and property value projections may vary from amounts show. Available credit will be less than projected if funds withdrawn from line-of-credit.

				Annual Totals				End of Year			
Yr	Age	SVC Fee	Payment	MIP	Interest	Loan Bal	Line of Credit	Prin. Limit	Property Value @ 4%	Property Value @ 8%
1	64	360	5,186	56	695	14,096	0	88,886	156,000	156,000
2	65	360	5,186	88	1,100	20,830	0	95,075	162,240	168,480
3	66	360	5,186	123	1,535	28,033	0	101,694	168,729	181,958
4	67	360	5,186	160	1,999	35,738	0	108,775	175,478	196,515
5	68	360	5,186	200	2,496	43,979	0	116,349	182,497	212,236
6	69	360	5,186	242	3,027	52,794	0	214,450	189,797	229,215
7	70	360	5,186	288	3,595	62,223	0	133,115	197,389	247,552
8	71	360	5,186	336	4,203	72,309	0	142,384	205,285	267,357
9	72	360	5,186	388	4,853	83,096	0	152,298	215,496	288,745
10	73	360	5,186	444	5,549	94,635	0	162,902	222,036	311,845
11	74	360	5,186	503	6,293	106,977	0	174,245	230,918	336,792
12	75	360	5,186	567	7,089	120,179	0	186,377	240,154	363,736
13	76	360	5,186	635	7,940	134,300	0	199,354	249,761	392,835
14	77	360	5,186	708	8,850	149,404	0	213,235	259,751	424,261
15	78	360	5,186	786	9,824	165,559	0	228,082	270,141	458,202
16	79	360	5,186	869	10,865	182,840	0	243,963	280,947	494,858
17	80	360	5,186	958	11,979	201,324	0	260,950	292,185	534,447
18	81	360	5,186	1,054	13,171	221,094	0	279,119	303,872	577,203
19	82	360	5,186	1,156	14,446	242,242	0	298,554	316,027	623,379
20	83	360	5,186	1,265	15,809	264,861	0	319,341	328,668	673,249
21	84	360	5,186	1,381	17,267	289,056	0	341,576	341,815	727,109
22	85	360	5,186	1,506	18,827	314,935	0	365,360	355,487	785,278
23	86	360	5,186	1,640	20,496	342,617	0	390,799	369,707	848,100
24	87	360	5,186	1,782	22,280	372,225	0	418,010	384,495	915,948
25	88	360	5,186	1,935	24,189	403,895	0	447,115	399,875	989,224
26	89	360	5,186	2,098	26,231	437,771	0	478,246	415,870	1,068,362
27	90	360	5,186	2,273	28,415	474,005	0	511,546	432,505	1,153,831
28	91	360	5,186	2,460	30,751	512,762	0	547,164	449,805	1,246,138
29	92	360	5,186	2,660	33,250	554,217	0	585,262	467,797	1,345,829
30	93	360	5,186	2,874	35,922	598,559	0	626,012	486,509	1,453,495
31	94	360	5,186	3,102	38,781	645,989	0	669,600	505,970	1,569,774
32	95	360	5,186	3,347	41,839	696,720	0	716,223	526,208	1,695,356
33	96	360	5,186	3,609	45,109	750,984	0	766,092	547,257	1,830,985
34	97	360	5,186	3,889	48,608	809,027	0	819,434	569,147	1,977,464
35	98	360	5,186	4,188	52,350	871,111	0	876,489	591,913	2,135,661
36	99	360	5,186	4,508	56,352	937,517	0	937,517	615,589	2,306,514

Figure A.2 Line of Credit, Home Value $150,000, Age 64
Home Equity Conversion Mortgage Insurance (HECM)

Borrower Name/Case Number:	Bill Bradley - Line of Credit	Refinance: No
	Variables	**Calculated**
Date of Closing:	9/1/2005	09/01/2005
Borrower's Birth Date:	10/10/1941	Age: 64
Expected Interest Rate:	6.250	6.250%
Property Appraised Value:	$150,000	$150,000
Maximum Claim Amount:	$150,000	$150,000
Principle Limit - Shared Premium Factor:		.554-19
Principal Limit:		$83,100.00
Upfront Premium:	FINANCED	$3,000.00
Other Closing Costs:	$4,800.00	$4,800.00
Initial Draw:	$0.00	$0.00
Monthly Servicing Fee:	$30.00	$4,887.94
Net Principal Limit:		$70,412.06
Line of Credit:	CALCULATE	$70,412.06
Monthly Payment:	$0.00	$0.00
Length of Term:	TENURE	TENURE

TOTAL ANNUAL LOAN COST RATE

LOAN TERMS

Age of youngest borrower:	64
Appraised Property Value:	$150,000 annually
Initial interest rate:	3.720%
Monthly advance:	$0.00
Initial Draw:	$0.00
Line of Credit:	$70,412.06
Length of Term:	

MONTHLY LOAN CHARGES

Monthly Servicing Fee:	$30.00
Mortgage Insurance:	0.5 %

OTHER CHARGES

Shared Appreciation:	None

INITIAL LOAN CHARGES

Closing Cost:	$4,800.00
Mortgage Insurance Premium:	$3,000.00
Annuity Cost:	None

REPAYMENT LIMITS

Net proceeds estimated at 93% of projected home sale

Appreciation Rate	DISCLOSURE PERIOD (Yrs.)			
	2	10	20	28
0%	16.09%	7.02%	5.83%	5.04%
4%	16.09%	7.02%	5.83%	5.45%
8%	16.09%	7.02%	5.83%	5.45%

The cost of any reverse mortgage loan depends on how long you keep the loan and how much your house appreciates in value. Generally, the longer you keep a reverse mortgage, the lower the total annual loan cost rate will be.

This table shows the estimated cost of your reverse mortgage loan, expressed as an annual rate. It illustrates the cost for your age, that life expectancy, and 1.4 times that life expectancy. The table also shows the cost of the loan, assuming the value of your home appreciates at three different rates: 0%, 4%, and 8%.

The total annual cost rates in this table are based on the total charges associated with this loan. These charges typically include principal, interest, closing costs, mortgage insurance premiums, annuity costs, and servicing costs (but not disposition costs—costs when you sell the home).

The rates in this table are estimates. Your actual cost may differ if, for example, the amount of your loan advances varies or the interest rate on your mortgage changes. You may receive projections of loan balances from counselors or lenders that are based on an expected average mortgage rate that differs from the initial interest rate.

Source: Seattle Mortgage

Figure A.2 Amortization Schedule—Annual Projections

Borrower Name/Case Number:	Bill Bradley - Line of Credit	Refinance:	No

Age of Youngest Borrower:	64	Initial Property Value:	$150,000
Expected Interest Rate:	6.25%	Beg. Mortgage Balance:	$7,800
Maximum Claim Amount:	$150,000	Initial Line of Credit:	$70,412.06
Initial Principal Limit:	$83,100	Monthly Payment:	$0.00
Initial Draw:	$0.00	Monthly Servicing Fee:	$30.00
Financed Closing Costs:	$7,800		

NOTE: Actual interest charges and property value projections may vary from amounts show.
Available credit will be less than projected if funds withdrawn from line-of-credit.

		Annual Totals					End of Year			
Yr	Age	SVC Fee	Payment	MIP	Interest	Loan Bal	Line of Credit	Prin. Limit	Property Value @ 4%	Property Value @ 8%
1	64	360	0	41	515	8,716	75,314	88,886	156,000	156,000
2	65	360	0	46	574	9,696	80,558	95,075	162,240	168,480
3	66	360	0	51	638	10,745	86,167	101,694	168,729	181,958
4	67	360	0	56	705	11,867	92,167	108,775	175,478	196,515
5	68	360	0	62	778	13,066	98,584	116,349	182,497	212,236
6	69	360	0	68	855	14,350	105,449	124,450	189,797	229,215
7	70	360	0	75	938	15,722	112,791	133,115	197,389	247,552
8	71	360	0	82	1,026	17,190	120,644	142,384	205,285	267,357
9	72	360	0	90	1,121	18,761	129,045	152,298	213,496	288,745
10	73	360	0	98	1,222	20,441	138,030	162,902	222,036	311,845
11	74	360	0	106	1,330	22,237	147,641	174,245	230,918	336,792
12	75	360	0	116	1,446	24,159	157,921	186,377	240,154	363,736
13	76	360	0	126	1,570	26,215	168,916	199,354	249,761	392,835
14	77	360	0	136	1,703	28,413	180,678	213,235	257,951	424,261
15	78	360	0	148	1,844	30,765	193,258	228,082	270,141	458,202
16	79	360	0	160	1,996	33,281	206,714	243,963	280,947	494,858
17	80	360	0	173	2,158	35,972	221,107	260,950	292,185	534,447
18	81	360	0	187	2,332	38,850	236,502	279,119	303,872	577,203
19	82	360	0	201	2,517	41,928	252,970	298,554	316,027	623,379
20	83	360	0	217	2,716	45,221	270,583	319,341	328,668	673,249
21	84	360	0	234	2,928	48,743	289,423	341,576	341,815	727,109
22	85	360	0	252	3,155	52,511	309,575	365,360	355,487	785,278
23	86	360	0	272	3,398	56,540	331,131	390,799	369,707	848,100
24	87	360	0	293	3,658	60,850	354,187	418,010	384,495	915,948
25	88	360	0	315	3,936	65,461	378,848	447,115	399,875	989,224
26	89	360	0	339	4,233	70,392	405,226	478,246	415,870	1,068,362
27	90	360	0	364	4,551	75,667	433,441	511,546	432,505	1,153,831
28	91	360	0	391	4,891	81,309	463,621	547,164	449,805	1,246,138
29	92	360	0	420	5,254	87,344	495,902	585,262	467,797	1,345,829
30	93	360	0	451	5,644	93,799	530,431	626,012	486,509	1,453,495
31	94	360	0	485	6,060	100,703	567,364	669,600	505,970	1,569,774
32	95	360	0	520	6,505	108,089	606,868	716,223	526,208	1,695,356
33	96	360	0	558	6,981	115,988	649,123	766,092	547,254	1,830,985
34	97	360	0	599	7,490	124,437	694,320	819,434	569,147	1,977,464
35	98	360	0	643	8,035	133,475	742,664	876,489	591,913	2,135,661
36	99	360	0	689	8,618	143,142	794,375	937,517	615,589	2,306,514

Borrower Name/Case Number:	Betty Boop – Tenure Total Draw	Refinance: No
	Variables	**Calculated**
Date of Closing:	9/1/2005	9/1/2005
Borrower's Birth Date:	10/10/1941	Age: 64
Expected Interest Rate:	6.250	6.250%
Property Appraised Value:	$150,000	$150,000
Maximum Claim Amount:	$150,000	$150,000
Prin Lim - Shared Prem Fac:		.554-19
Principal Limit:		$83,100.00
Upfront Premium:	FINANCED	$3,000.00
Other Closing Costs:	$4,800.00	$4,800.00
Initial Draw:	$70,412.06	$70,412.06
Monthly Servicing Fee:	$30.00	$4,887.94
Net Principal Limit:		$0.00
Line of Credit:	$0.00	$0.00
Monthly Payment:	CALCULATE	$0.00
Length of Term:	4 Years	4 Years

TOTAL ANNUAL LOAN COST RATE

LOAN TERMS

Age of youngest borrower:	64
Appraised Property Value: annually	$150,000
Initial interest rate:	3.720%
Monthly advance:	$0.00
Initial Draw:	$70,412.06
Line of Credit:	$0.00
Length of Term:	4 Years

INITIAL LOAN CHARGES

Closing Cost:	$4,800.00
Mortgage Insurance Premium:	$3,000.00
Annuity Cost:	None

MONTHLY LOAN CHARGES

Mo. Servicing Fee:	$30.00
Mortgage Insurance:	0.5 %

OTHER CHARGES

Shared Appreciation:	None

REPAYMENT LIMITS

Net proceeds estimated at 93% of projected home sale

Appreciation Rate	DISCLOSURE PERIOD (Yrs.)			
	2	10	20	28
0%	10.32%	5.70%	3.48%	2.47%
4%	10.32%	5.70%	5.08%	4.88%
8%	10.32%	5.70%	5.08%	4.88%

The cost of any reverse mortgage loan depends on how long you keep the loan and how much your house appreciates in value. Generally, the longer you keep a reverse mortgage, the lower the total annual loan cost rate will be.

This table shows the estimated cost of your reverse mortgage loan, expressed as an annual rate. It illustrates the cost for your age, that life expectancy, and 1.4 times that life expectancy. The table also shows the cost of the loan, assuming the value of your home appreciates at three different rates: 0%, 4%, and 8%.

The total annual cost rates in this table are based on the total charges associated with this loan. These charges typically include principal, interest, closing costs, mortgage insurance premiums, annuity costs, and servicing costs (but not disposition costs—costs when you sell the home).

The rates in this table are estimates. Your actual cost may differ if, for example, the amount of your loan advances varies or the interest rate on your mortgage changes. You may receive projections of loan balances from counselors or lenders that are based on an expected average mortgage rate that differs from the initial interest rate.

Source: Seattle Mortgage

Figure A.3 Amortization Schedule—Annual Projections

Borrower Name/Case Number:	Betty Boop - Tenure Total Draw	Refinance: No	
Age of Youngest Borrower:	64	Initial Property Value:	$150,000
Expected Interest Rate:	6.250%	Beg. Mortgage Balance:	$78,212
Maximum Claim Amount:	$150,000	Initial Line of Credit:	$0.00
Initial Principal Limit:	$83,100	Monthly Payment:	$0.00
Initial Draw:	$70,412.06	Monthly Servicing Fee:	$30.00
Financed Closing Costs:	$7,800		

NOTE: Actual interest charges and property value projections may vary from amounts show. Available credit will be less than projected if funds withdrawn from line-of-credit.

			Annual Totals				End of Year			
Yr	Age	SVC Fee	Payment	MIP	Interest	Loan Bal	Line of Credit	Prin. Limit	Property Value	Property Value
1	64	360	0	404	5,055	84,031	0	88,886	156,000	156,000
2	65	360	0	434	5,430	90,255	0	95,075	162,240	168,480
3	66	360	0	466	5,831	96,913	0	101,694	168,729	181,958
4	67	360	0	501	6,260	104,034	0	108,775	175,478	196,515
5	68	360	0	538	6,720	111,651	0	116,349	182,497	212,236
6	69	360	0	577	7,211	119,799	0	124,450	189,797	229,215
7	70	360	0	619	7,736	128,514	0	133,115	197,389	247,552
8	71	360	0	664	8,298	137,835	0	142,384	205,285	267,357
9	72	360	0	712	8,899	147,806	0	152,298	213,496	288,745
10	73	360	0	763	9,542	158,471	0	162,902	222,036	311,845
11	74	360	0	818	10,229	169,878	0	174,245	230,918	336,792
12	75	360	0	877	10,965	182,080	0	186,377	240,154	363,736
13	76	360	0	940	11,751	195,131	0	199,354	249,761	392,835
14	77	360	0	1,007	12,593	209,091	0	213,235	259,751	424,261
15	78	360	0	1,079	13,493	224,024	0	228,082	270,141	458,202
16	79	360	0	1,156	14,455	239,995	0	243,963	280,947	494,858
17	80	360	0	1,239	15,485	257,079	0	260,950	292,185	534,447
18	81	360	0	1,327	16,586	275,353	0	279,119	303,872	577,203
19	82	360	0	1,421	17,765	294,898	0	298,554	316,027	623,379
20	83	360	0	1,522	19,025	315,805	0	319,341	328,668	673,249
21	84	360	0	1,630	20,373	338,167	0	341,576	341,815	727,109
22	85	360	0	1,745	21,814	362,087	0	365,360	355,487	785,278
23	86	360	0	1,869	23,356	387,671	0	390,799	369,707	848,100
24	87	360	0	2,000	25,006	415,038	0	418,010	384,495	915,948
25	88	360	0	2,142	26,770	444,309	0	447,115	399,875	989,224
26	89	360	0	2,293	28,657	475,619	0	478,246	415,870	1,068,362
27	90	360	0	2,454	30,676	509,109	0	511,546	432,505	1,153,831
28	91	360	0	2,627	32,835	544,931	0	547,164	449,805	1,246,138
29	92	360	0	2,812	35,144	583,246	0	585,262	467,797	1,345,829
30	93	360	0	3,009	37,615	624,230	0	626,012	486,509	1,453,495
31	94	360	0	3,221	40,257	668,067	0	669,600	505,970	1,569,774
32	95	360	0	3,447	43,083	714,957	0	716,223	526,208	1,695,356
33	96	360	0	3,688	46,106	765,112	0	733,092	547,257	1,830,985
34	97	360	0	3,947	49,339	818,758	0	819,434	569,147	1,977,464
35	98	360	0	4,224	52,798	876,140	0	876,489	591,913	2,135,661
36	99	360	0	4,520	56,497	937,517	0	937,517	615,589	2,306,514

Figure A.4 Tenure Total Draw, $290,319 Maximum Claim, Age 77 Home Equity Conversion Mortgage Insurance (HECM)

Borrower Name/Case Number:	Dick Barnett-Tenure Total Draw	Refinance: No
	Variables	**Calculated**
Date of Closing:	9/1/2005	9/1/2005
Borrower's Birth Date:	10/10/1928	Age: 77
Expected Interest Rate:	6.250%	
Property Appraised Value:	$290,319	$290,319
Maximum Claim Amount:	$290,319	$290,319
Prin Lim - Shared Prem Fac:		.691-06
Principal Limit:		$200,610.43
Upfront Premium:	FINANCED	$5,806.38
Other Closing Costs:	$7,606.00	$7,606.00
Initial Draw:	$182,975.18	$182,975.18
Monthly Servicing Fee:	$30.00	$4,222.87
Net Principal Limit:		$0.00
Line of Credit:	CALCULATE	$0.00
Monthly Payment:	$0.00	$0.00
Length of Term:	TENURE	TENURE

TOTAL ANNUAL LOAN COST RATE

LOAN TERMS

Age of youngest borrower:	77
Appraised Property Value: annually	$290,319
Initial interest rate:	3.720%
Monthly advance:	$0.00
Initial Draw:	$182,975.18
Line of Credit:	$0.00
Length of Term:	TENURE

MONTHLY LOAN CHARGES

Mo. Servicing Fee:	$30.00
Mortgage Insurance:	0.5 %

OTHER CHARGES

Shared Appreciation:	None

INITIAL LOAN CHARGES

Closing Cost:	$7,606.00
Mortgage Insurance Premium:	$5,806.38
Annuity Cost:	None

REPAYMENT LIMITS

Net proceeds estimated at 93% of projected home sale

Appreciation Rate	DISCLOSURE PERIOD (Yrs.)			
	2	6	11	15
0%	8.16%	5.62%	3.60%	2.63%
4%	8.16%	5.62%	5.04%	4.85%
8%	8.16%	5.62%	5.04%	4.85%

The cost of any reverse mortgage loan depends on how long you keep the loan and how much your house appreciates in value. Generally, the longer you keep a reverse mortgage, the lower the total annual loan cost rate will be.

This table shows the estimated cost of your reverse mortgage loan, expressed as an annual rate. It illustrates the cost for your age, that life expectancy, and 1.4 times that life expectancy. The table also shows the cost of the loan, assuming the value of your home appreciates at three different rates: 0%, 4%, and 8%.

The total annual cost rates in this table are based on the total charges associated with this loan. These charges typically include principal, interest, closing costs, mortgage insurance premiums, annuity costs, and servicing costs (but not disposition costs—costs when you sell the home).

The rates in this table are estimates. Your actual cost may differ if, for example, the amount of your loan advances varies or the interest rate on your mortgage changes. You may receive projections of loan balances from counselors or lenders that are based on an expected average mortgage rate that differs from the initial interest rate.

Source: Seattle Mortgage

Figure A.4 Amortization Schedule—Annual Projections

Borrower Name/Case Number:	Dick Barnett-Tenure Total Draw	Refinance: No	
Age of Youngest Borrower:	77	Initial Property Value:	$290,319
Expected Interest Rate:	6.250%	Beg. Mortgage Balance:	$196,388
Maximum Claim Amount:	$290,319	Initial Line of Credit:	$0.00
Initial Principal Limit:	$200,610	Monthly Payment:	$0.00
Initial Draw:	$182,975.18	Monthly Servicing Fee:	$30.00
Financed Closing Costs:	$13,412		

NOTE: Actual interest charges and property value projections may vary from amounts show. Available credit will be less than projected if funds withdrawn from line-of-credit.

		Annual Totals					End of Year			
Yr	Age	SVC Fee	Payment	MIP	Interest	Loan Bal	Line of Credit	Prin. Limit	Property Value @ 4%	Property Value @8%
1	77	360	0	1,014	12,674	210,435	0	214,578	301,931	301,931
2	78	360	0	1,086	13,579	225,460	0	229,519	314,009	326,085
3	79	360	0	1,164	14,548	241,532	0	245,500	326,569	352,172
4	80	360	0	1,247	15,584	258,723	0	262,593	339,632	380,346
5	81	360	0	1,335	16,692	277,111	0	280,877	353,217	410,774
6	82	360	0	1,430	17,878	296,779	0	300,434	367,346	443,636
7	83	360	0	1,532	19,146	317,816	0	321,353	382,039	479,127
8	84	360	0	1,640	20,502	340,319	0	343,728	397,321	517,457
9	85	360	0	1,756	21,953	364,388	0	367,661	413,241	558,853
10	86	360	0	1,880	23,505	390,133	0	393,261	429,743	603,561
11	87	360	0	2,013	25,164	417,670	0	420,642	446,932	651,846
12	88	360	0	2,155	26,940	447,125	0	449,931	464,810	703,994
13	89	360	0	2,307	28,839	478,631	0	481,259	483,402	760,314
14	90	360	0	2,470	30,870	512,331	0	514,768	502,738	821,139
15	91	360	0	2,643	33,043	548,377	0	550,610	522,848	886,830
16	92	360	0	2,829	35,367	586,933	0	588,948	543,762	957,776
17	93	360	0	3,028	37,852	628,173	0	629,955	565,512	1,034,398
18	94	360	0	3,241	40,511	672,285	0	673,818	588,133	1,117,150
19	95	360	0	3,468	43,355	719,486	0	720,734	611,658	1,206,522
20	96	360	0	3,712	46,397	769,937	0	770,918	636,124	1,303,044
21	97	360	0	3,972	49,651	823,920	0	824,595	661,569	1,407,287
22	98	360	0	4,250	53,131	881,661	0	882,010	688,032	1,519,870
23	99	360	0	4,548	56,853	943,423	0	943,423	715,553	1,641,460

Borrower Name/Case Number:	Willis Reed – Line of Credit	Refinance: No
	Variables	**Calculated**
Date of Closing:	9/1/2005	9/1/2005
Borrower's Birth Date:	10/10/1923	Age: 82
Expected Interest Rate:	6.250%	
Property Appraised Value:	$290,319	$290,319
Maximum Claim Amount:	$290,319	$290,319
Prin Lim - Shared Prem Fac:		.746-05-
Principal Limit:		$216,577.97
Upfront Premium:	FINANCED	$5,806.38
Other Closing Costs:	$7,606.00	$7,606.00
Initial Draw:	$0.00	$0.00
Monthly Servicing Fee:	$30.00	$3,766.55
Net Principal Limit:		$199,399.04
Line of Credit:	CALCULATE	$199,399.04
Monthly Payment:	$0.00	$0.00
Length of Term:	TENURE	TENURE

TOTAL ANNUAL LOAN COST RATE

LOAN TERMS

Age of youngest borrower:	82
Appraised Property Value:	$290,319
Initial interest rate:	3.720%
Monthly advance:	$0.00
Initial Draw:	$0.00
Line of Credit:	$199,399.04
Length of Term:	TENURE

MONTHLY LOAN CHARGES

Mo. Servicing Fee:	$30.00
Mortgage Insurance:	0.5 % annually

OTHER CHARGES

Shared Appreciation:	None

INITIAL LOAN CHARGES

Closing Cost:	$7,606.00
Mortgage Insurance Premium:	$5,806.38
Annuity Cost:	None

REPAYMENT LIMITS

Net proceeds estimated at 93% of projected home sale

Appreciation Rate	DISCLOSURE PERIOD (Yrs.)			
	2	4	8	11
0%	11.34%	7.87%	6.16%	5.68%
4%	11.34%	7.87%	6.16%	5.68%
8%	11.34%	7.87%	6.16%	5.68%

The cost of any reverse mortgage loan depends on how long you keep the loan and how much your house appreciates in value. Generally, the longer you keep a reverse mortgage, the lower the total annual loan cost rate will be.

This table shows the estimated cost of your reverse mortgage loan, expressed as an annual rate. It illustrates the cost for your age, that life expectancy, and 1.4 times that life expectancy. The table also shows the cost of the loan, assuming the value of your home appreciates at three different rates: 0%, 4%, and 8%.

The total annual cost rates in this table are based on the total charges associated with this loan. These charges typically include principal, interest, closing costs, mortgage insurance premiums, annuity costs, and servicing costs (but not disposition costs— costs when you sell the home).

The rates in this table are estimates. Your actual cost may differ if, for example, the amount of your loan advances varies or the interest rate on your mortgage changes. You may receive projections of loan balances from counselors or lenders that are based on an expected average mortgage rate that differs from the initial interest rate.

Source: Seattle Mortgage

Figure A.5 Amortization Schedule—Annual Projections

Borrower Name/Case Number:	Willis Reed – Line of Credit	Refinance:	No

Age of Youngest Borrower:	82	Initial Property Value:	$290,319
Expected Interest Rate:	6.250%	Beg. Mortgage Balance:	$13,412
Maximum Claim Amount:	$290,319	Initial Line of Credit:	$199,399.04
Initial Principal Limit:	$216,578	Monthly Payment:	$0.00
Initial Draw:	$0.00	Monthly Servicing Fee:	$30.00
Financed Closing Costs:	$13,412		

NOTE: Actual interest charges and property value projections may vary from amounts show. Available credit will be less than projected if funds withdrawn from line-of-credit.

			-------Annual Totals-------				-------End of Year-------			
Yr	Age	SVC Fee	Payment	MIP	Interest	Loan Bal	Line of Credit	Prin. Limit	Property Value @ 4%	Property Value @ 8%
1	82	360	0	70	877	14,719	213,282	231,657	301,931	301,931
2	83	360	0	77	961	16,118	228,133	247,787	314,009	326,085
3	84	360	0	84	1,052	17,613	244,017	265,040	326,569	352,172
4	85	360	0	92	1,148	19,213	261,008	283,494	339,632	380,346
5	86	360	0	100	1,251	20,924	279,181	303,234	353,217	410,774
6	87	360	0	109	1,361	22,755	298,620	324,347	367,346	443,636
7	88	360	0	118	1,479	24,713	319,412	346,931	382,039	479,127
8	89	360	0	128	1,606	26,807	341,652	371,087	397,321	517,457
9	90	360	0	139	1,741	29,047	365,441	396,925	413,214	558,853
10	91	360	0	151	1,885	31,443	390,886	424,562	429,743	603,561
11	92	360	0	163	2,040	34,005	418,102	454,123	446,932	651,846
12	93	360	0	176	2,205	36,747	447,214	485,743	464,810	703,994
13	94	360	0	191	2,382	39,679	478,353	519,564	483,402	760,314
14	95	360	0	206	2,571	42,815	511,659	555,741	502,738	821,139
15	96	360	0	222	2,773	46,169	547,285	594,436	522,848	886,830
16	97	360	0	239	2,989	49,758	585,392	635,825	543,762	957,776
17	98	360	0	258	3,220	53,596	626,151	680,096	565,512	1,034,398
18	99	360	0	277	3,468	57,701	669,749	727,450	588,133	1,117,150

Figure A.6 Line of Credit, $290,319 Maximum Claim, Age 81 Home Equity Conversion Mortgage Insurance (HECM)

Borrower Name/Case Number:	Walt Frazier - Line of Credit	Refinance: No
	Variables	**Calculated**
Date of Closing:	9/1/2005	9/1/2005
Borrower's Birth Date:	10/10/1923	Age: 81
Expected Interest Rate:	6.250%	6.250%
Property Appraised Value:	$290,319	$290,319
Maximum Claim Amount:	$290,319	$290,319
Prin Lim - Shared Prem Fac:		.746-05-
Principal Limit:		$216,577.97
Upfront Premium:	FINANCED	$5,806.38
Other Closing Costs:	$7,606.00	$7,606.00
Initial Draw:	$0.00	$0.00
Monthly Servicing Fee:	$30.00	$3,766.55
Net Principal Limit:		$199,399.04
Line of Credit:	CALCULATE	$199,399.04
Monthly Payment:	$0.00	$0.00
Length of Term:	TENURE	TENURE

TOTAL ANNUAL LOAN COST RATE

LOAN TERMS

Age of youngest borrower:	81
Appraised Property Value: annually	$291,319
Initial interest rate:	3.720%
Monthly advance:	$0.00
Initial Draw:	$0.00
Line of Credit:	$199,399.04
Length of Term:	TENURE

MONTHLY LOAN CHARGES

Mo. Servicing Fee:	$30.00
Mortgage Insurance:	0.5 %

OTHER CHARGES

Shared Appreciation:	None

INITIAL LOAN CHARGES

Closing Cost:	$7,606.00
Mortgage Insurance Premium:	$5,806.38
Annuity Cost:	None

REPAYMENT LIMITS

Net proceeds estimated at 93% of projected home sale

Appreciation Rate	DISCLOSURE PERIOD (Yrs.)			
	2	4	8	11
0%	11.34%	7.87%	6.16%	5.68%
4%	11.34%	7.87%	6.16%	5.68%
8%	11.34%	7.87%	6.16%	5.68%

The cost of any reverse mortgage loan depends on how long you keep the loan and how much your house appreciates in value. Generally, the longer you keep a reverse mortgage, the lower the total annual loan cost rate will be.

This table shows the estimated cost of your reverse mortgage loan, expressed as an annual rate. It illustrates the cost for your age, that life expectancy, and 1.4 times that life expectancy. The table also shows the cost of the loan, assuming the value of your home appreciates at three different rates: 0%, 4%, and 8%.

The total annual cost rates in this table are based on the total charges associated with this loan. These charges typically include principal, interest, closing costs, mortgage insurance premiums, annuity costs, and servicing costs (but not disposition costs—costs when you sell the home).

The rates in this table are estimates. Your actual cost may differ if, for example, the amount of your loan advances varies or the interest rate on your mortgage changes. You may receive projections of loan balances from counselors or lenders that are based on an expected average mortgage rate that differs from the initial interest rate.

Source: Seattle Mortgage

Figure A.6 Amortization Schedule—Annual Projections

Borrower Name/Case Number:	Walt Frazier - Line of Credit	Refinance:	No

Age of Youngest Borrower:	81	Initial Property Value:	$290,319
Expected Interest Rate:	6.250%	Beg. Mortgage Balance:	$13,412
Maximum Claim Amount:	$290,319	Initial Line of Credit:	$199,399.04
Initial Principal Limit:	$216,578	Monthly Payment:	$0.00
Initial Draw:	$0.00	Monthly Servicing Fee:	$30.00
Financed Closing Costs:	$13,412		

NOTE: Actual interest charges and property value projections may vary from amounts show. Available credit will be less than projected if funds withdrawn from line-of-credit.

			-----Annual Totals-----				-----End of Year-----			
Yr	Age	SVC Fee	Payment	MIP	Interest	Loan Bal	Line of Credit	Prin. Limit	Property Value @ 4%	Property Value @ 8%
1	82	360	0	70	877	14,719	213,282	231,657	301,931	301,931
2	83	360	0	77	961	16,118	228,133	247,787	314,009	326,085
3	84	360	0	84	1,052	17,613	244,017	265,040	326,569	352,172
4	85	360	0	92	1,148	19,213	261,008	283,494	339,632	380,346
5	86	360	0	100	1,251	20,924	279,181	303,234	353,217	410,774
6	87	360	0	109	1,361	22,755	298,620	324,347	367,346	443,636
7	88	360	0	118	1,479	24,713	319,412	346,931	382,039	479,127
8	89	360	0	128	1,606	26,807	341,652	371,087	397,321	517,457
9	90	360	0	139	1,741	29,047	365,441	396,925	413,214	558,853
10	91	360	0	151	1,885	31,443	390,886	424,562	429,743	603,561
11	92	360	0	163	2,040	34,005	418,102	454,123	446,932	651,846
12	93	360	0	176	2,205	36,747	447,214	485,743	464,810	703,994
13	94	360	0	191	2,382	39,679	478,353	519,564	483,402	760,314
14	95	360	0	206	2,571	42,815	511,659	555,741	502,738	821,139
15	96	360	0	222	2,773	46,169	547,285	594,436	522,848	886,830
16	97	360	0	239	2,989	49,758	585,392	635,825	543,762	957,776
17	98	360	0	258	3,220	53,596	626,151	680,096	565,512	1,034,398
18	99	360	0	277	3,468	57,701	669,749	727,450	588,133	1,117,150

Figure A.7 Tenure Total Draw, $290,319 Maximum Claim, Age 81 Home Equity Conversion Mortgage Insurance (HECM)

	Bob Pettit – Tenure Total Draw	Refinance: No
Borrower Name/Case Number:		
	Variables	**Calculated**
Date of Closing:	9/1/2005	9/1/2005
Borrower's Birth Date:	10/10/1923	Age: 81
Expected Interest Rate:	6.250%	6.250%
Property Appraised Value:	$290,319	$290,319
Maximum Claim Amount:	$290,319	$290,319
Prin Lim - Shared Prem Fac:		.735-05-
Principal Limit:		$213,384.47
Upfront Premium:	FINANCED	$5,806.38
Other Closing Costs:	$7,606.00	$7,606.00
Initial Draw:	$196,101.60	$196,101.60
Monthly Servicing Fee:	$30.00	$3,870.49
Net Principal Limit:		$0.00
Line of Credit:	CALCULATE	$0.00
Monthly Payment:	$0.00	$0.00
Length of Term:	TENURE	TENURE

TOTAL ANNUAL LOAN COST RATE

LOAN TERMS

		MONTHLY LOAN CHARGES	
Age of youngest borrower:	81	Mo. Servicing Fee:	$30.00
Appraised Property Value:	$290,319	Mortgage Insurance:	0.5 %
annually			
Initial interest rate:	3.720%		
Monthly advance:	$0.00	**OTHER CHARGES**	
Initial Draw:	$196,101.60	Shared Appreciation:	None
Line of Credit:	$0.00		
Length of Term:	TENURE		

INITIAL LOAN CHARGES

		REPAYMENT LIMITS
Closing Cost:	$7,606.00	Net proceeds estimated at 93%
Mortgage Insurance Premium:	$5,806.38	of projected home sale
Annuity Cost:	None	

Appreciation Rate	DISCLOSURE PERIOD (Yrs.)			
	2	5	9	13
0%	7.90%	5.77%	3.62%	2.49%
4%	7.90%	5.77%	5.14%	4.89%
8%	7.90%	5.77%	5.14%	4.89%

The cost of any reverse mortgage loan depends on how long you keep the loan and how much your house appreciates in value. Generally, the longer you keep a reverse mortgage, the lower the total annual loan cost rate will be.

This table shows the estimated cost of your reverse mortgage loan, expressed as an annual rate. It illustrates the cost for your age, that life expectancy, and 1.4 times that life expectancy. The table also shows the cost of the loan, assuming the value of your home appreciates at three different rates: 0%, 4%, and 8%.

The total annual cost rates in this table are based on the total charges associated with this loan. These charges typically include principal, interest, closing costs, mortgage insurance premiums, annuity costs, and servicing costs (but not disposition costs—costs when you sell the home).

The rates in this table are estimates. Your actual cost may differ if, for example, the amount of your loan advances varies or the interest rate on your mortgage changes. You may receive projections of loan balances from counselors or lenders that are based on an expected average mortgage rate that differs from the initial interest rate.

Source: Seattle Mortgage

Figure A.7 Amortization Schedule—Annual Projections

Borrower Name/Case Number:	Bob Pettit – Tenure Total Draw	Refinance: No
Age of Youngest Borrower:	81	Initial Property Value: $290,319
Expected Interest Rate:	6.250%	Beg. Mortgage Balance: $209,514
Maximum Claim Amount:	$290,319	Initial Line of Credit: $0.00
Initial Principal Limit:	$213,384	Monthly Payment: $0.00
Initial Draw:	$196,101.60	Monthly Servicing Fee: $30.00
Financed Closing Costs:	$13,412.00	

NOTE: Actual interest charges and property value projections may vary from amounts show. Available credit will be less than projected if funds withdrawn from line-of-credit.

						Annual Totals				End of Year		
Yr	Age	SVC Fee	Payment	MIP	Interest	Loan Bal	Line of Credit	Prin. Limit	Property Value @ 4%	Property Value @ 8%
1	81	360	0	1,082	13,520	224,475	0	228,241	301,931	301,931
2	82	360	0	1,159	14,484	240,478	0	244,134	314,009	326,085
3	83	360	0	1,241	15,516	257,596	0	261,132	326,569	352,172
4	84	360	0	1,330	16,620	275,905	0	279,314	339,632	380,346
5	85	360	0	1,424	17,800	295,489	0	298,762	353,217	410,774
6	86	360	0	1,525	19,063	316,437	0	319,565	367,346	443,636
7	87	360	0	1,633	20,413	338,843	0	341,815	382,039	479,127
8	88	360	0	1,749	21,858	362,810	0	365,615	397,321	517,457
9	89	360	0	1,872	23,403	388,445	0	391,072	413,214	558,853
10	90	360	0	2,004	25,056	415,865	0	418,302	429,743	603,561
11	91	360	0	2,146	26,823	445,914	0	447,427	446,932	651,846
12	92	360	0	2,297	28,714	476,566	0	478,581	464,810	703,994
13	93	360	0	2,459	30,737	510,121	0	511,903	483,402	760,314
14	94	360	0	2,632	32,900	546,013	0	547,546	502,738	821,139
15	95	360	0	2,817	35,214	584,405	0	585,671	522,848	886,830
16	96	360	0	3,015	37,689	625,469	0	626,450	543,762	957,776
17	97	360	0	3,227	40,337	669,393	0	670,068	565,512	1,034,398
18	98	360	0	3,453	43,168	716,375	0	716,724	588,133	1,117,150
19	99	360	0	3,696	46,197	766,628	0	766,628	611,658	1,206,522

Figure A.8 Four-Year Term, $150,000 Home Value, Age 64 Home Equity Conversion Mortgage (HECM)

Borrower Name/Case Number:	Bob Pettit – Tenure Total Draw		Refinance: No
		Variables	Calculated
Date of Closing:		9/1/2005	9/1/2005
Borrower's Birth Date:		10/10/1923	Age: 81
Expected Interest Rate:		6.250%	6.250%
Property Appraised Value:		$290,319	$290,319
Maximum Claim Amount:		$290,319	$290,319
Prin Lim - Shared Prem Fac:			.735-05-
Principal Limit:			$213,384.47
Upfront Premium:		FINANCED	$5,806.38
Other Closing Costs:		$7,606.00	$7,606.00
Initial Draw:		$196,101.60	$196,101.60
Monthly Servicing Fee:		$30.00	$3,870.49
Net Principal Limit:			$0.00
Line of Credit:		CALCULATE	$0.00
Monthly Payment:		$0.00	$0.00
Length of Term:		TENURE	TENURE

TOTAL ANNUAL LOAN COST RATE

LOAN TERMS

Age of youngest borrower:	81
Appraised Property Value: annually	$290,319
Initial interest rate:	3.720%
Monthly advance:	$0.00
Initial Draw:	$196,101.60
Line of Credit:	$0.00
Length of Term:	TENURE

INITIAL LOAN CHARGES

Closing Cost:	$7,606.00
Mortgage Insurance Premium:	$5,806.38
Annuity Cost:	None

MONTHLY LOAN CHARGES

Mo. Servicing Fee:	$30.00
Mortgage Insurance:	0.5 %

OTHER CHARGES

Shared Appreciation:	None

REPAYMENT LIMITS

Net proceeds estimated at 93% of projected home sale

Appreciation Rate	DISCLOSURE PERIOD (Yrs.)			
	2	5	9	13
0%	7.90%	5.77%	3.62%	2.49%
4%	7.90%	5.77%	5.14%	4.89%
8%	7.90%	5.77%	5.14%	4.89%

The cost of any reverse mortgage loan depends on how long you keep the loan and how much your house appreciates in value. Generally, the longer you keep a reverse mortgage, the lower the total annual loan cost rate will be.

This table shows the estimated cost of your reverse mortgage loan, expressed as an annual rate. It illustrates the cost for your age, that life expectancy, and 1.4 times that life expectancy. The table also shows the cost of the loan, assuming the value of your home appreciates at three different rates: 0%, 4%, and 8%.

The total annual cost rates in this table are based on the total charges associated with this loan. These charges typically include principal, interest, closing costs, mortgage insurance premiums, annuity costs, and servicing costs (but not disposition costs— costs when you sell the home).

The rates in this table are estimates. Your actual cost may differ if, for example, the amount of your loan advances varies or the interest rate on your mortgage changes. You may receive projections of loan balances from counselors or lenders that are based on an expected average mortgage rate that differs from the initial interest rate.

Source: Seattle Mortgage

Figure A.8 Amortization Schedule—Annual Projections

Borrower Name/Case Number:	Elgin Baylor - 4 Year Term	Refinance: No

Age of Youngest Borrower:	64	Initial Property Value:	$150,000
Expected Interest Rate:	6.250	Beg. Mortgage Balance:	$7,800
Maximum Claim Amount:	$150,000	Initial Line of Credit:	$0.00
Initial Principal Limit:	$83,100	Monthly Payment:	$1,668.56
Initial Draw:	$0.00	Monthly Servicing Fee:	$30.00
Financed Closing Costs:	$7,800		

NOTE: Actual interest charges and property value projections may vary from amounts show. Available credit will be less than projected if funds withdrawn from line-of-credit.

			Annual Totals				End of Year			
Yr	Age	SVC Fee	Payment	MIP	Interest	Loan Bal	Line of Credit	Prin. Limit	Property Value @ 4%	Property Value @ 8%
1	64	360	20,023	97	1,207	29,486	0	88,886	156,000	156,000
2	65	360	20,023	208	2,605	52,683	0	95,075	162,240	168,480
3	66	360	20,023	328	4,101	77,495	0	101,694	168,729	181,958
4	67	360	20,023	456	5,701	104,034	0	108,775	175,478	196,515
5	68	360	0	538	6,720	111,651	0	116,349	182,497	212,236
6	69	360	0	577	7,211	119,799	0	124,450	189,797	229,215
7	70	360	0	619	7,736	128,514	0	133,115	197,389	247,552
8	71	360	0	664	8,298	137,835	0	142,384	205,285	267,357
9	72	360	0	712	8,899	147,806	0	152,298	213,496	288,745
10	73	360	0	763	9,542	158,471	0	162,902	222,036	311,845
11	74	360	0	818	10,229	169,878	0	174,245	230,918	336,792
12	75	360	0	877	10,965	182,080	0	186,377	240,154	363,736
13	76	360	0	940	11,751	195,131	0	199,354	249,761	392,835
14	77	360	0	1,007	12,593	209,091	0	213,235	259,751	424,261
15	78	360	0	1,079	13,493	224,024	0	228,082	270,141	458,202
16	79	360	0	1,156	14,455	239,995	0	243,963	280,947	494,858
17	80	360	0	1,239	15,485	257,079	0	260,950	292,185	534,447
18	81	360	0	1,327	16,586	275,353	0	279,119	303,872	577,203
19	82	360	0	1,421	17,765	294,898	0	298,554	316,027	623,379
20	83	360	0	1,522	19,025	315,805	0	319,341	328,668	673,249
21	84	360	0	1,630	20,373	338,167	0	341,576	341,815	727,109
22	85	360	0	1,745	21,814	362,087	0	365,360	355,487	785,278
23	86	360	0	1,869	23,356	387,671	0	390,799	369,707	848,100
24	87	360	0	2,000	25,006	415,038	0	418,010	384,495	915,948
25	88	360	0	2,142	26,770	444,309	0	447,115	399,875	989,224
26	89	360	0	2,293	28,657	475,619	0	478,246	415,870	1,068,362
27	90	360	0	2,454	30,676	509,109	0	511,546	432,505	1,153,831
28	91	360	0	2,627	32,835	544,931	0	547,164	449,805	1,246,138
29	92	360	0	2,812	35,144	583,246	0	585,262	467,797	1,345,829
30	93	360	0	3,009	37,615	624,230	0	626,012	486,509	1,453,495
31	94	360	0	3,221	40,257	668,067	0	669,600	505,970	1,569,774
32	95	360	0	3,447	43,083	714,957	0	716,223	526,208	1,695,356
33	96	360	0	3,688	46,106	765,112	0	766,092	547,257	1,830,985
34	97	360	0	3,947	49,339	818,758	0	819,434	569,147	1,977,464
35	98	360	0	4,224	52,798	876,140	0	876,489	591,913	2,135,661
36	99	360	0	4,520	56,497	937,517	0	937,517	615,589	2,306,514

LIBOR stands for London Inter Bank Offer Rate. It is the rate of interest at which banks offer to lend money to one another in the wholesale money markets in London. It is a standard financial index used in U.S. capital markets. In general, its changes have been smaller than changes in the prime rate.

Date	1-Month	3-Month	6-Month	1-Year
Jan-02	1.829	1.862	1.989	2.420
Feb-02	1.883	1.920	2.068	2.496
Mar-02	1.880	2.031	2.332	3.006
Apr-02	1.842	1.913	2.100	2.613
May-02	1.844	1.896	2.090	2.634
Jun-02	1.836	1.860	1.948	2.251
Jul-02	1.818	1.823	1.863	2.070
Aug-02	1.820	1.816	1.815	1.943
Sep-02	1.819	1.806	1.751	1.813
Oct-02	1.741	1.702	1.618	1.664
Nov-02	1.380	1.432	1.471	1.705
Dec-02	1.382	1.383	1.383	1.447
Jan-03	1.339	1.348	1.353	1.477
Feb-03	1.334	1.336	1.336	1.368
Mar-03	1.306	1.288	1.262	1.340
Apr-03	1.318	1.308	1.290	1.362
May-03	1.3189	1.2782	1.2232	1.2214
Jun-03	1.1232	1.1164	1.1239	1.2014
Jul-03	1.1036	1.1176	1.1507	1.2789
Aug-03	1.1170	1.1420	1.2098	1.4714
Sep-03	1.1214	1.1598	1.1795	1.2857
Oct-03	1.1201	1.1657	1.2207	1.4551
Nov-03	1.1157	1.1701	1.2297	1.4867
Dec-03	1.1195	1.1570	1.2192	1.4582
Jan-04	1.0982	1.1320	1.2107	1.4607
Feb-04	1.0973	1.1251	1.2026	1.3645
Mar-04	1.0914	1.1107	1.1595	1.3401
Apr-04	1.1007	1.1764	1.3682	1.8082
May-04	1.1089	1.3082	1.5789	2.0764
Jun-04	1.3582	1.6039	1.9420	2.4682

Figure A.10 10-Year Constant Maturity Index

HECM loans are tied to the One-Year Constant Maturity Treasury Index and the 10-Year Treasury Constant Maturity Index. For the HECM monthly adjustable-rate mortgage, the key rate is the One-Year gauge while the HECM annual adjustable-rate mortgage moves according to the 10-Year Index. Here is a look at how the 10-Year Index has moved over time.

.Date	Rate	Date	Rate	Date	Rate
01/1997	6.58	03/2000	6.26	06/2003	3.33
02/1997	6.42	04/2000	5.99	07/2003	3.98
03/1997	6.69	05/2000	6.44	08/2003	4.45
04/1997	6.89	06/2000	6.10	09/2003	4.27
05/1997	6.71	07/2000	6.05	10/2003	4.29
06/1997	6.49	08/2000	5.83	11/2003	4.30
07/1997	6.22	09/2000	5.80	12/2003	4.27
08/1997	6.30	10/2000	5.74	01/2004	4.15
09/1997	6.21	11/2000	5.72	02/2004	4.08
10/1997	6.03	12/2000	5.24	03/2004	3.83
11/1997	5.88	01/2001	5.16	04/2004	4.35
12/1997	5.81	02/2001	5.10	05/2004	4.72
01/1998	5.54	03/2001	4.89	06/2004	4.73
02/1998	5.57	04/2001	5.14		
03/1998	5.65	05/2001	5.39		
04/1998	5.64	06/2001	5.28		
05/1998	5.65	07/2001	5.24		
06/1998	5.50	08/2001	4.97		
07/1998	5.46	09/2001	4.73		
08/1998	5.34	10/2001	4.57		
09/1998	4.81	11/2001	4.65		
10/1998	4.53	12/2001	5.09		
11/1998	4.83	01/2002	5.04		
12/1998	4.65	02/2002	4.91		
01/1999	4.72	03/2002	5.28		
02/1999	5.00	04/2002	5.21		
03/1999	5.23	05/2002	5.16		
04/1999	5.18	06/2002	4.93		
05/1999	5.54	07/2002	4.65		
06/1999	5.90	08/2002	4.26		
07/1999	5.79	09/2002	3.87		
08/1999	5.94	10/2002	3.94		
09/1999	5.92	11/2002	4.05		
10/1999	6.11	12/2002	4.03		
11/1999	6.03	01/2003	4.05		
12/1999	6.28	02/2003	3.90		
01/2000	6.66	03/2003	3.81		
02/2000	6.52	04/2003	3.96		
		05/2003	3.57		

Figure A.11 One-Year Constant Maturity Index

HECM loans are tied to the One-Year Constant Maturity Treasury Index and the 10-Year Treasury Constant Maturity Index. For the HECM monthly adjustable-rate mortgage, the key rate is the One-Year gauge while the HECM annual adjustable-rate mortgage moves according to the 10-Year Index. Here is a look at how the One-Year Index has moved over time.

Date	Average Monthly	Monthly Change	Yearly Change
1999 01	4.51	-0.12	-0.73
1999 02	4.70	2.28	-0.61
1999 03	4.78	0.96	-0.61
1999 04	4.69	-1.08	-0.69
1999 05	4.85	1.92	-0.59
1999 06	5.10	3.00	-0.31
1999 07	5.03	-0.84	-0.33
1999 08	5.20	2.04	-0.01
1999 09	5.25	0.60	0.54
1999 10	5.43	2.16	1.31
1999 11	5.55	1.44	1.02
1999 12	5.84	3.48	1.32
2000 02	6.22	1.20	1.52
2000 03	6.22	0.00	1.44
2000 04	6.15	-0.84	1.46
2000 05	6.33	2.16	1.48
2000 06	6.17	-1.92	1.07
2000 07	6.08	-1.08	1.05
2000 08	6.18	1.20	0.98
2000 09	6.13	-0.60	0.88
2000 10	6.01	-1.44	0.58
2000 11	6.09	0.96	0.54
2000 12	5.60	-5.88	-0.24
2001 01	4.81	-9.48	-1.31
2001 02	4.68	-1.56	-1.54
2001 03	4.30	-4.56	-1.92
2001 04	3.98	-3.84	-2.17
2001 05	3.78	-2.40	-2.55
2001 06	3.58	-2.40	-2.59
2001 07	3.62	0.48	-2.46
2001 08	3.47	-1.80	-2.71
2001 09	2.82	-7.80	-3.31
2001 10	2.33	-5.88	-3.68
2001 11	2.18	-1.80	-3.91
2001 12	2.22	0.48	-3.38
2002 01	2.16	-0.72	-2.65
2002 02	2.23	0.84	-2.45
2002 03	2.57	4.08	-1.73
2002 04	2.48	-1.08	-1.50
2002 05	2.35	-1.56	-1.43
2002 06	2.20	-1.80	-1.38
2002 07	1.96	-2.88	-1.66
2002 08	1.76	-2.40	-1.71
2002 09	1.72	-0.48	-1.10
2002 10	1.65	-0.84	-0.68
2002 11	1.49	-1.92	-0.69
2002 12	1.45	-0.48	-0.77
2003 01	1.36	-1.08	-0.80
2003 02	1.30	-0.72	-0.93
2003 03	1.24	-0.72	-1.33
2003 04	1.27	0.36	-1.21
2003 05	1.18	-1.08	-1.17
2003 06	1.01	-2.04	-1.19
2003 07	1.12	1.32	-0.84
2003 08	1.31	2.28	-0.45
2003 09	1.24	-0.84	-0.48
2003 10	1.25	0.12	-0.40
2003 11	1.34	1.08	-0.15
2003 12	1.31	-0.36	-0.14
2004 01	1.24	-0.84	-0.12
2004 02	1.24	0.00	-0.06
2004 03	1.19	-0.60	-0.05
2004 04	1.43	2.88	0.16
2004 05	1.78	4.20	0.60
2004 06	2.12	4.08	1.11

Reverse Mortgage Lenders, Helpful Forms, and Resources

Reverse Mortgage Lenders Home Keeper, HECM and Cash Account Programs

The following list, provided by the United States Department of Housing and Urban Development and the National Association of Reverse Mortgage Lenders, includes most of the U.S. lenders offering the Fannie Mae Home Keeper Mortgage and the FHA Home Equity Conversion Mortgage (HECM). The "Big Three" national lenders—Financial Freedom, Seattle Mortgage and Wells Fargo have a presence in nearly every state and are listed only at the top of this section along with Carteret Mortgage and Allied Home Mortgage. Some individual lenders service more than one state. Financial Freedom's "jumbo" products are available through its state representatives and "brokered" through many of the other lenders listed below.

National:

FINANCIAL FREEDOM SENIOR
FUNDING CORP.
7595 Irvine Center Drive, Suite 250
Irvine, CA 92618
Telephone: (888) REVERSE; (888) 738-3773
E-Mail: sales@financialfreedom.com
www.financialfreedom.com

SEATTLE MORTGAGE CO.
601 108th Avenue NE, Suite 700
Bellevue, WA 98004
Telephone: (800) 233-4601
E-Mail: inquiry@smcreverse.com
www.seattlemortgage.com

WELLS FARGO HOME MORTGAGE
600 Northern Shores Lane
Greensboro, NC 27455-3441
Telephone: (800) 543-5642; (800) 336-7359
www.reversemortgages.net

CARTERET MORTGAGE CORP.
6211 Centreville Road, Suite 800
Centreville, VA 20121
Telephone: 1-877-227-8373

ALLIED HOME MORTGAGE CORP.
611 Pinemont
Houston, TX 77092
1-800-520-0057

Alabama:

AMERICAN REVERSE MORTGAGE CORP
212 14th Ct NW
Birmingham, AL 35215
Telephone: (352) 867-1111
Fax Number: (352) 369-5985
E-Mail: Info@AmericanReverse.com

BANK INDEPENDENT
710 S Montgomery Ave
Sheffield, AL 35660
Telephone: (256) 386-5000

CENTURA BANK
1585 Southlake Parkway
Morrow, GA 30260
Telephone: (404) 495-6834
Fax Number: (404) 495-6818

EAGLE MORTGAGE INC
204 W North Street
Poplarville, MS 39470
Telephone: (601) 795-8881
Fax Number: (601) 795-0840

EVERBANK
6984 Flowery Branch Road
Cummings, GA 30041
Telephone: (812) 949-2883

HIBERNIA NATIONAL BANK
11130 Industriplex Blvd
Baton Rouge, LA 70809
Telephone: (504) 381-2372

HOME FEDERAL SAVINGS BANK TN
515 Market St
Knoxville, TN 37902
Telephone: (615) 546-0330

HOMESOUTH MORTGAGE SERVICES INC
200 Cahaba Park Circle Ste 125
Birmingham, AL 35242
Telephone: (205) 591-5055
Fax Number: (205) 591-5053

MCGOWIN KING MORTGAGE LLC
9 Office Park Circle Ste 117
Birmingham, AL 35223
Telephone: (205) 879-7775

SHELTER MORTGAGE COMPANY LLC
3350 Northlake Pkwy, Suite B
Atlanta, GA 30345
Telephone: (678) 279-9000
Fax Number: (678) 279-2000

TRUSTMARK NATIONAL BANK
277 East Pearl
Jackson, MS 39201
Telephone: (601) 354-5150

Alaska:

FINANCIAL FREEDOM SENIOR FUNDING CORP.
Telephone: 1-888-REVERSE/1-888-738-3773
E-Mail: sales@financialfreedom.com

SEATTLE MORTGAGE CO.
Telephone: 1-800-233-4601
E-Mail: inquiry@smcreverse.com

WELLS FARGO HOME MORTGAGE
Telephone: 1-800-336-7359
E-Mail: Reverse_ProgConn@WellsFargo.com

Arizona:

COLONIAL MORTGAGE AND
INVESTMENT
8715 W Union Hills Dr Ste 103
Peoria, AZ 85382
Telephone: (602) 995-3990
Fax Number: (602) 995-9424

COMMUNITY LENDING INC
1990 W. Camelback Rd., 218
Phoenix, AZ 85015
Telephone: (602) 393-2890
Fax Number: (602) 393-2895

FARWEST MORTGAGE BANKERS INC
16824 Ave. of Fountains
Fountain Hills, AZ 85268
Telephone: (480) 816-4564
Fax Number: (480) 816-4563

HOME ACCESS CAPITAL INC
2111 E Highland Ave. Suite 440
Phoenix, AZ 85016
Telephone: (602) 234-2230
Fax Number: (602) 234-2234

PACIFIC COAST MORTGAGE INC
6300 E Thomas Rd Ste 200
Scottsdale, AZ 85251
Telephone: (480) 949-0707
Fax Number: (480) 949-5252

PRIME CAPITAL INC
5357 E Pima
Tucson, AZ 85712
Telephone: (602) 296-1600

PRIME SOURCE MORTGAGE INC
7100 E Lincoln Drive Ste B120
Scottsdale, AZ 85253
Telephone: (480) 998-2882

SCME MORTGAGE BANKERS INC
6265 Greenwich Drive Ste 200
San Diego, CA 92122
Telephone: (858) 558-2700

SKOFED MORTGAGE FUNDING CORP
2610 So. Jones Blvd, Suite #1
Las Vegas, NV 89146
Telephone: (702) 362-2626
Fax Number: (702) 362-6500

SUN AMERICAN MORTGAGE CO
444 South Greenfield Road
Mesa, AZ 85206
Telephone: (602) 832-4343

ZIONS FIRST NATIONAL BANK
255 N Admiral Blvd Rd
Salt Lake City, UT 84116
Telephone: (801) 273-3000
Fax Number: (801) 273-3035

Arkansas:

ALLIED HOME MORTGAGE CAPITAL
CORPORATION
2524 Crestwood Avenue Ste-5
N Little Rock, AR 72116
Telephone: (501) 758-1931

BANK OF SALEM
202 Church Street
Salem, AR 72576
Telephone: (501) 895-2591

EAGLE MORTGAGE INC
204 W North Street
Poplarville, MS 39470
Telephone: (601) 795-8881
Fax Number: (601) 795-0840

FIRST CONTINENTAL MTG CORP
POB 4095 450 Southwest Drive
Jonesboro, AR 72403
Telephone: (501) 932-6756

TRUSTMARK NATIONAL BANK
277 East Pearl
Jackson, MS 39201
Telephone: (601) 354-5150

California:

AMERICAN MORTGAGE
PROFESSIONALS INC
465 East Grand Avenue
Escondido, CA 92025
Telephone: (760) 743-8922
Fax Number: (760) 740-9417

AMERIFUND FINANCIAL INC
3920 E. Coronado St #101
Anaheim, CA 92807
Telephone: (714) 632-0111
Fax Number: (714) 632-0101

AMS FINANCIAL INC
615 First Street
Benicia, CA 94510
Telephone: (707) 746-4920

BENN REALTY SERVICES INC
44444 16th Street West Ste 203
Lancaster, CA 93534
Telephone: (661) 945-6829

CALIFORNIA REVERSE MORTGAGE CO
4399 Arden Way
Sacramento, CA 95864
Telephone: (916) 971-9500
Fax Number: (916) 971-0955

CARROLLTON MORTGAGE CO
121 E Orangeburg Ave Ste 1
Modesto, CA 95350
Telephone: (209) 526-6200

CEDAR FINANCIAL NETWORK
901 Campisi Way Suite 205
Campell, CA 95008
Telephone: (408) 879-9011

CENTRAL COAST HOME LOANS
7901 San Miguel Canyon Road
Prunedale, CA 93907
Telephone: (831) 663-0391

CENTRAL PACIFIC MORTGAGE CO
7777 Alvarado Road 302
La Mesa, CA 91941
Telephone: (619) 433-3170
Fax Number: (619) 433-3180

CLARION MORTGAGE CAPITAL INC
17772 East 17th Street Ste 208
Tustin, CA 92780
Telephone: (303) 843-0777

COACHELLA VALLEY MORTGAGE CTR
73-200 El Paseo Suite 2C
Palm Desert, CA 92260
Telephone: (760) 773-2811
Fax Number: (760) 773-2814

DOUGLAS MORTGAGE INC
11344 Coloma Rd Suite 880
Gold River, CA 95670
Telephone: (916) 853-0220

EAST WEST MORTGAGE COMPANY
21616 Rose Lane
Woodland, CA 95695
Telephone: (820) 758-0936

FARWEST MORTGAGE BANKERS INC
261 South Lakeview Avenue
Placentia, CA 92680
Telephone: (714) 579-1177

FIRST MUTUAL MORTGAGE INC
10681 Foothill Blvd Ste 101
Rancho Cucamonga, CA 91730
Telephone: (909) 989-7455

FRONTIER MORTGAGE CORPORATION
1801 East 14th Street
San Leandro, CA 94577
Telephone: (510) 895-5969
Fax Number: (510) 895-5971
E-Mail: robertmotta@frontier4loans.com

FULLERTON MORTGAGE AND ESCROW
501 Mission Avenue
Oceanside, CA 92049
Telephone: (619) 966-3632

HOME MORTGAGE FINANCIAL INC
1801D E Parkcourt Pl Ste 203
Santa Ana, CA 92701
Telephone: (714) 560-8430

LENDERS DEPOT INC
27450 Ynez Rd Ste 320
Temecula, CA 92591
Telephone: (909) 296-3322

METROCITIES MORTGAGE LLC
15301 Ventura Blvd., D300
Sherman Oaks, CA 91403
Telephone: (818) 981-0606
Fax Number: (818) 981-2953
E-Mail: cwight@metrociti.com

MONTEREY COAST MORTGAGE CORP
80 Garden Court Suite 270
Monterey, CA 93940
Telephone: (831) 655-1644
Fax Number: (831) 655-8591

MORTGAGE STORE FINANCIAL INC
727 W 7th Street #850
Los Angeles, CA 90017
Telephone: (213) 234-2400

NEIGHBORS FINANCIAL CORP
1314 H Street Suite-100
Sacramento, CA 95814
Telephone: (916) 732-2340
Fax Number: (916) 732-2345

NORTHWEST FINANCIAL GROUP INC
2986 Bechelli Lane Suite 200
Redding, CA 96002
Telephone: (530) 223-2950

PACIFIC HOME LENDING
536 Pearl Street
Monterey, CA 93940
Telephone: (831) 648-8080

PACIFIC REPUBLIC MORTGAGE
CORPORATION
7339 Pacific Avenue
Stockton, CA 95207
Telephone: (209) 474-6161
Fax Number: (209) 474-6911

PENCO FINANCIAL INC
21015 Pathfinder Road Ste 111
Diamond Bar, CA 91765
Telephone: (909) 612-5300
Fax Number: (909) 861-5927

REVERSE MORTGAGES OF CA IN
407 S Clovis Ave Ste 106
Fresno, CA 93727
Telephone: (559) 252-5555
Fax Number: (559) 255-5503

SCME MORTGAGE BANKERS INC
6363 Greenwich Drive, #150
San Diego, CA 92122
Telephone: (858) 558-3397
Fax Number: (858) 558-2716

SENIOR FINANCE CENTER
1585 Heartwood Drive, Suite C
McKinleyville, CA 95519
Telephone: (707) 839-7500
Fax Number: (707) 839-7600

SENIOR FUNDING ASSOCIATES
22151 Ventura Blvd. Suite 202
Woodland Hills, CA 91364
Telephone: (818) 999-2665
Fax Number: (818) 999-1211
E-Mail: seniorfunding@sbcglobal.net

SENIOR'S REVERSE MORTGAGE INC
1485 Enea Court Ste 1330
Concord, CA 94520
Telephone: (925) 370-9339
Fax Number: (925) 370-9449

SEQUOIA PACIFIC MORTGAGE CO
1002 Mendocino Ave
Santa Rosa, CA 95401
Telephone: (707) 575-3220
Fax Number: (707) 575-1751

SKY VALLEY FINANCIAL INC
1090 Adams St Ste L
Benicia, CA 94510
Telephone: (707) 557-9944

U S FINANCIAL MORTGAGE
CORPORATION
735 Sunrise Ave Suite 210
Roseville, CA 95661
Telephone: (916) 781-6713

WAUSAU MORTGAGE CORPORATION
140 Gregory Lane, Ste. 190
Pleasant Hill, CA 94523
Telephone: (925) 521-1521
Fax Number: (925) 521-1522

Colorado:

ACADEMY MORTGAGE LLC
4502 E 115th Avenue
Thornton, CO 80233
Telephone: (303) 280-0356

ALLIANCE GUARANTY MORTGAGE
CORP
2821 S Parker Rd #605
Aurora, CO 80014
Telephone: (303) 785-2800
Fax Number: (303) 785-0089

CAPITAL ACCESS MORTGAGE
7900 E Union Ave Ste 150
Denver, CO 80237
Telephone: (303) 691-0691
Fax Number: (303) 691-0791

CLARION MORTGAGE CAPITAL INC
9034 East Easter Place Ste 204
Englewood, CO 80112
Telephone: (303) 843-0777

FARWEST MORTGAGE BANKERS INC
4940 Lakeshore Drive
Littleton, CO 80123
Telephone: (303) 795-9329

LIBERTY FINANCIAL GROUP INC
2121 S Oneida Street Suite 470
Denver, CO 80224
Telephone: (303) 691-2626
Fax Number: (303) 691-2298

MOUNTAIN PACIFIC MORTGAGE CO
375 Horsetooth, Bldg. 6, #201
Fort Collins, CO 80525
Telephone: (970) 204-4509
Fax Number: (970) 204-1068

ROCKY MOUNTAIN MUTUAL
MORTGAGE INCORPOR
7550 West Yale Ave Ste B100
Denver, CO 80227
Telephone: (303) 989-3299

UNIVERSAL LENDING CORPORATION
6775 E Evans Avenue
Denver, CO 80224
Telephone: (303) 758-3336

ZIONS FIRST NATIONAL BANK
255 N Admiral Blvd Rd
Salt Lake City, UT 84116
Telephone: (801) 273-3000
Fax Number: (801) 273-3035

Connecticut:

AMSTON MORTGAGE
711 Middletown Road Suite 8
Colchester, CT 06415
Telephone: (800) 625-8633
Fax Number: (860) 365-0001

BNY MORTGAGE COMPANY LLC
57 Jefferson Street
Milford, MA 01757
Telephone: (508) 422-9589
Fax Number: (508) 422-9592

CAMBRIDGE HOME CAPITAL LLC
80 Cuttermill Road Ste 408
Great Neck, NY 11021
Telephone: (516) 829-5700
Fax Number: (516) 829-5777

CONCORD MORTGAGE CORP
25 Melville Park Rd
Melville, NY 11747
Telephone: (631) 756-0700
Fax Number: (631) 756-0900

CONTINENTAL FUNDING CORP
7 Cabot Place 2nd Floor
Stoughton, MA 02072
Telephone: (781) 344-4846
Fax Number: (781) 344-1841

EAST WEST MORTGAGE COMPANY
189 Hartford Ave Ste 1
Bellingham, MA 02019
Telephone: (508) 966-5250
Fax Number: (508) 966-5251

EQUITY AMERICA MORTGAGE SVCS
INC
340 Granite St
Manchester, NH 03102
Telephone: (603) 625-2820

EVERHOME MORTGAGE COMPANY
8100 Nations Way
Jacksonville, FL 32256
Telephone: (904) 281-6000

FAIRFIELD COUNTY BANK CORP
374 Main Street
Ridgefield, CT 06877
Telephone: (203) 438-6518

FAST TRACK FUNDING CORP
247 W Old Country Road
Hicksville, NY 11801
Telephone: (516) 938-6600

FEDERAL MORTGAGE AND
INVESTMENT CORP
1111 Clifton Avenue
Clifton, NJ 07013
Telephone: (973) 777-7784

FREEDOM CHOICE MORTGAGE
30 East Main Street
Avon, CT 06001
Telephone: (203) 677-0127

HOME MORTGAGE LOAN COMPANY
393 Center Street
Auburn, ME 04210
Telephone: (207) 946-2820

KASTLE MORTGAGE CORPORATION
77 West Main Street
Freehold, NJ 07728
Telephone: (732) 845-5444

M AND T MORTGAGE CORPORATION
Northway 10 Executive Park
Clifton Park, NY 12065
Telephone: (518) 877-3500

MORTGAGE FINANCIAL SERVICES INC
170 Main St Suite 108
Tewksbury, MA 01876
Telephone: (978) 863-9555

NEW JERSEY HOME FUNDING GROUP
LLC
457 Route 79
Morganville, NJ 07751
Telephone: (732) 970-9210

NEW JERSEY HSNG MTG FIN AGEN
637 South Clinton Avenue
Trenton, NJ 08650
Telephone: (609) 278-7400

OCEANFIRST BANK
975 Hooper Avenue
Toms River, NJ 08753
Telephone: (732) 240-4500

REAL ESTATE MORTGAGE NETWORK
INC
70 Grand Avenue
River Edge, NJ 07661
Telephone: (201) 498-9300
Fax Number: (201) 498-9377

RHODE ISLAND HSG MTGE FIN CORP
44 Washington Street
Providence, RI 02903
Telephone: (401) 751-5566

SOUTHERN STAR MORTGAGE CORP
90 Merrick Avenue Suite 204
East Meadow, NY 11554
Telephone: (516) 712-4400
Fax Number: (516) 794-2116

SUPERIOR MORTGAGE CORP
1395 Route 539
Tuckerton, NJ 08087
Telephone: (609) 294-2854
Fax Number: (609) 294-0620

USA FINANCIAL RESOURCES INC
66 Medford Avenue
Patchogue, NY 11772
Telephone: (516) 758-9200

WEBSTER BANK
609 West Johnson Avenue
Cheshire, CT 06410
Telephone: (888) 681-7788

Delaware:

AAKO INC
3569 Bristol Pike Bldg No 2
Bensalem, PA 19020
Telephone: (215) 633-8080
Fax Number: (215) 633-8088

ACADEMY MORTGAGE LLC
5602 Baltimore National Pk 401
Baltimore, MD 21228
Telephone: (410) 788-7070

AGENCY FOR CONSUMER EQUITY
MORTGAGE INC
101 Executive Blvd. 1st Floor
Elmsford, NY 10523
Telephone: (800) 881-2954
Fax Number: (914) 682-0521

ALBION FINANCIAL INC
1873 Route 70 East Ste 302-D
Cherry Hill, NJ 08003
Telephone: (856) 424-4367

ALLIED HOME MORTGAGE CAPITAL
CORPORATION
12 W. Green St.
Middletown, DE 19709
Telephone: (302) 376-9815
Fax Number: (302) 376-9816

BNY MORTGAGE COMPANY LLC
385 Rifle Camp Road
West Paterson, NJ 07424
Telephone: (800) 299-3133
Fax Number: (973) 247-4391

CAMBRIDGE HOME CAPITAL LLC
80 Cuttermill Road Ste 408
Great Neck, NY 11021
Telephone: (516) 829-5700
Fax Number: (516) 829-5777

CARDINAL FINANCIAL COMPANY
444 Jacksonville Road
Warminster, PA 18974
Telephone: (215) 293-6800
Fax Number: (215) 293-6807

COMMERCE BANK NA
17000 Horizon Way
Mt Laurell, NJ 08054
Telephone: (732) 747-1999
Fax Number: (732) 450-0737

FEDERAL MORTGAGE AND
INVESTMENT CORP
1111 Clifton Avenue
Clifton, NJ 07013
Telephone: (973) 777-7784

FIDELITY AND TRUST MORTGAGE INC
7229 Hanover Parkway, Suite C
Greenbelt, MD 20770
Telephone: (301) 313-9100
Fax Number: (301) 313-0900

FIRST MARINER BANK
3301 Boston Street
Baltimore, MD 21224
Telephone: (410) 558-4118
Fax Number: (410) 342-0489

FIRST MONEY GROUP INC
1777 Reisterstown Rd Suite 230
Baltimore, MD 21208
Telephone: (410) 653-6909

HOME CONSULTANTS INC
661 Northern Blvd
Clarks Summit, PA 18411
Telephone: (570) 586-7863
Fax Number: (570) 586-7865

INTERCHANGE BANK
Park 80 West—Plaza Two
Saddle Brook, NJ 07663
Telephone: (201) 703-2246

KASTLE MORTGAGE CORPORATION
77 West Main Street
Freehold, NJ 07728
Telephone: (732) 845-5444

M AND T MORTGAGE CORPORATION
2270 Erin Court
Lancaster, PA 17604
Telephone: (717) 397-5548
Fax Number: (717) 397-2643

MORTGAGE MONEY MART INC
1199 Amboy Avenue
Edison, NJ 08837
Telephone: (732) 548-9423

NATIONRESIDENTIAL MORTGAGE
BANKING CORP
One Rabro Drive
Hauppauge, NY 11788
Telephone: (516) 232-1133

NEW JERSEY HSNG MTG FIN AGEN
637 South Clinton Avenue
Trenton, NJ 08650
Telephone: (609) 278-7400

OCEANFIRST BANK
975 Hooper Avenue
Toms River, NJ 08753
Telephone: (732) 240-4500

RCRBL ENTERPRISES LTD
1123 Old Town Road
Coram, NY 11727
Telephone: (631) 736-7700

REAL ESTATE MORTGAGE NETWORK
INC
70 Grand Avenue
River Edge, NJ 07661
Telephone: (201) 498-9300
Fax Number: (201) 498-9377

SAVINGS FIRST MORTGAGE LLC
100 Painters Mill Road Ste 800
Owings Mills, MD 21117
Telephone: (410) 654-8800

SOUTHERN STAR MORTGAGE CORP
90 Merrick Avenue Suite 204
East Meadow, NY 11554
Telephone: (516) 712-4400
Fax Number: (516) 794-2116

SUPERIOR MORTGAGE CORP
1395 Route 539
Tuckerton, NJ 08087
Telephone: (609) 294-2854
Fax Number: (609) 294-0620

USA FINANCIAL RESOURCES INC
66 Medford Avenue
Patchogue, NY 11772
Telephone: (516) 758-9200

District of Columbia:

AAKO INC
3569 Bristol Pike Bldg No 2
Bensalem, PA 19020
Telephone: (215) 633-8080
Fax Number: (215) 633-8088

ACADEMY MORTGAGE LLC
5602 Baltimore National Pk 401
Baltimore, MD 21228
Telephone: (410) 788-7070

ALBION FINANCIAL INC
1873 Route 70 East Ste 302-D
Cherry Hill, NJ 08003
Telephone: (856) 424-4367

ALL PENNSYLVANIA REVERSE
MORTGAGE INC
4085 Route 8
Allison Park, PA 15101
Telephone: (412) 963-6062

CENTURA BANK
133 S Franklin Street
Rocky Mount, NC 27804
Telephone: (919) 454-6053

COMMERCE BANK NA
17000 Horizon Way
Mt Laurell, NJ 08054
Telephone: (732) 747-1999
Fax Number: (732) 450-0737

EAST WEST MORTGAGE COMPANY
1568 Spring Hill Rd Ste 100
McLean, VA 22102
Telephone: (703) 442-0150

EVERBANK
4010 Jefferson Woods Drive
Powhatan, VA 23129
Telephone: (804) 403-3380

EVERHOME MORTGAGE COMPANY
8100 Nations Way
Jacksonville, FL 32256
Telephone: (904) 281-6000

FIDELITY AND TRUST MORTGAGE INC
7229 Hanover Parkway, Suite C
Greenbelt, MD 20770
Telephone: (301) 313-9100
Fax Number: (301) 313-0900

FIDELITY AND TRUST MORTGAGE INC
115-22 Aikens Center
Martinsburg, WV 25401
Telephone: (304) 260-9433
Fax Number: (301) 260-9434

FIRST MARINER BANK
3301 Boston Street
Baltimore, MD 21224
Telephone: (410) 558-4118
Fax Number: (410) 342-0489

FIRST MONEY GROUP INC
1777 Reisterstown Rd Suite 230
Baltimore, MD 21208
Telephone: (410) 653-6909

LUMINA MORTGAGE COMPANY INC
219 Racine Drive Suite A
Wilmington, NC 28403
Telephone: (910) 452-3555
Fax Number: (910) 452-9929

M AND T MORTGAGE CORPORATION
601 Dresher Road, Ste 150
Horsham, PA 19044
Telephone: (215) 956-7030
Fax Number: (215) 956-7029

MORTGAGE MOBILITY LLC
1094 Second Street Pike
Richboro, PA 18954
Telephone: (215) 357-4900
Fax Number: (215) 364-1927

NEW JERSEY HSNG MTG FIN AGEN
637 South Clinton Avenue
Trenton, NJ 08650
Telephone: (609) 278-7400

PEOPLES TRUST MORTGAGE LLC
3920 Plank Road Suite 200
Fredericksburg, VA 22407
Telephone: (540) 548-8749

S AND T BANK
800 Philadelphia Street
Indiana, PA 15701
Telephone: (800) 325-2265

SAVINGS FIRST MORTGAGE LLC
100 Painters Mill Road Ste 800
Owings Mills, MD 21117
Telephone: (410) 654-8800

SENIORS FIRST MORTGAGE COMPANY
LLC
4525 South Avenue Suite 301
Virginia Beach, VA 23452
Telephone: (757) 671-6000

SUPERIOR MORTGAGE CORP
1395 Route 539
Tuckerton, NJ 08087
Telephone: (609) 294-2854
Fax Number: (609) 294-0620

UNITED FIRST MORTGAGE INC
1503 Santa Rosa Road Ste 109
Richmond, VA 23229
Telephone: (804) 282-5631

Florida:

AMERICA'S MORTGAGE BROKER LLC
3153 US Highway 98 North
Lakeland, FL 33805
Telephone: (863) 686-8899
Fax Number: (863) 688-4628

AMERICA'S SENIOR FIN'L SRVCS INC
10800 Biscayne Blvd Ste 500
Miami Shores, FL 33161
Telephone: (800) 760-5363
Fax Number: (305) 556-8640

AMERICAN REVERSE MORTGAGE CORP
605 SW First Avenue
Ocala, FL 34474
Telephone: (352) 867-1111
Fax Number: (352) 369-5985

AMSTAR MORTGAGE CORPORATION
6349 103rd Street
Jacksonville, FL 32210
Telephone: (904) 573-8893

CENTURA BANK
1401 N. Federal Highway
Boca Raton, FL 33432
Telephone: (561) 362-7956
Fax Number: (561) 362-7955

CENTURA BANK
2 South Orange, Suite 100
Orlando, FL 32801
Telephone: (407) 835-7888
Fax Number: (407) 835-1663

CIRCLE MORTGAGE CORPORATION
6600 Taft Street Fourth Floor
Hollywood, FL 33024
Telephone: (954) 981-6800
Fax Number: (954) 981-9099

EVERBANK
8100 Nations Way
Jacksonville, FL 32256
Telephone: (904) 281-6390

EVERHOME MORTGAGE COMPANY
8100 Nations Way
Jacksonville, FL 32256
Telephone: (904) 281-6000

FIRST COMMUNITY BANK OF ORANGE
CITY
2240 South Volusia Avenue
Orange City, FL 32763
Telephone: (904) 775-3115

FIRST FLORIDA INTERNATL MTG
815 Emmett Street
Kissimmee, FL 34741
Telephone: (407) 933-0567

FIRST MARINER BANK
499 E Sheridan Street
Dania Beach, FL 33004
Telephone: (800) 879-7041
Fax Number: (877) 522-7146

FIRST NATIONAL BANK OF FLORIDA
900 Goodlette Road North
Naples, FL 34102
Telephone: (239) 573-2211
Fax Number: (239) 573-2527

GMAC MORTGAGE CORPORATION
500 West Cypress Creek Road
Ft. Lauderdale, FL 33309
Telephone: (954) 771-4420
Fax Number: (954) 771-4490

GMAC MORTGAGE CORPORATION
9425 Sunset Drive
Miami, FL 33173
Telephone: (305) 412-4622
Fax Number: (305) 412-7882

HAYHURST MORTGAGE INC
6839 Main Street
Miami Lakes, FL 33014
Telephone: (954) 441-7374
Fax Number: (954) 441-7376

INDEPENDENT BANK OF OCALA
60 S W 17th Street
Ocala, FL 32674
Telephone: (904) 622-2377

MORTGAGE SERVICES INC
7999 North Federal Highway Ste
Boca Raton, FL 33487
Telephone: (561) 988-9988
Fax Number: (561) 988-9971

MORTGAGE TRUST COMPANY
2642 Bee Ridge Road
Sarasota, FL 34239
Telephone: (941) 925-1990

NATIONS FINANCIAL INC
10769-12 Beach Blvd
Jacksonville, FL 32246
Telephone: (904) 482-1600
Fax Number: (904) 764-0078

REAL ESTATE MORTGAGE NETWORK
INC
1673 Main St
Dunedin, FL 34698
Telephone: (727) 736-6065
Fax Number: (727) 736-4266

SAFEWAY MORTGAGE INC
2655 South Cobb Drive Suite 1
Smyrna, GA 30080
Telephone: (770) 434-9486

SEMINOLE FUNDING INC
9410 Seminole Boulevard
Seminole, FL 33772
Telephone: (727) 392-1906
Fax Number: (727) 392-1969

SGB CORPORATION
1 S 660 Midwest Rd. #100
Oakbrook Terrace, IL 60181
Telephone: (630) 916-9299
Fax Number: (630) 916-1299

SHELTER MORTGAGE COMPANY LLC
3350 Northlake Pkwy, Suite B
Atlanta, GA 30345
Telephone: (678) 279-9000
Fax Number: (678) 279-2000

STATEWIDE MORTGAGE OUTLET INC
8921 W Atlantic Blvd Ste M
Coral Springs, FL 33071
Telephone: (954) 346-9400
Fax Number: (954) 346-9773

STERLING MORTGAGE SVCS INC
729 South Federal Hwy Ste 200
Stuart, FL 34994
Telephone: (407) 288-5251

SUPERIOR MORTGAGE CORP
15310 Amberly Dr, Suit 318
Tampa, FL 33647
Telephone: (813) 558-2041
Fax Number: (813) 994-8472

THIRD COMMUNITY MORTGAGE CORP
12730 New Brittany Blvd #428
Fort Myers, FL 33907
Telephone: (239) 939-9655
Fax Number: (239) 939-9755

U S FINANCIAL MORTGAGE
CORPORATION
735 Sunrise Ave Suite 210
Roseville, CA 95661
Telephone: (916) 781-6713

Georgia:

AMERICAN REVERSE MORTGAGE CORP
605 SW First Avenue
Ocala, FL 34474
Telephone: (352) 867-1111
Fax Number: (352) 369-5985
E-Mail: info@americanreverse.com

AMSTAR MORTGAGE CORPORATION
6349 103rd Street
Jacksonville, FL 32210
Telephone: (904) 573-8893

ANCIENT CITY MORTGAGE
1100-4 Ponce de Leon Blvd S
St Johns, FL 32084
Telephone: (904) 826-0096
Fax Number: (904) 826-0260

ARENCIBIA FINANCIAL SVCS INC
1820 Riggins Road
Tallahassee, FL 32308
Telephone: (850) 877-3990
Fax Number: (850) 877-3999

BANK INDEPENDENT
710 S Montgomery Ave
Sheffield, AL 35660
Telephone: (256) 386-5000

CENTURA BANK
1585 Southlake Parkway
Morrow, GA 30260
Telephone: (404) 495-6834

EVERBANK
6984 Flowery Branch Road
Cummings, GA 30041
Telephone: (812) 949-2883

EVERHOME MORTGAGE COMPANY
8100 Nations Way
Jacksonville, FL 32256
Telephone: (904) 281-6000

FRANKLIN FUNDING INC
147 Wappoo Creek Drive Ste 105
Charleston, SC 29412
Telephone: (843) 762-2218

HIBERNIA NATIONAL BANK
11130 Industriplex Blvd
Baton Rouge, LA 70809
Telephone: (504) 381-2372

HOME BUILDERS MORTGAGE CORP
678 B St Andrews Blvd
Charleston, SC 29407
Telephone: (843) 556-4643

HOME FEDERAL SAVINGS BANK TN
515 Market St
Knoxville, TN 37902
Telephone: (615) 546-0330

HOMEOWNERS MORTGAGE
ENTERPRISES INC
2530 Devine Street
Columbia, SC 29205
Telephone: (803) 765-9037

HOMESOUTH MORTGAGE SERVICES
INC
200 Cahaba Park Circle Ste 125
Birmingham, AL 35242
Telephone: (205) 591-5055
Fax Number: (205) 591-5053

INDEPENDENT BANK OF OCALA
60 S W 17th Street
Ocala, FL 32674
Telephone: (904) 622-2377

MCGOWIN KING MORTGAGE LLC
9 Office Park Circle Ste 117
Birmingham, AL 35223
Telephone: (205) 879-7775

MORTGAGE CAPITAL INVESTORS INC
7901 N. Ocean Blvd.
Myrtle Beach, SC 29572
Telephone: (843) 449-8004
Fax Number: (843) 449-8206

MORTGAGE SOUTH OF TENNESSEE
409 S Germantown Rd
Chattanooga, TN 37411
Telephone: (423) 624-3878

NATIONS FINANCIAL INC
10769-12 Beach Blvd
Jacksonville, FL 32246
Telephone: (904) 482-1600
Fax Number: (904) 764-0078

SAFEWAY MORTGAGE INC
2655 South Cobb Drive Suite 1
Smyrna, GA 30080
Telephone: (770) 434-9486

SHELTER MORTGAGE COMPANY LLC
3350 Northlake Pkwy, Suite B
Atlanta, GA 30345
Telephone: (678) 279-9000
Fax Number: (678) 279-2000
E-Mail: ffmatl@aol.com

TARA MORTGAGE CORPORATION
4300 Bayou Blvd Ste 1
Pensacola, FL 32503
Telephone: (850) 474-0011

Hawaii:

HOMESTREET BANK
601 Union Street
Seattle, WA 98101
Telephone: (206) 623-3050
Fax Number: (206) 389-6306

U S FINANCIAL MORTGAGE
CORPORATION
735 Sunrise Ave Suite 210
Roseville, CA 95661
Telephone: (916) 781-6713

Idaho:

MORTGAGE PLACE LLC
5593 N Glenwood
Boise, ID 83714
Telephone: (208) 472-8877
Fax Number: (208) 472-8879

FAIRWAY INDEPENDENT MORTGAGE
CORPORATION
2404 East Amity Avenue
Nampa, ID 83686
Telephone: (208) 467-9663

FSI MORTGAGE LLC
1858 East 1st Street
Idaho Falls, ID 83401
Telephone: (208) 529-6643

INTERMOUNTAIN MORTGAGE CO INC
3333 2nd Avenue North Ste 250
Billings, MT 59101
Telephone: (406) 252-2600
Fax Number: (406) 237-0187

INVESTORS WEST MORTGAGE
814 N 8th Street
Boise, ID 83702
Telephone: (208) 345-8153

IRELAND BANK
33 Bannock Ave
Malad City, ID 83252
Telephone: (208) 766-2211

PREMIER MORTGAGE RESOURCES LLC
16 12th Ave S
Nampa, ID 83651
Telephone: (208) 562-1777
Fax Number: (208) 362-6208

ZIONS FIRST NATIONAL BANK
255 N Admiral Blvd Rd
Salt Lake City, UT 84116
Telephone: (801) 273-3000
Fax Number: (801) 273-3035

Illinois:

AAA MORTGAGE CORP
717 N McCarthy Road
Appleton, WI 54913
Telephone: (920) 830-0600

AMERICAN HOME MORTGAGE CORP
915 West 175th Suite-3W
Homewood, IL 60430
Telephone: (708) 647-7909

AMERICAN MORTGAGE SERVICE
415 Glensprings Dr. Suite 203
Cincinnati, OH 45246
Telephone: (513) 674-8900
Fax Number: (513) 674-8906

AMERIFUND FINANCIAL INC
50 Crestwood Executive Ctr Ste
Saint Louis, MO 63126
Telephone: (866) 839-7700
Fax Number: (866) 839-7701

ASPEN MORTGAGE CORPORATION
651 N Washington
Naperville, IL 60563
Telephone: (630) 983-3600

BEST MORTGAGE AND FINANCIAL
GROUP
1217 North Kings Highway
Cape Girardeau, MO 63701
Telephone: (573) 334-9900

CENTIER BANK
600 East 84th Avenue
Merrillville, IN 46410
Telephone: (219) 659-0043

CLA MORTGAGE INC
7280 S. 13th Street #103
Oak Creek, WI 53154
Telephone: (414) 570-8811
Fax Number: (414) 570-8822

COLE TAYLOR BANK
5501 West 79th Street
Burbank, IL 60459
Telephone: (800) 613-7778
Fax Number: (630) 801-8580

CREDIT UNION MORTGAGE COMPANY
555 W Crosstown Pkwy Ste 401
Kalamazoo, MI 49008
Telephone: (616) 349-1021
Fax Number: (616) 349-0420

DOW MORTGAGE COMPANY
1600 Plainfield Rd
Crest Hill, IL 60435
Telephone: (815) 730-9400
Fax Number: (815) 730-0800

EVERBANK
2550 West Golf Road #100
Rollingsmeadows, IL 60008
Telephone: (847) 439-5500

EVERHOME MORTGAGE COMPANY
8100 Nations Way
Jacksonville, FL 32256
Telephone: (904) 281-6000

FIRST CENTENNIAL MORTGAGE
11 North Edgelawn Avenue
Avrora, IL 60506
Telephone: (630) 906-7315

FIRST MIDWEST BANK
300 Park Blvd—Suite 400
Itasc, IL 60143
Telephone: (815) 774-2165
Fax Number: (815) 774-2070

GSF MORTGAGE CORPORATION
999 N Plaza Dr Ste 710
Schaumburg, IL 60173
Telephone: (847) 605-8244
Fax Number: (262) 373-1641

HOMEOWNERS MORTGAGE SERVICE
INC
11555 N Meridian St Ste 160
Carmel, IN 46032
Telephone: (317) 580-2250

JAMES B NUTTER AND COMPANY
4153 Broadway
Kansas City, MO 64111
Telephone: (816) 531-2345

LIBERTY MORTGAGE INC
509 W McKinley Ave
Mishawaka, IN 46545
Telephone: (574) 257-0629

METRO MORTGAGE CO INC
6657 Odana Road
Madison, WI 53719
Telephone: (608) 829-3000

MORTGAGE NETWORK INC
70 East 91st St., Ste 109,
Indianapolis, IN 46240
Telephone: (317) 706-1114
Fax Number: (317) 706-1115

OSWEGO COMMUNITY BANK
10 N Madison St
Oswego, IL 60543
Telephone: (630) 554-3411

SENIORS EQUITY INCOME INC
6910 N Main St-14 Bldg 22-B
Granger, IN 46530
Telephone: (219) 272-0710

SGB CORPORATION
1 S 660 Midwest Rd. #100
Oakbrook Terrace, IL 60181
Telephone: (630) 916-9299
Fax Number: (630) 916-1299

Indiana:

ALBION FINANCIAL INC
5930 Lovers Lane
Portage, MI 49002
Telephone: (616) 383-1330

AMERICAN HOME MORTGAGE CORP
915 West 175th Suite-3W
Homewood, IL 60430
Telephone: (708) 647-7909

AMERICAN MORTGAGE SERVICE CO
415 Glensprings Dr. Suite 203
Cincinnati, OH 45246
Telephone: (513) 674-8900
Fax Number: (513) 674-8906

AMERICAN REVERSE MORTGAGE CORP
2101 South Hamilton Road, #110
Columbus, OH 43232
Telephone: (614) 577-1440
Fax Number: (614) 577-1442

AMERISTATE BANCORP INC
7925 Graceland St
Dayton, OH 45459
Telephone: (937) 434-9900
Fax Number: (937) 434-9922

ASPEN MORTGAGE CORPORATION
651 N Washington
Naperville, IL 60563
Telephone: (630) 983-3600

CUSTOM MORTGAGE INC
1712 N Meridian St Suite 200
Indianapolis, IN 46202
Telephone: (317) 920-5400

DOW MORTGAGE COMPANY
1600 Plainfield Rd
Crest Hill, IL 60435
Telephone: (815) 730-9400
Fax Number: (815) 730-0800

EVANS FINANCIAL SERVICES
4115 Mannheim Road Ste 100
Jasper, IN 47546
Telephone: (812) 634-7283
Fax Number: (812) 634-9760

EVERBANK
2550 West Golf Road #100
Rollings Meadows, IL 60008
Telephone: (847) 439-5500

EVERHOME MORTGAGE COMPANY
8100 Nations Way
Jacksonville, FL 32256
Telephone: (904) 281-6000

FIRST CENTENNIAL MORTGAGE
11 North Edgelawn Avenue
Avrora, IL 60506
Telephone: (630) 906-7315

FIRST COMMUNITY MORTGAGE INC
9352 Main Street
Montgomery, OH 45242
Telephone: (513) 791-3429
Fax Number: (513) 791-3547

FIRST MIDWEST BANK
300 Park Blvd—Suite 400
Itasc, IL 60143
Telephone: (815) 774-2165
Fax Number: (815) 774-2070

GSF MORTGAGE CORPORATION
999 N Plaza Dr Ste 710
Schaumburg, IL 60173
Telephone: (847) 605-8244
Fax Number: (262) 373-1641

HOMEOWNERS MORTGAGE SERVICE INC
11555 N Meridian St Ste 160
Carmel, IN 46032
Telephone: (317) 580-2250

LIBERTY MORTGAGE INC
509 W McKinley Ave
Mishawaka, IN 46545
Telephone: (574) 257-0629

MORTGAGE NETWORK INC
70 East 91st St., Ste 109,
Indianapolis, IN 46240
Telephone: (317) 706-1114
Fax Number: (317) 706-1115

MORTGAGE SERVICES INC
1801 E Empire Suite 2
Bloomington, IL 61704
Telephone: (309) 662-6693
Fax Number: (309) 663-0818

OSWEGO COMMUNITY BANK
10 N Madison St
Oswego, IL 60543
Telephone: (630) 554-3411

PARK NATIONAL BANK
50 North Third St
Newark, OH 43055
Telephone: (614) 349-8451

PEOPLES TRUST MORTGAGE LLC
837 Donaldson Road
Erlanger, KY 41018
Telephone: (859) 372-3540
Fax Number: (859) 372-3548

RESIDENTIAL MORTGAGE SERVS INC
191 Kentucky Avenue
Lexington, KY 40502
Telephone: (606) 252-5626

SENIORS EQUITY INCOME INC
6910 N Main St-14 Bldg 22-B
Granger, IN 46530
Telephone: (219) 272-0710

SGB CORPORATION
1 S 660 Midwest Rd. #100
Oakbrook Terrace, IL 60181
Telephone: (630) 916-9299
Fax Number: (630) 916-1299

SOUTHERN OHIO MORTGAGE LLC
912 Senate Dr
Dayton, OH 45459
Telephone: (937) 435-7277
Fax Number: (937) 435-5707

STOCK YARDS BANK MORTGAGE
COMPANY
1040 E Main Street
Louisville, KY 40206
Telephone: (502) 582-2571

Iowa:

ALLIANCE GUARANTY MORTGAGE
CORP
11414 West Center Suite-137
Omaha, NE 68114
Telephone: (800) 474-5726

CENTENNIAL MORTGAGE AND
FUNDING
250 Prairie Center Dr Ste 100
Eden Prairie, MN 55344
Telephone: (952) 826-0025
Fax Number: (952) 826-0027

DISCOVER MORTGAGE CORP
1500 South Hwy 100 Ste 360
Minneapolis, MN 55416
Telephone: (612) 546-0424

FARWEST MORTGAGE BANKERS INC
1532 Aspen Drive
Eagan, MN 55122
Telephone: (651) 994-1088

FIRST UNITED BANK
430 NW Fourth St
Faribault, MN 55021
Telephone: (507) 334-2201
Fax Number: (507) 334-2205

HOMESTEAD MORTGAGE
CORPORATION
4105 N Lexington Ave Ste 100
Arden Hills, MN 55126
Telephone: (612) 490-5555

JAMES B NUTTER AND COMPANY
4153 Broadway
Kansas City, MO 64111
Telephone: (816) 531-2345

JOHN DEERE COMMUNITY C U
1827 Ansborough Avenue
Waterloo, IA 50701
Telephone: (319) 274-7562

LIBERTY FIRST CREDIT UNION
501 North 46th Street
Lincoln, NE 68503
Telephone: (402) 464-8347

MORTGAGE AUTHORITY INC
9557 W 87th Street
Overland Park, KS 66212
Telephone: (913) 648-9000
Fax Number: (913) 648-9009

MORTGAGE SERVICES INC
2921 S 168th Street
Omaha, NE 68130
Telephone: (402) 330-9388
Fax Number: (402) 330-9382

MOUNTAIN PACIFIC MORTGAGE CO
1201 E 32nd St, Suite E
Joplin, MO 64804
Telephone: (417) 623-0500
Fax Number: (417) 623-0990

PEOPLES TRUST MORTGAGE LLC
1750 Weir Drive
Woodbury, MN 55125
Telephone: (651) 714-7171
Fax Number: (651) 714-7177

WESTERN NATIONAL BANK DULUTH
5629 Grand Ave
Duluth, MN 55807
Telephone: (218) 723-1000

Kansas:

ALLIANCE GUARANTY MORTGAGE
CORP
11414 West Center Suite-137
Omaha, NE 68114
Telephone: (800) 474-5726

AMERIFUND FINANCIAL INC
50 Crestwood Executive Ctr Ste
Saint Louis, MO 63126
Telephone: (866) 839-7700
Fax Number: (866) 839-7701

BEST MORTGAGE AND FINANCIAL
GROUP
1217 North Kings Highway
Cape Girardeau, MO 63701
Telephone: (573) 334-9900

JAMES B NUTTER AND COMPANY
4153 Broadway
Kansas City, MO 64111
Telephone: (816) 531-2345

JOHN DEERE COMMUNITY C U
1827 Ansborough Avenue
Waterloo, IA 50701
Telephone: (319) 274-7562

LIBERTY FIRST CREDIT UNION
501 North 46th Street
Lincoln, NE 68503
Telephone: (402) 464-8347

MORTGAGE AUTHORITY INC
9557 W 87th Street
Overland Park, KS 66212
Telephone: (913) 648-9000
Fax Number: (913) 648-9009

MORTGAGE SERVICES INC
2921 S 168th Street
Omaha, NE 68130
Telephone: (402) 330-9388
Fax Number: (402) 330-9382

MOUNTAIN PACIFIC MORTGAGE CO
1201 E 32nd St, Suite E
Joplin, MO 64804
Telephone: (417) 623-0500
Fax Number: (417) 623-0990

Kentucky:

AMERICAN REVERSE MORTGAGE CORP
2101 South Hamilton Road, #110
Columbus, OH 43232
Telephone: (614) 577-1440
Fax Number: (614) 577-1442

CENTIER BANK
600 East 84th Avenue
Merrillville, IN 46410
Telephone: (219) 659-0043

CENTURA BANK
133 S Franklin Street
Rocky Mount, NC 27804
Telephone: (919) 454-6053

CUSTOM MORTGAGE INC
1712 N Meridian St Suite 200
Indianapolis, IN 46202
Telephone: (317) 920-5400

FIDELITY AND TRUST MORTGAGE INC
115-22 Aikens Center
Martinsburg, WV 25401
Telephone: (304) 260-9433
Fax Number: (301) 260-9434

FIRST COMMUNITY MORTGAGE INC
9352 Main Street
Montgomery, OH 45242
Telephone: (513) 791-3429
Fax Number: (513) 791-3547

HOME FEDERAL SAVINGS BANK TN
515 Market St
Knoxville, TN 37902
Telephone: (615) 546-0330

HOMEOWNERS MORTGAGE SERVICE
INC
11555 N Meridian St Ste 160
Carmel, IN 46032
Telephone: (317) 580-2250

LIBERTY MORTGAGE INC
509 W McKinley Ave
Mishawaka, IN 46545
Telephone: (574) 257-0629

MORTGAGE NETWORK INC
70 East 91st St., Ste 109,
Indianapolis, IN 46240
Telephone: (317) 706-1114
Fax Number: (317) 706-1115

MORTGAGE SOUTH OF TENNESSEE
409 S Germantown Rd
Chattanooga, TN 37411
Telephone: (423) 624-3878

PEOPLES TRUST MORTGAGE LLC
837 Donaldson Road
Erlanger, KY 41018
Telephone: (859) 372-3540
Fax Number: (859) 372-3548

RESIDENTIAL MORTGAGE CORP
1332 Andrea St
Bowling Green, KY 42104
Telephone: (502) 842-7773

RESIDENTIAL MORTGAGE SERVS INC
191 Kentucky Avenue
Lexington, KY 40502
Telephone: (606) 252-5626

SENIORS EQUITY INCOME INC
6910 N Main St-14 Bldg 22-B
Granger, IN 46530
Telephone: (219) 272-0710

SOUTHERN OHIO MORTGAGE LLC
912 Senate Dr
Dayton, OH 45459
Telephone: (937) 435-7277
Fax Number: (937) 435-5707

Louisiana:

AMERIPLEX MORTGAGE COMPANY
3341 B Winthrop Avenue
Fort Worth, TX 76116
Telephone: (817) 732-8200
Fax Number: (817) 732-8787

BANK OF NEW ORLEANS
1600 Veterans Blvd
Metairie, LA 70005
Telephone: (504) 834-1190
Fax Number: (504) 834-7777

BANK OF SALEM
1801 Central Avenue Suite C
Hot Springs, AR 71901
Telephone: (501) 624-7685

CENTRAL PACIFIC MORTGAGE CO
1500 N Norwood Ste 301
Hurst, TX 76054
Telephone: (817) 282-8733
Fax Number: (817) 268-5859

COACHELLA VALLEY MORTGAGE CTR
4422 FM 1960 West Suite 120
Houston, TX 77068
Telephone: (281) 444-4345

COMMUNITY HOME LOAN LLC
11000 Richmond Ave.
Houston, TX 77042
Telephone: (281) 657-0472
Fax Number: (281) 657-0484

FIRST CONTINENTAL MTG CORP
POB 4095 450 Southwest Drive
Jonesboro, AR 72403
Telephone: (501) 932-6756

FIRST FEDERAL BANK OF LOUISIANA
1135 Lake Shore Dr
Lake Charles, LA 70601
Telephone: (337) 433-3611

FIRST UNIVERSAL MORTGAGE INC
1615 N Hampton Road Ste 180
De Soto, TX 75115
Telephone: (972) 228-8282

GDG MORTGAGE INC
440 Benmar Suite 2250
Houston, TX 77060
Telephone: (281) 445-4380

GRIFFIN FINANCIAL MORTGAGE LLC
1701 River Run Suite 308
Fort Worth, TX 76107
Telephone: (817) 338-1708

HIBERNIA NATIONAL BANK
11130 Industriplex Blvd
Baton Rouge, LA 70809
Telephone: (504) 381-2372

LANDMARK MORTGAGE
CORPORATION
732 Behrman Highway Suite I
Gretna, LA 70056
Telephone: (504) 392-3861

METAIRIE BANK AND TRUST CO
3344 Metairie Road
Metairie, LA 70001
Telephone: (504) 834-6330
Fax Number: (504) 832-3235

REALTY MORTGAGE CORPORATION
112 Bedford Road #116
Bedford, TX 76022
Telephone: (817) 285-8084
Fax Number: (817) 285-9151

RELIANCE MORTGAGE CO
8115 Preston Rd Ste 800
Dallas, TX 75225
Telephone: (214) 360-9000
Fax Number: (214) 853-4130

REVERSE MORTGAGE OF TEXAS INC
13455 Noel Road Suite 1000
Dallas, TX 75240
Telephone: (214) 418-7924
Fax Number: (972) 407-0534

SECURE FINANCIAL SERVICES
2500 West Loop South Ste 350
Houston, TX 77027
Telephone: (713) 355-9955
Fax Number: (713) 355-9999

SOUTHSIDE BANK
1201 South Beckam
Tyler, TX 75701
Telephone: (903) 531-7111

STANDARD MORTGAGE CORPORATION
701 Poydras St No 300 Plaza
New Orleans, LA 70139
Telephone: (504) 581-7721

SUPERIOR MORTGAGE AND EQUITY
160 Dowlen Road
Beaumont, TX 77706
Telephone: (409) 866-7743

TRUSTMARK NATIONAL BANK
277 East Pearl
Jackson, MS 39201
Telephone: (601) 354-5150

UNITED COMPANIES MORTGAGE CORP
5841 S Sherwood Forest Blvd
Baton Rouge, LA 70816
Telephone: (225) 292-5010
Fax Number: (225) 293-4355

WHITNEY NATIONAL BANK
228 St Charles Avenue
New Orleans, LA 70130
Telephone: (504) 838-6400

Maine:

AMSTON MORTGAGE
711 Middletown Road Suite 8
Colchester, CT 06415
Telephone: (800) 625-8633
Fax Number: (860) 365-0001

BNY MORTGAGE COMPANY LLC
57 Jefferson Street
Milford, MA 01757
Telephone: (508) 422-9589
Fax Number: (508) 422-9592

CONTINENTAL FUNDING CORP
7 Cabot Place 2nd Floor
Stoughton, MA 02072
Telephone: (781) 344-4846
Fax Number: (781) 344-1841

EAST WEST MORTGAGE COMPANY
189 Hartford Ave Ste 1
Bellingham, MA 02019
Telephone: (508) 966-5250
Fax Number: (508) 966-5251

EQUITY AMERICA MORTGAGE SVCS
INC
340 Granite St
Manchester, NH 03102
Telephone: (603) 625-2820

FAIRFIELD COUNTY BANK CORP
374 Main Street
Ridgefield, CT 06877
Telephone: (203) 438-6518

FREEDOM CHOICE MORTGAGE
30 East Main Street
Avon, CT 06001
Telephone: (203) 677-0127

GMAC MORTGAGE CORPORATION
3 Executive Park Dr Ste 310
Bedford, NH 03110
Telephone: (603) 668-0778

HOME MORTGAGE LOAN COMPANY
393 Center Street
Auburn, ME 04210
Telephone: (207) 946-2820

MCLAUGHLIN FINANCIAL INC
90 Highland Ave
Salem, MA 01970
Telephone: (978) 744-6016

MORTGAGE FINANCIAL SERVICES INC
170 Main St Suite 108
Tewksbury, MA 01876
Telephone: (978) 863-9555

PROVIDIAN NATIONAL BANK
295 Main Street
Tilton, NH 03276
Telephone: (603) 286-4348

WEBSTER BANK
609 West Johnson Avenue
Cheshire, CT 06410
Telephone: (888) 681-7788

Maryland:

AAKO INC
3569 Bristol Pike Bldg No 2
Bensalem, PA 19020
Telephone: (215) 633-8080
Fax Number: (215) 633-8088

ACADEMY MORTGAGE LLC
5602 Baltimore National Pk 401
Baltimore, MD 21228
Telephone: (410) 788-7070

ALBION FINANCIAL INC
1873 Route 70 East Ste 302-D
Cherry Hill, NJ 08003
Telephone: (856) 424-4367

ALL PENNSYLVANIA REVERSE
MORTGAGE INC
4085 Route 8
Allison Park, PA 15101
Telephone: (412) 963-6062

BNY MORTGAGE COMPANY LLC
385 Rifle Camp Road
West Paterson, NJ 07424
Telephone: (800) 299-3133
Fax Number: (973) 247-4391

CARDINAL FINANCIAL COMPANY
444 Jacksonville Road
Warminster, PA 18974
Telephone: (215) 293-6800
Fax Number: (215) 293-6807

CENTURA BANK
133 S Franklin Street
Rocky Mount, NC 27804
Telephone: (919) 454-6053

COMMERCE BANK NA
17000 Horizon Way
Mt Laurell, NJ 08054
Telephone: (732) 747-1999
Fax Number: (732) 450-0737

EAST WEST MORTGAGE COMPANY
1568 Spring Hill Rd Ste 100
McLean, VA 22102
Telephone: (703) 442-0150

EVERBANK
4010 Jefferson Woods Drive
Powhatan, VA 23129
Telephone: (804) 403-3380

EVERHOME MORTGAGE COMPANY
8100 Nations Way
Jacksonville, FL 32256
Telephone: (904) 281-6000

FEDERAL MORTGAGE AND
INVESTMENT CORP
1111 Clifton Avenue
Clifton, NJ 07013
Telephone: (973) 777-7784

FIDELITY AND TRUST MORTGAGE INC
7229 Hanover Parkway, Suite C
Greenbelt, MD 20770
Telephone: (301) 313-9100
Fax Number: (301) 313-0900

FIRST MARINER BANK
3301 Boston Street
Baltimore, MD 21224
Telephone: (410) 558-4118
Fax Number: (410) 342-0489

FIRST MONEY GROUP INC
1777 Reisterstown Rd Suite 230
Baltimore, MD 21208
Telephone: (410) 653-6909

INTERCHANGE BANK
Park 80 West-Plaza Two
Saddle Brook, NJ 07663
Telephone: (201) 703-2246

MORTGAGE CAPITAL INVESTORS INC
6571 Edsall Road
Springfield, VA 22151
Telephone: (703) 941-0711
Fax Number: (703) 256-3118

MORTGAGE MONEY MART INC
1199 Amboy Avenue
Edison, NJ 08837
Telephone: (732) 548-9423

NEW JERSEY HOME FUNDING GROUP
LLC
457 Route 79
Morganville, NJ 07751
Telephone: (732) 970-9210

NEW JERSEY HSNG MTG FIN AGEN
637 South Clinton Avenue
Trenton, NJ 08650
Telephone: (609) 278-7400

OCEANFIRST BANK
975 Hooper Avenue
Toms River, NJ 08753
Telephone: (732) 240-4500

PEOPLES TRUST MORTGAGE LLC
3920 Plank Road Suite-200
Fredericksburg, VA 22407
Telephone: (540) 548-8749

REAL ESTATE MORTGAGE NETWORK
INC
70 Grand Avenue
River Edge, NJ 07661
Telephone: (201) 498-9300
Fax Number: (201) 498-9377

S AND T BANK
800 Philadelphia Street
Indiana, PA 15701
Telephone: (800) 325-2265

SAVINGS FIRST MORTGAGE LLC
100 Painters Mill Road Ste 800
Owings Mills, MD 21117
Telephone: (410) 654-8800

SENIORS FIRST MORTGAGE COMPANY
LLC
4525 South Avenue Suite 301
Virginia Beach, VA 23452
Telephone: (757) 671-6000

SUPERIOR MORTGAGE CORP
1395 Route 539
Tuckerton, NJ 08087
Telephone: (609) 294-2854
Fax Number: (609) 294-0620

UNITED FIRST MORTGAGE INC
1503 Santa Rosa Road Ste-109
Richmond, VA 23229
Telephone: (804) 282-5631

WEST PENN FIN SERVICE CTR INC
1800 Smallman Street
Pittsburgh, PA 15222
Telephone: (704) 948-1993

Massachusetts:

ACADEMY MORTGAGE CORPORATION
4055 South 700 East Suite 200
Salt Lake City, UT 84107
Telephone: (801) 261-4860

AMSTON MORTGAGE
711 Middletown Road Suite 8
Colchester, CT 06415
Telephone: (800) 625-8633
Fax Number: (860) 365-0001

BNY MORTGAGE COMPANY LLC
57 Jefferson Street
Milford, MA 01757
Telephone: (508) 422-9589
Fax Number: (508) 422-9592

CAMBRIDGE HOME CAPITAL LLC
80 Cuttermill Road Ste 408
Great Neck, NY 11021
Telephone: (516) 829-5700
Fax Number: (516) 829-5777

CONCORD MORTGAGE CORP
25 Melville Park Rd
Melville, NY 11747
Telephone: (631) 756-0700
Fax Number: (631) 756-0900

CONTINENTAL FUNDING CORP
7 Cabot Place 2nd Floor
Stoughton, MA 02072
Telephone: (781) 344-4846
Fax Number: (781) 344-1841

EAST WEST MORTGAGE COMPANY
189 Hartford Ave Ste 1
Bellingham, MA 02019
Telephone: (508) 966-5250
Fax Number: (508) 966-5251

EQUITY AMERICA MORTGAGE SVCS
INC
340 Granite St
Manchester, NH 03102
Telephone: (603) 625-2820

EVERHOME MORTGAGE COMPANY
8100 Nations Way
Jacksonville, FL 32256
Telephone: (904) 281-6000

FAIRFIELD COUNTY BANK CORP
374 Main Street
Ridgefield, CT 06877
Telephone: (203) 438-6518

FEDERAL MORTGAGE AND
INVESTMENT CORP
1111 Clifton Avenue
Clifton, NJ 07013
Telephone: (973) 777-7784

FREEDOM CHOICE MORTGAGE
30 East Main Street
Avon, CT 06001
Telephone: (203) 677-0127

GMAC MORTGAGE CORPORATION
3 Executive Park Dr Ste 310
Bedford, NH 03110
Telephone: (603) 668-0778

HOME MORTGAGE LOAN COMPANY
393 Center Street
Auburn, ME 04210
Telephone: (207) 946-2820

INTERCHANGE BANK
Park 80 West-Plaza Two
Saddle Brook, NJ 07663
Telephone: (201) 703-2246

MORTGAGE FINANCIAL SERVICES INC
170 Main St Suite 108
Tewksbury, MA 01876
Telephone: (978) 863-9555

MORTGAGE MONEY MART INC
1199 Amboy Avenue
Edison, NJ 08837
Telephone: (732) 548-9423

NATIONRESIDENTIAL MORTGAGE
BANKING CORP
One Rabro Drive
Hauppauge, NY 11788
Telephone: (516) 232-1133

NEW JERSEY HOME FUNDING GROUP
LLC
457 Route 79
Morganville, NJ 07751
Telephone: (732) 970-9210

PROVIDIAN NATIONAL BANK
295 Main Street
Tilton, NH 03276
Telephone: (603) 286-4348

REAL ESTATE MORTGAGE NETWORK
INC
70 Grand Avenue
River Edge, NJ 07661
Telephone: (201) 498-9300
Fax Number: (201) 498-9377

RHODE ISLAND HSG MTGE FIN CORP
44 Washington Street
Providence, RI 02903
Telephone: (401) 751-5566

SOUTHERN STAR MORTGAGE CORP
90 Merrick Avenue Suite 204
East Meadow, NY 11554
Telephone: (516) 712-4400
Fax Number: (516) 794-2116

USA FINANCIAL RESOURCES INC
66 Medford Avenue
Patchogue, NY 11772
Telephone: (516) 758-9200

WEBSTER BANK
609 West Johnson Avenue
Cheshire, CT 06410
Telephone: (888) 681-7788

Michigan:

ALBION FINANCIAL INC
5930 Lovers Lane
Portage, MI 49002
Telephone: (616) 383-1330

AMERICAN HOME MORTGAGE CORP
915 West 175th Suite 3W
Homewood, IL 60430
Telephone: (708) 647-7909

AMERICAN MIDWEST MTG CORP
6363 York Road
Parma Heights, OH 44130
Telephone: (216) 884-5000

AMERICAN REVERSE MORTGAGE CORP
2101 South Hamilton Road, #110
Columbus, OH 43232
Telephone: (614) 577-1440
Fax Number: (614) 577-1442

ASPEN MORTGAGE CORPORATION
651 N Washington
Naperville, IL 60563
Telephone: (630) 983-3600

CREDIT UNION MORTGAGE COMPANY
555 W Crosstown Pkwy Ste 401
Kalamazoo, MI 49008
Telephone: (616) 349-1021
Fax Number: (616) 349-0420

CUSTOM MORTGAGE INC
1712 N Meridian St Suite 200
Indianapolis, IN 46202
Telephone: (317) 920-5400

DOW MORTGAGE COMPANY
1600 Plainfield Rd
Crest Hill, IL 60435
Telephone: (815) 730-9400
Fax Number: (815) 730-0800

EVERBANK
1755 W Big Beaver Road
Troy, MI 48084
Telephone: (847) 439-5500

EVERHOME MORTGAGE COMPANY
8100 Nations Way
Jacksonville, FL 32256
Telephone: (904) 281-6000

EXCEL MORTGAGE CORPORATION
6100 Rockside Woods Blvd 225
Independence, OH 44131
Telephone: (216) 573-8090

FIRST ALLIANCE MORTGAGE CO
32100 Telegraph Road Suite-205
Bingham Farms, MI 48025
Telephone: (248) 433-9626
Fax Number: (248) 433-1210

FIRST CENTENNIAL MORTGAGE
11 North Edgelawn Avenue
Aurora, IL 60506
Telephone: (630) 906-7315

FIRST FEDERAL SAVINGS AND LOAN
601 Clinton Street
Defiance, OH 43510
Telephone: (419) 782-5015

FIRST FINANCIAL MORTGAGE CORP
200 North Center Suite 202
Northville, MI 48167
Telephone: (810) 347-7440

FIRST MIDWEST BANK
300 Park Blvd—Suite 400
Itasc, IL 60143
Telephone: (815) 774-2165
Fax Number: (815) 774-2070

GSF MORTGAGE CORPORATION
999 N Plaza Dr Ste 710
Schaumburg, IL 60173
Telephone: (847) 605-8244
Fax Number: (262) 373-1641

LIBERTY MORTGAGE INC
509 W McKinley Ave
Mishawaka, IN 46545
Telephone: (574) 257-0629

MORTGAGE CORP OHIO
110 E. Wilson Bridge Rd #220
Worthington, OH 43085
Telephone: (614) 431-3499
Fax Number: (614) 431-2697

OSWEGO COMMUNITY BANK
10 N Madison St
Oswego, IL 60543
Telephone: (630) 554-3411

PARK NATIONAL BANK
50 North Third St
Newark, OH 43055
Telephone: (614) 349-8451

PARK PLACE MORTGAGE CORP
38807 Ann Arbor Rd., Suite 3
Livonia, MI 48150
Telephone: (734) 542-1700
Fax Number: (734) 542-1054

PROFESSIONAL FINANCIAL MTG INC
16165 W 12 Mile Road
Southfield, MI 48076
Telephone: (810) 557-3230

REAL ESTATE MORTGAGE CORP
20325 Center Ridge Road,
Rocky River, OH 44116
Telephone: (440) 356-5363
Fax Number: (440) 356-3633

SENIOR REVERSE MORTGAGE LTD
4935 Dorr St
Toledo, OH 43615
Telephone: (419) 537-0015
Fax Number: (419) 537-0737

SENIORS EQUITY INCOME INC
6910 N Main St-14 Bldg 22-B
Granger, IN 46530
Telephone: (219) 272-0710

SGB CORPORATION
1 S 660 Midwest Rd. #100
Oakbrook Terrace, IL 60181
Telephone: (630) 916-9299
Fax Number: (630) 916-1299

SIGNATURE MORTGAGE CORP
4194 Fulton Rd NW
Canton, OH 44718
Telephone: (330) 491-1986

THIRD COMMUNITY MORTGAGE CORP
112 S. Water St. Suite C
Kent, OH 44240
Telephone: (330) 346-0380
Fax Number: (330) 346-0870

Minnesota:

CENTENNIAL MORTGAGE AND
FUNDING
250 Prairie Center Dr Ste 100
Eden Prairie, MN 55344
Telephone: (952) 826-0025
Fax Number: (952) 826-0027

CLA MORTGAGE INC
7280 S. 13th Street #103
Oak Creek, WI 53154
Telephone: (414) 570-8811
Fax Number: (414) 570-8822

DISCOVER MORTGAGE CORP
1500 South Hwy 100 Ste 360
Minneapolis, MN 55416
Telephone: (612) 546-0424

FARWEST MORTGAGE BANKERS INC
1532 Aspen Drive
Eagan, MN 55122
Telephone: (651) 994-1088

FIRST UNITED BANK
430 NW Fourth St
Faribault, MN 55021
Telephone: (507) 334-2201
Fax Number: (507) 334-2205

GATE CITY BANK
500 2nd Ave. North
Fargo, ND 58102
Telephone: (701) 293-2400

HOMESTEAD MORTGAGE
CORPORATION
4105 N Lexington Ave Ste 100
Arden Hills, MN 55126
Telephone: (612) 490-5555

JOHN DEERE COMMUNITY C U
1827 Ansborough Avenue
Waterloo, IA 50701
Telephone: (319) 274-7562

M AND I MARSHALL AND ILSLEY BANK
6625 Lyndale Ave South
Richfield, MN 55423
Telephone: (612) 798-3139
Fax Number: (612) 798-3137

METRO MORTGAGE CO INC
6657 Odana Road
Madison, WI 53719
Telephone: (608) 829-3000

MORTGAGE PLUS FINANCIAL CORP
199 Coon Rapids Blvd Suite 110
Coon Rapids, MN 55433
Telephone: (763) 786-7587

PEOPLES TRUST MORTGAGE LLC
1750 Weir Drive
Woodbury, MN 55125
Telephone: (651) 714-7171
Fax Number: (651) 714-7177

WESTERN NATIONAL BANK DULUTH
5629 Grand Ave
Duluth, MN 55807
Telephone: (218) 723-1000

Mississippi:

AMERICAN REVERSE MORTGAGE CORP
212 14th Ct NW
Birmingham, AL 35215
Telephone: (352) 867-1111
Fax Number: (352) 369-5985

BANK OF NEW ORLEANS
1600 Veterans Blvd
Metairie, LA 70005
Telephone: (504) 834-1190
Fax Number: (504) 834-7777

BANK OF SALEM
202 Church Street
Salem, AR 72576
Telephone: (501) 895-2591

EAGLE MORTGAGE INC
204 W North Street
Poplarville, MS 39470
Telephone: (601) 795-8881
Fax Number: (601) 795-0840

FIRST FEDERAL BANK OF LOUISIANA
1135 Lake Shore Dr
Lake Charles, LA 70601
Telephone: (337) 433-3611

HIBERNIA NATIONAL BANK
11130 Industriplex Blvd
Baton Rouge, LA 70809
Telephone: (504) 381-2372

HOMESOUTH MORTGAGE SERVICES
INC
200 Cahaba Park Circle Ste 125
Birmingham, AL 35242
Telephone: (205) 591-5055
Fax Number: (205) 591-5053

LANDMARK MORTGAGE
CORPORATION
732 Behrman Highway Suite I
Gretna, LA 70056
Telephone: (504) 392-3861

METAIRIE BANK AND TRUST CO
3344 Metairie Road
Metairie, LA 70001
Telephone: (504) 834-6330
Fax Number: (504) 832-3235

STANDARD MORTGAGE CORPORATION
701 Poydras St No 300 Plaza
New Orleans, LA 70139

TRUSTMARK NATIONAL BANK
277 East Pearl
Jackson, MS 39201
Telephone: (601) 354-5150

UNITED COMPANIES MORTGAGE
CORP
5841 S Sherwood Forest Blvd
Baton Rouge, LA 70816
Telephone: (225) 292-5010
Fax Number: (225) 293-4355

WHITNEY NATIONAL BANK
228 St Charles Avenue
New Orleans, LA 70130
Telephone: (504) 838-6400

Missouri:

AMERIFUND FINANCIAL INC
50 Crestwood Executive Ctr Ste
Saint Louis, MO 63126
Telephone: (866) 839-7700
Fax Number: (866) 839-7701

BANK OF SALEM
202 Church Street
Salem, AR 72576
Telephone: (501) 895-2591

BEST MORTGAGE AND FINANCIAL
GROUP
1217 North Kings Highway
Cape Girardeau, MO 63701
Telephone: (573) 334-9900

COLE TAYLOR BANK
5501 West 79th Street
Burbank, IL 60459
Telephone: (800) 613-7778
Fax Number: (630) 801-8580

JAMES B NUTTER AND COMPANY
4153 Broadway
Kansas City, MO 64111
Telephone: (816) 531-2345

MORTGAGE AUTHORITY INC
9557 W 87th Street
Overland Park, KS 66212
Telephone: (913) 648-9000
Fax Number: (913) 648-9009

MORTGAGE SERVICES INC
1801 E Empire Suite 2
Bloomington, IL 61704
Telephone: (309) 662-6693
Fax Number: (309) 663-0818

MOUNTAIN PACIFIC MORTGAGE CO
1201 E 32nd St, Suite E
Joplin, MO 64804
Telephone: (417) 623-0500
Fax Number: (417) 623-0990

SGB CORPORATION
1 S 660 Midwest Rd. #100
Oakbrook Terrace, IL 60181
Telephone: (630) 916-9299
Fax Number: (630) 916-1299

Montana:

MORTGAGE PLACE LLC
5593 N Glenwood
Boise, ID 83714
Telephone: (208) 472-8877
Fax Number: (208) 472-8879

EVERHOME MORTGAGE COMPANY
8100 Nations Way
Jacksonville, FL 32256
Telephone: (904) 281-6000

FAIRWAY INDEPENDENT MORTGAGE
CORPORATION
2404 East Amity Avenue
Nampa, ID 83686
Telephone: (208) 467-9663

FSI MORTGAGE LLC
1858 East 1st Street
Idaho Falls, ID 83401
Telephone: (208) 529-6643

HOMESTREET BANK
601 Union Street
Seattle, WA 98101
Telephone: (206) 623-3050
Fax Number: (206) 389-6306

INTERMOUNTAIN MORTGAGE CO INC
3333 2nd Avenue North Ste 250
Billings, MT 59101
Telephone: (406) 252-2600
Fax Number: (406) 237-0187

INVESTORS WEST MORTGAGE
814 N 8th Street
Boise, ID 83702
Telephone: (208) 345-8153

IRELAND BANK
33 Bannock Ave
Malad City, ID 83252
Telephone: (208) 766-2211

PREMIER MORTGAGE RESOURCES LLC
16 12th Ave S
Nampa, ID 83651
Telephone: (208) 562-1777
Fax Number: (208) 362-6208

Nebraska:

ALLIANCE GUARANTY MORTGAGE
CORP
11414 West Center Suite-137
Omaha, NE 68114
Telephone: (800) 474-5726

JAMES B NUTTER AND COMPANY
4153 Broadway
Kansas City, MO 64111
Telephone: (816) 531-2345

JOHN DEERE COMMUNITY C U
1827 Ansborough Avenue
Waterloo, IA 50701
Telephone: (319) 274-7562

LIBERTY FIRST CREDIT UNION
501 North 46th Street
Lincoln, NE 68503
Telephone: (402) 464-8347

MORTGAGE AUTHORITY INC
9557 W 87th Street
Overland Park, KS 66212
Telephone: (913) 648-9000
Fax Number: (913) 648-9009

MORTGAGE SERVICES INC
2921 S 168th Street
Omaha, NE 68130
Telephone: (402) 330-9388
Fax Number: (402) 330-9382

MOUNTAIN PACIFIC MORTGAGE CO
1201 E 32nd St, Suite E
Joplin, MO 64804
Telephone: (417) 623-0500
Fax Number: (417) 623-0990

Nevada:

ACADEMY MORTGAGE CORPORATION
3670 Grant Drive, #105
Reno, NV 89509
Telephone: (775) 825-4545
Fax Number: (775) 825-2504

COACHELLA VALLEY MORTGAGE CTR
73-200 El Paseo Suite 2C
Palm Desert, CA 92260
Telephone: (760) 773-2811
Fax Number: (760) 773-2814

COLONIAL MORTGAGE AND
INVESTMENT
8715 W Union Hills Dr Ste 103
Peoria, AZ 85382
Telephone: (602) 995-3990
Fax Number: (602) 995-9424

COMMUNITY LENDING INC
1990 W. Camelback Rd., 218
Phoenix, AZ 85015
Telephone: (602) 393-2890
Fax Number: (602) 393-2895

EAST WEST MORTGAGE COMPANY
21616 Rose Lane
Woodland, CA 95695
Telephone: (820) 758-0936

FARWEST MORTGAGE BANKERS INC
16824 Ave. of Fountains
Fountain Hills, AZ 85268
Telephone: (480) 816-4564
Fax Number: (480) 816-4563

FRONTIER MORTGAGE CORPORATION
1801 East 14th Street
San Leandro, CA 94577
Telephone: (510) 895-5969
Fax Number: (510) 895-5971

HOME ACCESS CAPITAL INC
2111 E Highland Ave. Suite 440
Phoenix, AZ 85016
Telephone: (602) 234-2230
Fax Number: (602) 234-2234

JAYNA INC
800 N Rainbow Blvd Suite 100
Las Vegas, NV 89107
Telephone: (702) 948-5077
Fax Number: (702) 948-5077

LENDERS DEPOT INC
27450 Ynez Rd Ste 320
Temecula, CA 92591
Telephone: (909) 296-3322

PACIFIC COAST MORTGAGE INC
6300 E Thomas Rd Ste 200
Scottsdale, AZ 85251
Telephone: (480) 949-0707
Fax Number: (480) 949-5252

PRIME SOURCE MORTGAGE INC
7100 E Lincoln Drive Ste B120
Scottsdale, AZ 85253
Telephone: (480) 998-2882

SKOFED MORTGAGE FUNDING CORP
2610 So. Jones Blvd, Suite #1
Las Vegas, NV 89146
Telephone: (702) 362-2626
Fax Number: (702) 362-6500

SUN AMERICAN MORTGAGE CO
444 South Greenfield Road
Mesa, AZ 85206
Telephone: (602) 832-4343

ZIONS FIRST NATIONAL BANK
255 N Admiral Blvd Rd
Salt Lake City, UT 84116
Telephone: (801) 273-3000
Fax Number: (801) 273-3035

New Hampshire:

AMSTON MORTGAGE
711 Middletown Road Suite 8
Colchester, CT 06415
Telephone: (800) 625-8633
Fax Number: (860) 365-0001

BNY MORTGAGE COMPANY LLC
57 Jefferson Street
Milford, MA 01757
Telephone: (508) 422-9589
Fax Number: (508) 422-9592

CARTERET MORTGAGE CORPORATION
31 Tokenel Drive
Londonderry, NH 03053
Telephone: (603) 434-1555

CONTINENTAL FUNDING CORP
7 Cabot Place 2nd Floor
Stoughton, MA 02072
Telephone: (781) 344-4846
Fax Number: (781) 344-1841

EAST WEST MORTGAGE COMPANY
189 Hartford Ave Ste 1
Bellingham, MA 02019
Telephone: (508) 966-5250
Fax Number: (508) 966-5251

EQUITY AMERICA MORTGAGE SVCS
INC
340 Granite St
Manchester, NH 03102
Telephone: (603) 625-2820

FAIRFIELD COUNTY BANK CORP
374 Main Street
Ridgefield, CT 06877
Telephone: (203) 438-6518

FINANCIAL FREEDOM SENIOR
FUNDING CORP
41 Tomlinson Ave
Plainville, CT 06062
Telephone: (860) 747-3704

FREEDOM CHOICE MORTGAGE
30 East Main Street
Avon, CT 06001
Telephone: (203) 677-0127

HOME MORTGAGE LOAN COMPANY
393 Center Street
Auburn, ME 04210
Telephone: (207) 946-2820

M AND T MORTGAGE CORPORATION
Northway 10 Executive Park
Clifton Park, NY 12065
Telephone: (518) 877-3500

MCLAUGHLIN FINANCIAL INC
90 Highland Ave
Salem, MA 01970
Telephone: (978) 744-6016

MORTGAGE FINANCIAL SERVICES INC
170 Main St Suite 108
Tewksbury, MA 01876
Telephone: (978) 863-9555

PROVIDIAN NATIONAL BANK
295 Main Street
Tilton, NH 03276
Telephone: (603) 286-4348

RHODE ISLAND HSG MTGE FIN CORP
44 Washington Street
Providence, RI 02903
Telephone: (401) 751-5566

WEBSTER BANK
609 West Johnson Avenue
Cheshire, CT 06410
Telephone: (888) 681-7788

New Jersey:

AAKO INC
3569 Bristol Pike Bldg No 2
Bensalem, PA 19020
Telephone: (215) 633-8080
Fax Number: (215) 633-8088

ACADEMY MORTGAGE LLC
5602 Baltimore National Pk 401
Baltimore, MD 21228
Telephone: (410) 788-7070

AGENCY FOR CONSUMER EQUITY
MORTGAGE INC
101 Executive Blvd. 1st Floor
Elmsford, NY 10523
Telephone: (800) 881-2954
Fax Number: (914) 682-0521

ALBION FINANCIAL INC
1873 Route 70 East Ste 302-D
Cherry Hill, NJ 08003
Telephone: (856) 424-4367

AMSTON MORTGAGE
711 Middletown Road Suite 8
Colchester, CT 06415
Telephone: (800) 625-8633
Fax Number: (860) 365-0001

BNY MORTGAGE COMPANY LLC
57 Jefferson Street
Milford, MA 01757
Telephone: (508) 422-9589
Fax Number: (508) 422-9592

BNY MORTGAGE COMPANY LLC
385 Rifle Camp Road
West Paterson, NJ 07424
Telephone: (800) 299-3133
Fax Number: (973) 247-4391

CAMBRIDGE HOME CAPITAL LLC
80 Cuttermill Road Ste 408
Great Neck, NY 11021
Telephone: (516) 829-5700
Fax Number: (516) 829-5777

CARDINAL FINANCIAL COMPANY
444 Jacksonville Road
Warminster, PA 18974
Telephone: (215) 293-6800
Fax Number: (215) 293-6807

CENTURA BANK
133 S Franklin Street
Rocky Mount, NC 27804
Telephone: (919) 454-6053

COMMERCE BANK NA
17000 Horizon Way
Mt Laurell, NJ 08054
Telephone: (732) 747-1999
Fax Number: (732) 450-0737

CONCORD MORTGAGE CORP
25 Melville Park Rd
Melville, NY 11747
Telephone: (631) 756-0700
Fax Number: (631) 756-0900

CONTINENTAL FUNDING CORP
7 Cabot Place 2nd Floor
Stoughton, MA 02072
Telephone: (781) 344-4846
Fax Number: (781) 344-1841

EAST WEST MORTGAGE COMPANY
189 Hartford Ave Ste 1
Bellingham, MA 02019
Telephone: (508) 966-5250
Fax Number: (508) 966-5251

EAST WEST MORTGAGE COMPANY
1568 Spring Hill Rd Ste 100
McLean, VA 22102
Telephone: (703) 442-0150

EVERHOME MORTGAGE COMPANY
8100 Nations Way
Jacksonville, FL 32256
Telephone: (904) 281-6000

FAIRFIELD COUNTY BANK CORP
374 Main Street
Ridgefield, CT 06877
Telephone: (203) 438-6518

FAST TRACK FUNDING CORP
247 W Old Country Road
Hicksville, NY 11801
Telephone: (516) 938-6600

FEDERAL MORTGAGE AND
INVESTMENT CORP
1111 Clifton Avenue
Clifton, NJ 07013
Telephone: (973) 777-7784

FIDELITY AND TRUST MORTGAGE INC
7229 Hanover Parkway, Suite C
Greenbelt, MD 20770
Telephone: (301) 313-9100
Fax Number: (301) 313-0900

FIRST MARINER BANK
3301 Boston Street
Baltimore, MD 21224
Telephone: (410) 558-4118
Fax Number: (410) 342-0489

FIRST MONEY GROUP INC
1777 Reisterstown Rd Suite 230
Baltimore, MD 21208
Telephone: (410) 653-6909

FREEDOM CHOICE MORTGAGE
30 East Main Street
Avon, CT 06001
Telephone: (203) 677-0127

HOME CONSULTANTS INC
661 Northern Boulevard
Clarks Summit, PA 18411
Telephone: (570) 586-7863
Fax Number: (570) 586-7865

INTERCHANGE BANK
Park 80 West-Plaza Two
Saddle Brook, NJ 07663
Telephone: (201) 703-2246

KASTLE MORTGAGE CORPORATION
77 West Main Street
Freehold, NJ 07728
Telephone: (732) 845-5444

M AND T MORTGAGE CORPORATION
2270 Erin Court
Lancaster, PA 17604
Telephone: (717) 397-5548
Fax Number: (717) 397-2643

MCLAUGHLIN FINANCIAL INC
90 Highland Ave
Salem, MA 01970
Telephone: (978) 744-6016

MORTGAGE FINANCIAL SERVICES INC
170 Main St Suite 108
Tewksbury, MA 01876
Telephone: (978) 863-9555

MORTGAGE MOBILITY LLC
1094 Second Street Pike
Richboro, PA 18954
Telephone: (215) 357-4900
Fax Number: (215) 364-1927

MORTGAGE MONEY MART INC
1199 Amboy Avenue
Edison, NJ 08837
Telephone: (732) 548-9423

NATIONRESIDENTIAL MORTGAGE
BANKING CORP
One Rabro Drive
Hauppauge, NY 11788
Telephone: (516) 232-1133

NEW JERSEY HOME FUNDING GROUP
LLC
457 Route 79
Morganville, NJ 07751
Telephone: (732) 970-9210

NEW JERSEY HSNG MTG FIN AGEN
637 South Clinton Avenue
Trenton, NJ 08650
Telephone: (609) 278-7400

OCEANFIRST BANK
975 Hooper Avenue
Toms River, NJ 08753
Telephone: (732) 240-4500

PEOPLES TRUST MORTGAGE LLC
3920 Plank Road Suite-200
Fredericksburg, VA 22407
Telephone: (540) 548-8749

RCRBL ENTERPRISES LTD
1123 Old Town Road
Coram, NY 11727
Telephone: (631) 736-7700

REAL ESTATE MORTGAGE NETWORK
INC
70 Grand Avenue
River Edge, NJ 07661
Telephone: (201) 498-9300
Fax Number: (201) 498-9377

SAVINGS FIRST MORTGAGE LLC
100 Painters Mill Road Ste 800
Owings Mills, MD 21117
Telephone: (410) 654-8800

SEATTLE MORTGAGE COMPANY
301 Elmwood Avenue
Feasterville, PA 19053
Telephone: (215) 953-8786
Fax Number: (888) 748-9300

SENIORS FIRST MORTGAGE COMPANY
LLC
4525 South Avenue Suite 301
Virginia Beach, VA 23452
Telephone: (757) 671-6000

SOUTHERN STAR MORTGAGE CORP
90 Merrick Avenue Suite 204
East Meadow, NY 11554
Telephone: (516) 712-4400
Fax Number: (516) 794-2116

SUPERIOR MORTGAGE CORP
1395 Route 539
Tuckerton, NJ 08087
Telephone: (609) 294-2854
Fax Number: (609) 294-0620

UNITED FIRST MORTGAGE INC
1503 Santa Rosa Road Ste 109
Richmond, VA 23229
Telephone: (804) 282-5631

USA FINANCIAL RESOURCES INC
66 Medford Avenue
Patchogue, NY 11772
Telephone: (516) 758-9200

WEBSTER BANK
609 West Johnson Avenue
Cheshire, CT 06410
Telephone: (888) 681-7788

New Mexico:

A D S MORTGAGE CORP
3809 Atrisco Dr NW Suite A
Albuquerque, NM 87120
Telephone: (505) 299-2373

ALETHES LLC
2112 Traywood Dr
El Paso, TX 79935
Telephone: (915) 591-6868
Fax Number: (915) 591-6869

LEWALLEN MORTGAGE INC
10701 Montgomery NE—Suite A
Albuquerque, NM 87111
Telephone: (505) 293-9300
Fax Number: (505) 294-1974

MAJOR MORTGAGE
1421 Luisa Street, Suite N
Santa Fe, NM 87501
Telephone: (505) 989-7050
Fax Number: (505) 989-7057

SOUTHWEST FUNDING LP
8848 Greenville Avenue
Dallas, TX 75243
Telephone: (214) 221-5215
Fax Number: (214) 221-5470

New York:

AAKO INC
3569 Bristol Pike Bldg No 2
Bensalem, PA 19020
Telephone: (215) 633-8080
Fax Number: (215) 633-8088

AGENCY FOR CONSUMER EQUITY
MORTGAGE INC
101 Executive Blvd. 1st Floor
Elmsford, NY 10523
Telephone: (800) 881-2954
Fax Number: (914) 682-0521

ALBION FINANCIAL INC
1873 Route 70 East Ste 302-D
Cherry Hill, NJ 08003
Telephone: (856) 424-4367

ALL PENNSYLVANIA REVERSE
MORTGAGE INC
4085 Route 8
Allison Park, PA 15101
Telephone: (412) 963-6062

AMERICAN MIDWEST MTG CORP
6363 York Road
Parma Heights, OH 44130
Telephone: (216) 884-5000

AMSTON MORTGAGE
711 Middletown Road Suite 8
Colchester, CT 06415
Telephone: (800) 625-8633
Fax Number: (860) 365-0001

BNY MORTGAGE COMPANY LLC
440 Mamaroneck Ave 2nd Floor
Harrison, NY 10528
Telephone: (800) 299-3133
Fax Number: (914) 899-6491

CAMBRIDGE HOME CAPITAL LLC
80 Cuttermill Road Ste 408
Great Neck, NY 11021
Telephone: (516) 829-5700
Fax Number: (516) 829-5777

CARDINAL FINANCIAL COMPANY
444 Jacksonville Road
Warminster, PA 18974
Telephone: (215) 293-6800
Fax Number: (215) 293-6807

COMMERCE BANK NA
17000 Horizon Way
Mt Laurell, NJ 08054
Telephone: (732) 747-1999
Fax Number: (732) 450-0737

COMMUNITY HOME EQU CONV CORP
160 Linden Oaks Drive
Rochester, NY 14625
Telephone: (716) 389-1324
Fax Number: (716) 383-4209

CONCORD MORTGAGE CORP
25 Melville Park Rd
Melville, NY 11747
Telephone: (631) 756-0700
Fax Number: (631) 756-0900

CONTINENTAL FUNDING CORP
7 Cabot Place 2nd Floor
Stoughton, MA 02072
Telephone: (781) 344-4846
Fax Number: (781) 344-1841

EAST WEST MORTGAGE COMPANY
189 Hartford Ave Ste 1
Bellingham, MA 02019
Telephone: (508) 966-5250
Fax Number: (508) 966-5251

EXCEL MORTGAGE CORPORATION
6100 Rockside Woods Blvd 225
Independence, OH 44131
Telephone: (216) 573-8090

FAIRFIELD COUNTY BANK CORP
374 Main Street
Ridgefield, CT 06877
Telephone: (203) 438-6518

FAST TRACK FUNDING CORP
247 W Old Country Road
Hicksville, NY 11801
Telephone: (516) 938-6600

FEDERAL MORTGAGE AND
INVESTMENT CORP
1111 Clifton Avenue
Clifton, NJ 07013
Telephone: (973) 777-7784

FIRST FEDERAL SAVINGS AND LOAN
601 Clinton Street
Defiance, OH 43510
Telephone: (419) 782-5015

FREEDOM CHOICE MORTGAGE
30 East Main Street
Avon, CT 06001
Telephone: (203) 677-0127

HOME CONSULTANTS INC
661 Northern Boulevard
Clarks Summit, PA 18411
Telephone: (570) 586-7863
Fax Number: (570) 586-7865

INTERCHANGE BANK
Park 80 West-Plaza Two
Saddle Brook, NJ 07663
Telephone: (201) 703-2246

KASTLE MORTGAGE CORPORATION
77 West Main Street
Freehold, NJ 07728
Telephone: (732) 845-5444

M AND T MORTGAGE CORPORATION
Northway 10 Executive Park
Clifton Park, NY 12065
Telephone: (518) 877-3500

MCLAUGHLIN FINANCIAL INC
90 Highland Ave
Salem, MA 01970
Telephone: (978) 744-6016

MORTGAGE FINANCIAL SERVICES INC
170 Main St Suite 108
Tewksbury, MA 01876
Telephone: (978) 863-9555

MORTGAGE MOBILITY LLC
1094 Second Street Pike
Richboro, PA 18954
Telephone: (215) 357-4900
Fax Number: (215) 364-1927

MORTGAGE MONEY MART INC
1199 Amboy Avenue
Edison, NJ 08837
Telephone: (732) 548-9423

MORTGAGE NOW INC
750 W. Resource Drive, #300
Brooklyn Hts., OH 44131
Telephone: (216) 635-0000
Fax Number: (216) 635-1111

NATIONRESIDENTIAL MORTGAGE
BANKING CORP
One Rabro Drive
Hauppauge, NY 11788
Telephone: (516) 232-1133

NEW JERSEY HOME FUNDING GROUP
LLC
457 Route 79
Morganville, NJ 07751
Telephone: (732) 970-9210

NEW JERSEY HSNG MTG FIN AGEN
637 South Clinton Avenue
Trenton, NJ 08650
Telephone: (609) 278-7400

OCEANFIRST BANK
975 Hooper Avenue
Toms River, NJ 08753
Telephone: (732) 240-4500

RCRBL ENTERPRISES LTD
1123 Old Town Road
Coram, NY 11727
Telephone: (631) 736-7700

REAL ESTATE MORTGAGE CORP
20325 Center Ridge Road,
Rocky River, OH 44116
Telephone: (440) 356-5363
Fax Number: (440) 356-3633

REAL ESTATE MORTGAGE NETWORK
INC
70 Grand Avenue
River Edge, NJ 07661
Telephone: (201) 498-9300
Fax Number: (201) 498-9377

RHODE ISLAND HSG MTGE FIN CORP
44 Washington Street
Providence, RI 02903
Telephone: (401) 751-5566

S AND T BANK
800 Philadelphia Street
Indiana, PA 15701
Telephone: (800) 325-2265

SENIOR REVERSE MORTGAGE LTD
4935 Dorr St
Toledo, OH 43615
Telephone: (419) 537-0015
Fax Number: (419) 537-0737

SIGNATURE MORTGAGE CORP
4194 Fulton Rd NW
Canton, OH 44718
Telephone: (330) 491-1986

SOUTHERN STAR MORTGAGE CORP
90 Merrick Avenue Suite 204
East Meadow, NY 11554
Telephone: (516) 712-4400
Fax Number: (516) 794-2116

SUPERIOR MORTGAGE CORP
1395 Route 539
Tuckerton, NJ 08087
Telephone: (609) 294-2854
Fax Number: (609) 294-0620

THIRD COMMUNITY MORTGAGE CORP
112 S. Water St. Suite C
Kent, OH 44240
Telephone: (330) 346-0380
Fax Number: (330) 346-0870

USA FINANCIAL RESOURCES INC
66 Medford Avenue
Patchogue, NY 11772
Telephone: (516) 758-9200

WEBSTER BANK
609 West Johnson Avenue
Cheshire, CT 06410
Telephone: (888) 681-7788

WEST PENN FIN SERVICE CTR INC
1800 Smallman Street
Pittsburgh, PA 15222
Telephone: (704) 948-1993

North Carolina:

CENTURA BANK
133 S Franklin Street
Rocky Mount, NC 27804
Telephone: (919) 454-6053

EVERBANK
5512 Livonia Cover
North Charleston, SC 29420
Telephone: (843) 552-5011

FRANKLIN FUNDING INC
147 Wappoo Creek Drive Ste 105
Charleston, SC 29412
Telephone: (843) 762-2218

HOME BUILDERS MORTGAGE CORP
678 B St Andrews Blvd
Charleston, SC 29407
Telephone: (843) 556-4643

HOME FEDERAL SAVINGS BANK TN
515 Market St
Knoxville, TN 37902
Telephone: (615) 546-0330

HOMEOWNERS MORTGAGE
ENTERPRISES INC
2530 Devine Street
Columbia, SC 29205
Telephone: (803) 765-9037

LUMINA MORTGAGE COMPANY INC
219 Racine Drive Suite A
Wilmington, NC 28403
Telephone: (910) 452-3555
Fax Number: (910) 452-9929

MORTGAGE CAPITAL INVESTORS INC
7901 N. Ocean Blvd.
Myrtle Beach, SC 29572
Telephone: (843) 449-8004
Fax Number: (843) 449-8206

MORTGAGE SOUTH OF TENNESSEE
409 S Germantown Rd
Chattanooga, TN 37411
Telephone: (423) 624-3878

OLDE TOWN MORTGAGE LLC
412-B N Gum St
Summerville, SC 29483
Telephone: (843) 832-0944

PEOPLES TRUST MORTGAGE LLC
3920 Plank Road Suite-200
Fredericksburg, VA 22407
Telephone: (540) 548-8749

SENIORS FIRST MORTGAGE COMPANY
LLC
4525 South Avenue Suite 301
Virginia Beach, VA 23452
Telephone: (757) 671-6000

THE MORTGAGE MALL INC
615 South New Hope Rd Ste 100
Gastonia, NC 28054
Telephone: (704) 866-4089

UNITED FIRST MORTGAGE INC
1503 Santa Rosa Road Ste-109
Richmond, VA 23229
Telephone: (804) 282-5631

North Dakota:

CENTENNIAL MORTGAGE AND FUNDING
250 Prairie Center Dr Ste 100
Eden Prairie, MN 55344
Telephone: (952) 826-0025
Fax Number: (952) 826-0027

DISCOVER MORTGAGE CORP
1500 South Hwy 100 Ste 360
Minneapolis, MN 55416
Telephone: (612) 546-0424

FARWEST MORTGAGE BANKERS INC
1532 Aspen Drive
Eagan, MN 55122
Telephone: (651) 994-1088

FIRST UNITED BANK
430 NW Fourth St
Faribault, MN 55021
Telephone: (507) 334-2201
Fax Number: (507) 334-2205

GATE CITY BANK
500 2nd Ave. North
Fargo, ND 58102
Telephone: (701) 293-2400

HOMESTEAD MORTGAGE
CORPORATION
4105 N Lexington Ave Ste 100
Arden Hills, MN 55126
Telephone: (612) 490-5555

M AND I MARSHALL AND ILSLEY BANK
6625 Lyndale Ave South
Richfield, MN 55423
Telephone: (612) 798-3139
Fax Number: (612) 798-3137

MORTGAGE PLUS FINANCIAL CORP
199 Coon Rapids Blvd Suite 110
Coon Rapids, MN 55433
Telephone: (763) 786-7587

PEOPLES TRUST MORTGAGE LLC
1750 Weir Drive
Woodbury, MN 55125
Telephone: (651) 714-7171
Fax Number: (651) 714-7177

WESTERN NATIONAL BANK DULUTH
5629 Grand Ave
Duluth, MN 55807
Telephone: (218) 723-1000

Ohio:

AMERICAN MIDWEST MTG CORP
6363 York Road
Parma Heights, OH 44130
Telephone: (216) 884-5000

AMERICAN MORTGAGE SERVICE CO
415 Glensprings Dr. Suite 203
Cincinnati, OH 45246
Telephone: (513) 674-8900
Fax Number: (513) 674-8906

AMERICAN REVERSE MORTGAGE CORP
2101 South Hamilton Road, #110
Columbus, OH 43232
Telephone: (614) 577-1440
Fax Number: (614) 577-1442

AMERISTATE BANCORP INC
7925 Graceland St
Dayton, OH 45459
Telephone: (937) 434-9900
Fax Number: (937) 434-9922

CUSTOM MORTGAGE INC
1712 N Meridian St Suite 200
Indianapolis, IN 46202
Telephone: (317) 920-5400

EVERBANK
1755 W Big Beaver Road
Troy, MI 48084
Telephone: (847) 439-5500

EXCEL MORTGAGE CORPORATION
6100 Rockside Woods Blvd 225
Independence, OH 44131
Telephone: (216) 573-8090

FIDELITY AND TRUST MORTGAGE INC
115-22 Aikens Center
Martinsburg, WV 25401
Telephone: (304) 260-9433
Fax Number: (301) 260-9434

FIRST COMMUNITY MORTGAGE INC
9352 Main Street
Montgomery, OH 45242
Telephone: (513) 791-3429
Fax Number: (513) 791-3547

FIRST FEDERAL SAVINGS AND LOAN
601 Clinton Street
Defiance, OH 43510
Telephone: (419) 782-5015

FIRST FINANCIAL MORTGAGE CORP
200 North Center Suite 202
Northville, MI 48167
Telephone: (810) 347-7440

HOMEOWNERS MORTGAGE SERVICE
INC
11555 N Meridian St Ste 160
Carmel, IN 46032
Telephone: (317) 580-2250

LIBERTY MORTGAGE INC
509 W McKinley Ave
Mishawaka, IN 46545
Telephone: (574) 257-0629

MORTGAGE CORP OHIO
110 E. Wilson Bridge Rd #220
Worthington, OH 43085
Telephone: (614) 431-3499
Fax Number: (614) 431-2697

MORTGAGE NETWORK INC
70 East 91st St., Ste 109
Indianapolis, IN 46240
Telephone: (317) 706-1114
Fax Number: (317) 706-1115

MORTGAGE NOW INC
750 W. Resource Drive, #300
Brooklyn Hts., OH 44131
Telephone: (216) 635-0000
Fax Number: (216) 635-1111

PARK NATIONAL BANK
50 North Third St
Newark, OH 43055
Telephone: (614) 349-8451

PARK PLACE MORTGAGE CORP
38807 Ann Arbor Rd., Suite 3
Livonia, MI 48150
Telephone: (734) 542-1700
Fax Number: (734) 542-1054

PEOPLES TRUST MORTGAGE LLC
837 Donaldson Road
Erlanger, KY 41018
Telephone: (859) 372-3540
Fax Number: (859) 372-3548

PILLAR FINANCIAL CORPORATION
3129 Dixie Highway
Waterford, MI 48328
Telephone: (248) 674-8171

PROFESSIONAL FINANCIAL MTG INC
16165 W 12 Mile Road
Southfield, MI 48076
Telephone: (810) 557-3230

REAL ESTATE MORTGAGE CORP
20325 Center Ridge Road
Rocky River, OH 44116
Telephone: (440) 356-5363
Fax Number: (440) 356-3633

RESIDENTIAL MORTGAGE CORP
1332 Andrea St
Bowling Green, KY 42104
Telephone: (502) 842-7773

RESIDENTIAL MORTGAGE SERVS INC
191 Kentucky Avenue
Lexington, KY 40502
Telephone: (606) 252-5626

S AND T BANK
800 Philadelphia Street
Indiana, PA 15701
Telephone: (800) 325-2265

SENIOR REVERSE MORTGAGE LTD
4935 Dorr St
Toledo, OH 43615
Telephone: (419) 537-0015
Fax Number: (419) 537-0737

SENIORS EQUITY INCOME INC
6910 N Main St-14 Bldg 22-B
Granger, IN 46530
Telephone: (219) 272-0710

SGB CORPORATION
1 S 660 Midwest Rd. #100
Oakbrook Terrace, IL 60181
Telephone: (630) 916-9299
Fax Number: (630) 916-1299

SIGNATURE MORTGAGE CORP
4194 Fulton Rd NW
Canton, OH 44718
Telephone: (330) 491-1986

SOUTHERN OHIO MORTGAGE LLC
912 Senate Dr
Dayton, OH 45459
Telephone: (937) 435-7277
Fax Number: (937) 435-5707

STOCK YARDS BANK MORTGAGE
COMPANY
1040 E Main Street
Louisville, KY 40206
Telephone: (502) 582-2571

THIRD COMMUNITY MORTGAGE CORP
112 S. Water St. Suite C
Kent, OH 44240
Telephone: (330) 346-0380
Fax Number: (330) 346-0870

WEST PENN FIN SERVICE CTR INC
1800 Smallman Street
Pittsburgh, PA 15222
Telephone: (704) 948-1993

Oklahoma:

AMERIPLEX MORTGAGE COMPANY
3341 B Winthrop Avenue
Fort Worth, TX 76116
Telephone: (817) 732-8200
Fax Number: (817) 732-8787

BANK OF SALEM
708 Texas Street
Sulphur Springs, TX 75482
Telephone: (800) 667-9270
Fax Number: (903) 885-0231

CENTRAL PACIFIC MORTGAGE CO
17000 Dallas Parkway Ste 229
Dallas, TX 75248
Telephone: (972) 380-6288
Fax Number: (972) 380-0971

CENTRAL PACIFIC MORTGAGE CO
1500 N Norwood Ste 301
Hurst, TX 76054
Telephone: (817) 282-8733
Fax Number: (817) 268-5859

EVERHOME MORTGAGE COMPANY
8100 Nations Way
Jacksonville, FL 32256
Telephone: (904) 281-6000

FIRST COMMERCIAL BANK
7308 NW Expressway
Oklahoma City, OK 73132
Telephone: (405) 722-8810
Fax Number: (405) 721-7162

FIRST UNIVERSAL MORTGAGE INC
1615 N Hampton Road Ste 180
De Soto, TX 75115
Telephone: (972) 228-8282

GRIFFIN FINANCIAL MORTGAGE LLC
1701 River Run Suite 308
Fort Worth, TX 76107
Telephone: (817) 338-1708

HIBERNIA NATIONAL BANK
2318 Richmond Road
Texarkana, TX 75504
Telephone: (903) 838-2800

JUDITH O SMITH MORTGAGE GROUP INC
6125 Interstate 20 Ste 140
Ft Worth, TX 76132
Telephone: (817) 294-7887

MERCANTILE FUNDING
CORPORATION
300 North Coit Road Suite 235
Richardson, TX 75080
Telephone: (972) 661-9988
Fax Number: (972) 661-9989

REALTY MORTGAGE CORPORATION
1014 W. Broadway
Ardmore, OK 73401
Telephone: (580) 223-1948
Fax Number: (580) 223-2646

RELIANCE MORTGAGE CO
8115 Preston Rd Ste 800
Dallas, TX 75225
Telephone: (214) 360-9000
Fax Number: (214) 853-4130

REVERSE MORTGAGE OF TEXAS INC
13455 Noel Road Suite 1000
Dallas, TX 75240
Telephone: (214) 418-7924
Fax Number: (972) 407-0534

SGB CORPORATION
1 S 660 Midwest Rd. #100
Oakbrook Terrace, IL 60181
Telephone: (630) 916-9299
Fax Number: (630) 916-1299

SOUTHSIDE BANK
1201 South Beckam
Tyler, TX 75701
Telephone: (903) 531-7111

SOUTHWEST FUNDING LP
1100 E Pleasant Run Dr 110
Desoto, TX 75115
Telephone: (972) 230-3900

WR STARKEY MORTGAGE LLP
5055 W Park Blvd, Ste 300
Plano, TX 75093
Telephone: (972) 599-5210
Fax Number: (972) 599-5277

Oregon:

AMERIFUND FINANCIAL INC
8833 Pacific Ave. Ste. G
Tacoma, WA 98444
Telephone: (253) 535-4770
Fax Number: (413) 556-7432

BANK OF THE CASCADES
1070 NW Bond St Ste 100
Bend, OR 97701
Telephone: (541) 385-9933
Fax Number: (541) 385-9936

CAPSTONE INC
1313 NE 134th St Ste 220
Vancouver, WA 98685
Telephone: (360) 574-3599

EAGLE HOME MORTGAGE INC
34709 9th Avenue South #A-600
Federal Way, WA 98003
Telephone: (253) 874-2520
Fax Number: (253) 874-2606

FINANCIAL ADVANTAGE CORP
2709 Wetmore Avenue
Everett, WA 98201
Telephone: (425) 953-4021
Fax Number: (425) 303-8164

FRONTIER BANK
332 SW Everett Mall Way
Everett, WA 98204
Telephone: (206) 514-0798

GOLDEN EMPIRE MORTGAGE INC
508 North Main Street
Milton Freewater, OR 97862
Telephone: (509) 301-5626
Fax Number: (509) 525-5627

HOMESTREET BANK
601 Union Street
Seattle, WA 98101
Telephone: (206) 623-3050
Fax Number: (206) 389-6306

INVESTORS WEST MORTGAGE
814 N 8th Street
Boise, ID 83702
Telephone: (208) 345-8153

JUSLYN ENTERPRISES INC
401 West 17th Street
Vancouver, WA 98660
Telephone: (360) 944-9004

LANDMARK MORTGAGE COMPANY
10415 SE Stark Ste D
Portland, OR 97216
Telephone: (503) 255-3995

LOAN SERVICES INC
451 SW 10th St Ste 201
Renton, WA 98055
Telephone: (425) 793-8880
Fax Number: (425) 793-8888

MERIT FINANCIAL INC
13905 NE 128th Street
Kirkland, WA 98034
Telephone: (425) 605-1350
Fax Number: (425) 605-6406

NORMANDY MORTGAGE INC
15525 1st Ave SO Suite 1
Seattle, WA 98148
Telephone: (206) 242-3900

NORTHERN MORTGAGE INC
11020 South Tacoma Way #A
Lakewood, WA 98499
Telephone: (253) 512-1169
Fax Number: (253) 512-1125

PACIFIC REPUBLIC MORTGAGE
CORPORATION
1322 E. McAndrews Rd. #101
Medford, OR 97504
Telephone: (541) 770-2727
Fax Number: (541) 773-9748

PACIFIC REPUBLIC MORTGAGE
CORPORATION
10220 SW Greenburg Road #135
Portland, OR 97223
Telephone: (503) 244-8554
Fax Number: (503) 244-8526

SUNSET MORTGAGE COMPANY
10365 SE Sunnyside Rd Ste-330
Clackamas, OR 97015
Telephone: (503) 698-5800

SUNSET MORTGAGE COMPANY
4230 Galewood Street Suite 200
Lake Oswego, OR 97035
Telephone: (503) 635-7393
Fax Number: (503) 635-5992

SUNSET WEST MORTGAGE
5400 Carillon Point
Kirkland, WA 98033
Telephone: (425) 576-0502
Fax Number: (425) 576-0907

U S FINANCIAL MORTGAGE
CORPORATION
34004-B Texas Street
Albany, OR 97321
Telephone: (541) 928-5579
Fax Number: (541) 928-2196

UNITED FINANCIAL MORTGAGE CORP
2020 SW Fourth Avenue
Portland, OR 97201
Telephone: (360) 423-9032
Fax Number: (360) 423-9093

UNITED MORTGAGE CORP OF
AMERICA
328 N Olympic Avenue
Arlington, WA 98223
Telephone: (360) 403-9378

WAUSAU MORTGAGE CORPORATION
3025 112th Ave NE
Bellevue, WA 98004
Telephone: (425) 216-2979
Fax Number: (425) 452-0089

ZIONS FIRST NATIONAL BANK
255 N Admiral Blvd Rd
Salt Lake City, UT 84116
Telephone: (801) 273-3000
Fax Number: (801) 273-3035

Pennsylvania:

AAKO INC
3569 Bristol Pike Bldg No 2
Bensalem, PA 19020
Telephone: (215) 633-8080
Fax Number: (215) 633-8088

ACADEMY MORTGAGE LLC
5602 Baltimore National Pk 401
Baltimore, MD 21228
Telephone: (410) 788-7070

ALBION FINANCIAL INC
1873 Route 70 East Ste 302-D
Cherry Hill, NJ 08003
Telephone: (856) 424-4367

ALL PENNSYLVANIA REVERSE
MORTGAGE INC
4085 Route 8
Allison Park, PA 15101
Telephone: (412) 963-6062

AMERICAN MIDWEST MTG CORP
6363 York Road
Parma Heights, OH 44130
Telephone: (216) 884-5000

CAMBRIDGE HOME CAPITAL LLC
80 Cuttermill Road Ste 408
Great Neck, NY 11021
Telephone: (516) 829-5700
Fax Number: (516) 829-5777

CARDINAL FINANCIAL COMPANY
444 Jacksonville Road
Warminster, PA 18974
Telephone: (215) 293-6800
Fax Number: (215) 293-6807

COMMERCE BANK NA
17000 Horizon Way
Mt Laurell, NJ 08054
Telephone: (732) 747-1999
Fax Number: (732) 450-0737

CONCORD MORTGAGE CORP
25 Melville Park Rd
Melville, NY 11747
Telephone: (631) 756-0700
Fax Number: (631) 756-0900

EAST WEST MORTGAGE COMPANY
1568 Spring Hill Rd Ste 100
McLean, VA 22102
Telephone: (703) 442-0150

FEDERAL MORTGAGE AND
INVESTMENT CORP
1111 Clifton Avenue
Clifton, NJ 07013
Telephone: (973) 777-7784

FIDELITY AND TRUST MORTGAGE INC
115-22 Aikens Center
Martinsburg, WV 25401
Telephone: (304) 260-9433
Fax Number: (301) 260-9434

FIRST MARINER BANK
3301 Boston Street
Baltimore, MD 21224
Telephone: (410) 558-4118
Fax Number: (410) 342-0489

FIRST MONEY GROUP INC
1777 Reisterstown Rd Suite 230
Baltimore, MD 21208
Telephone: (410) 653-6909

INTERCHANGE BANK
Park 80 West-Plaza Two
Saddle Brook, NJ 07663
Telephone: (201) 703-2246

KASTLE MORTGAGE CORPORATION
77 West Main Street
Freehold, NJ 07728
Telephone: (732) 845-5444

M AND T MORTGAGE CORPORATION
601 Dresher Road, Ste 150
Horsham, PA 19044
Telephone: (215) 956-7030
Fax Number: (215) 956-7029

M AND T MORTGAGE CORPORATION
2270 Erin Court
Lancaster, PA 17604
Telephone: (717) 397-5548
Fax Number: (717) 397-2643

MORTGAGE CAPITAL INVESTORS INC
6571 Edsall Road
Springfield, VA 22151
Telephone: (703) 941-0711
Fax Number: (703) 256-3118

MORTGAGE CORP OHIO
110 E. Wilson Bridge Rd #220
Worthington, OH 43085
Telephone: (614) 431-3499
Fax Number: (614) 431-2697

MORTGAGE MOBILITY LLC
1094 Second Street Pike
Richboro, PA 18954
Telephone: (215) 357-4900
Fax Number: (215) 364-1927

MORTGAGE MONEY MART INC
1199 Amboy Avenue
Edison, NJ 08837
Telephone: (732) 548-9423

NATIONRESIDENTIAL MORTGAGE
BANKING CORP
One Rabro Drive
Hauppauge, NY 11788
Telephone: (516) 232-1133

NEW JERSEY HOME FUNDING GROUP
LLC
457 Route 79
Morganville, NJ 07751
Telephone: (732) 970-9210

NEW JERSEY HSNG MTG FIN AGEN
637 South Clinton Avenue
Trenton, NJ 08650
Telephone: (609) 278-7400

OCEANFIRST BANK
975 Hooper Avenue
Toms River, NJ 08753
Telephone: (732) 240-4500

PARK NATIONAL BANK
50 North Third St
Newark, OH 43055
Telephone: (614) 349-8451

PEOPLES TRUST MORTGAGE LLC
3920 Plank Road Suite 200
Fredericksburg, VA 22407
Telephone: (540) 548-8749

REAL ESTATE MORTGAGE NETWORK
INC
70 Grand Avenue
River Edge, NJ 07661
Telephone: (201) 498-9300
Fax Number: (201) 498-9377

S AND T BANK
800 Philadelphia Street
Indiana, PA 15701
Telephone: (800) 325-2265

SAVINGS FIRST MORTGAGE LLC
100 Painters Mill Road Ste 800
Owings Mills, MD 21117
Telephone: (410) 654-8800

SENIORS FIRST MORTGAGE COMPANY
LLC
4525 South Avenue Suite 301
Virginia Beach, VA 23452
Telephone: (757) 671-6000

SOUTHERN STAR MORTGAGE CORP
90 Merrick Avenue Suite 204
East Meadow, NY 11554
Telephone: (516) 712-4400
Fax Number: (516) 794-2116

SUPERIOR MORTGAGE CORP
1395 Route 539
Tuckerton, NJ 08087
Telephone: (609) 294-2854
Fax Number: (609) 294-0620

UNITED FIRST MORTGAGE INC
1503 Santa Rosa Road Ste-109
Richmond, VA 23229
Telephone: (804) 282-5631

USA FINANCIAL RESOURCES INC
66 Medford Avenue
Patchogue, NY 11772
Telephone: (516) 758-9200

WEBSTER BANK
609 West Johnson Avenue
Cheshire, CT 06410
Telephone: (888) 681-7788

WEST PENN FIN SERVICE CTR INC
1800 Smallman Street
Pittsburgh, PA 15222
Telephone: (704) 948-1993

Rhode Island:

AGENCY FOR CONSUMER EQUITY
MORTGAGE INC
101 Executive Blvd. 1st Floor
Elmsford, NY 10523
Telephone: (800) 881-2954
Fax Number: (914) 682-0521

BNY MORTGAGE COMPANY LLC
57 Jefferson Street
Milford, MA 01757
Telephone: (508) 422-9589
Fax Number: (508) 422-9592

CAMBRIDGE HOME CAPITAL LLC
80 Cuttermill Road Ste 408
Great Neck, NY 11021
Telephone: (516) 829-5700
Fax Number: (516) 829-5777

CONCORD MORTGAGE CORP
25 Melville Park Rd
Melville, NY 11747
Telephone: (631) 756-0700
Fax Number: (631) 756-0900

CONTINENTAL FUNDING CORP
7 Cabot Place 2nd Floor
Stoughton, MA 02072
Telephone: (781) 344-4846
Fax Number: (781) 344-1841

EAST WEST MORTGAGE COMPANY
189 Hartford Ave Ste 1
Bellingham, MA 02019
Telephone: (508) 966-5250
Fax Number: (508) 966-5251

EQUITY AMERICA MORTGAGE SVCS
INC
340 Granite St
Manchester, NH 03102
Telephone: (603) 625-2820

FAIRFIELD COUNTY BANK CORP
374 Main Street
Ridgefield, CT 06877
Telephone: (203) 438-6518

FAST TRACK FUNDING CORP
247 W Old Country Road
Hicksville, NY 11801
Telephone: (516) 938-6600

FREEDOM CHOICE MORTGAGE
30 East Main Street
Avon, CT 06001
Telephone: (203) 677-0127

GMAC MORTGAGE CORPORATION
3 Executive Park Dr Ste 310
Bedford, NH 03110
Telephone: (603) 668-0778

MCLAUGHLIN FINANCIAL INC
90 Highland Ave
Salem, MA 01970
Telephone: (978) 744-6016

MORTGAGE FINANCIAL SERVICES INC
170 Main St Suite 108
Tewksbury, MA 01876
Telephone: (978) 863-9555

PROVIDIAN NATIONAL BANK
295 Main Street
Tilton, NH 03276
Telephone: (603) 286-4348

RCRBL ENTERPRISES LTD
1123 Old Town Road
Coram, NY 11727
Telephone: (631) 736-7700

RHODE ISLAND HSG MTGE FIN CORP
44 Washington Street
Providence, RI 02903
Telephone: (401) 751-5566

SOUTHERN STAR MORTGAGE CORP
90 Merrick Avenue Suite 204
East Meadow, NY 11554
Telephone: (516) 712-4400
Fax Number: (516) 794-2116

USA FINANCIAL RESOURCES INC
66 Medford Avenue
Patchogue, NY 11772
Telephone: (516) 758-9200

WEBSTER BANK
609 West Johnson Avenue
Cheshire, CT 06410
Telephone: (888) 681-7788

South Carolina:

CENTURA BANK
133 S Franklin Street
Rocky Mount, NC 27804
Telephone: (919) 454-6053

EVERBANK
5512 Livonia Cover
North Charleston, SC 29420
Telephone: (843) 552-5011

EVERHOME MORTGAGE COMPANY
8100 Nations Way
Jacksonville, FL 32256
Telephone: (904) 281-6000

FRANKLIN FUNDING INC
147 Wappoo Creek Drive Ste 105
Charleston, SC 29412
Telephone: (843) 762-2218

HOME BUILDERS MORTGAGE CORP
678 B St Andrews Blvd
Charleston, SC 29407
Telephone: (843) 556-4643

HOME FEDERAL SAVINGS BANK TN
515 Market St
Knoxville, TN 37902
Telephone: (615) 546-0330

HOMEOWNERS MORTGAGE
ENTERPRISES INC
2530 Devine Street
Columbia, SC 29205
Telephone: (803) 765-9037

LUMINA MORTGAGE COMPANY INC
219 Racine Drive Suite A
Wilmington, NC 28403
Telephone: (910) 452-3555
Fax Number: (910) 452-9929

MORTGAGE CAPITAL INVESTORS INC
7901 N. Ocean Blvd.
Myrtle Beach, SC 29572
Telephone: (843) 449-8004
Fax Number: (843) 449-8206

MORTGAGE CAPITAL INVESTORS INC
6571 Edsall Road
Springfield, VA 22151
Telephone: (703) 941-0711
Fax Number: (703) 256-3118

MORTGAGE SOUTH OF TENNESSEE
409 S Germantown Rd
Chattanooga, TN 37411
Telephone: (423) 624-3878

OLDE TOWNE MORTGAGE LLC
412-B N Gum St
Summerville, SC 29483
Telephone: (843) 832-0944

SAFEWAY MORTGAGE INC
2655 South Cobb Drive Suite 1
Smyrna, GA 30080
Telephone: (770) 434-9486

SHELTER MORTGAGE COMPANY LLC
3350 Northlake Pkwy, Suite B
Atlanta, GA 30345
Telephone: (678) 279-9000
Fax Number: (678) 279-2000

THE MORTGAGE MALL INC
615 South New Hope Rd Ste 100
Gastonia, NC 28054
Telephone: (704) 866-4089

TRUSTMARK NATIONAL BANK
277 East Pearl
Jackson, MS 39201
Telephone: (601) 354-5150

South Dakota:

CENTENNIAL MORTGAGE AND
FUNDING
250 Prairie Center Dr Ste 100
Eden Prairie, MN 55344
Telephone: (952) 826-0025
Fax Number: (952) 826-0027

DISCOVER MORTGAGE CORP
1500 South Hwy 100 Ste 360
Minneapolis, MN 55416
Telephone: (612) 546-0424

FARWEST MORTGAGE BANKERS INC
1532 Aspen Drive
Eagan, MN 55122
Telephone: (651) 994-1088

FIRST UNITED BANK
430 NW Fourth St
Faribault, MN 55021
Telephone: (507) 334-2201
Fax Number: (507) 334-2205

GATE CITY BANK
500 2nd Ave. North
Fargo, ND 58102
Telephone: (701) 293-2400

HOMESTEAD MORTGAGE
CORPORATION
4105 N Lexington Ave Ste 100
Arden Hills, MN 55126
Telephone: (612) 490-5555

JOHN DEERE COMMUNITY C U
1827 Ansborough Avenue
Waterloo, IA 50701
Telephone: (319) 274-7562

M AND I MARSHALL AND ILSLEY BANK
6625 Lyndale Ave South
Richfield, MN 55423
Telephone: (612) 798-3139
Fax Number: (612) 798-3137

MORTGAGE PLUS FINANCIAL CORP
199 Coon Rapids Blvd Suite 110
Coon Rapids, MN 55433
Telephone: (763) 786-7587

PEOPLES TRUST MORTGAGE LLC
1750 Weir Drive
Woodbury, MN 55125
Telephone: (651) 714-7171
Fax Number: (651) 714-7177

WESTERN NATIONAL BANK DULUTH
5629 Grand Ave
Duluth, MN 55807
Telephone: (218) 723-1000

Tennessee:

AMERICAN REVERSE MORTGAGE CORP
212 14th Ct NW
Birmingham, AL 35215
Telephone: (352) 867-1111
Fax Number: (352) 369-5985
E-Mail: Info@AmericanReverse.com

BANK INDEPENDENT
710 S Montgomery Ave
Sheffield, AL 35660
Telephone: (256) 386-5000

BANK OF SALEM
1801 Central Avenue Suite C
Hot Springs, AR 71901
Telephone: (501) 624-7685

CENTURA BANK
133 S Franklin Street
Rocky Mount, NC 27804
Telephone: (919) 454-6053

EAGLE MORTGAGE INC
204 W North Street
Poplarville, MS 39470
Telephone: (601) 795-8881
Fax Number: (601) 795-0840

EVERBANK
6984 Flowery Branch Road
Cummings, GA 30041
Telephone: (812) 949-2883

FIRST CONTINENTAL MTG CORP
POB 4095 450 Southwest Drive
Jonesboro, AR 72403
Telephone: (501) 932-6756

FRANKLIN FUNDING INC
147 Wappoo Creek Drive Ste 105
Charleston, SC 29412
Telephone: (843) 762-2218

GLL AND ASSOCIATES INC
4550 Country Club Road
Winston Salem, NC 27104
Telephone: (336) 760-4911
Fax Number: (336) 760-6338

HIBERNIA NATIONAL BANK
11130 Industriplex Blvd
Baton Rouge, LA 70809
Telephone: (504) 381-2372

HOME BUILDERS MORTGAGE CORP
678 B St Andrews Blvd
Charleston, SC 29407
Telephone: (843) 556-4643

HOME FEDERAL SAVINGS BANK TN
515 Market St
Knoxville, TN 37902
Telephone: (615) 546-0330

HOMEOWNERS MORTGAGE
ENTERPRISES INC
2530 Devine Street
Columbia, SC 29205
Telephone: (803) 765-9037

HOMESOUTH MORTGAGE SERVICES INC
200 Cahaba Park Circle Ste 125
Birmingham, AL 35242
Telephone: (205) 591-5055
Fax Number: (205) 591-5053

LUMINA MORTGAGE COMPANY INC
219 Racine Drive Suite A
Wilmington, NC 28403
Telephone: (910) 452-3555
Fax Number: (910) 452-9929

MORTGAGE CAPITAL INVESTORS INC
7901 N. Ocean Blvd.
Myrtle Beach, SC 29572
Telephone: (843) 449-8004
Fax Number: (843) 449-8206

MORTGAGE SOUTH OF TENNESSEE
409 S Germantown Rd
Chattanooga, TN 37411
Telephone: (423) 624-3878

OLDE TOWNE MORTGAGE LLC
412-B N Gum St
Summerville, SC 29483
Telephone: (843) 832-0944

PEOPLES TRUST MORTGAGE LLC
837 Donaldson Road
Erlanger, KY 41018
Telephone: (859) 372-3540
Fax Number: (859) 372-3548

PEOPLES TRUST MORTGAGE LLC
3920 Plank Road Suite 200
Fredericksburg, VA 22407
Telephone: (540) 548-8749

RESIDENTIAL MORTGAGE CORP
1332 Andrea St
Bowling Green, KY 42104
Telephone: (502) 842-7773

RESIDENTIAL MORTGAGE SERVS INC
191 Kentucky Avenue
Lexington, KY 40502
Telephone: (606) 252-5626

SENIORS FIRST MORTGAGE COMPANY
LLC
4525 South Avenue Suite 301
Virginia Beach, VA 23452
Telephone: (757) 671-6000

SHELTER MORTGAGE COMPANY LLC
3350 Northlake Pkwy, Suite B
Atlanta, GA 30345
Telephone: (678) 279-9000
Fax Number: (678) 279-2000
E-Mail: ffmatl@aol.com

STOCK YARDS BANK MORTGAGE
COMPANY
1040 E Main Street
Louisville, KY 40206
Telephone: (502) 582-2571

TRUSTMARK NATIONAL BANK
277 East Pearl
Jackson, MS 39201
Telephone: (601) 354-5150

UNITED FIRST MORTGAGE INC
1503 Santa Rosa Road Ste-109
Richmond, VA 23229
Telephone: (804) 282-5631

Texas:

ALETHES LLC
3700 RR 620 South Ste A
Austin, TX 78734
Telephone: (512) 401-0522
Fax Number: (512) 401-9115

AMERIPLEX MORTGAGE COMPANY
3341 B Winthrop Avenue
Fort Worth, TX 76116
Telephone: (817) 732-8200
Fax Number: (817) 732-8787

BANK OF SALEM
708 Texas Street
Sulphur Springs, TX 75482
Telephone: (800) 667-9270
Fax Number: (903) 885-0231

CENTRAL PACIFIC MORTGAGE CO
17000 Dallas Parkway Ste 229
Dallas, TX 75248
Telephone: (972) 380-6288
Fax Number: (972) 380-0971

COACHELLA VALLEY MORTGAGE CTR
4422 FM 1960 West Suite 120
Houston, TX 77068
Telephone: (281) 444-4345

COMMUNITY HOME LOAN LLC
11000 Richmond Ave.
Houston, TX 77042
Telephone: (281) 657-0472
Fax Number: (281) 657-0484

COMMUNITY HOME LOAN LLC
3730 Kirby Drive, Suite 1200
Houston, TX 77098
Telephone: (713) 831-6828
Fax Number: (713) 831-6829

DIVERSIFIED FINANCIAL SOLUTIONS
LLC
12000 Westheimer, Suite 225
Houston, TX 77077
Telephone: (713) 771-1000
Fax Number: (713) 771-8181

FIRST COMMERCIAL BANK
7308 NW Expressway
Oklahoma City, OK 73132
Telephone: (405) 722-8810
Fax Number: (405) 721-7162

FIRST UNIVERSAL MORTGAGE INC
1615 N Hampton Road Ste 180
De Soto, TX 75115
Telephone: (972) 228-8282

GDG MORTGAGE INC
440 Benmar Suite 2250
Houston, TX 77060
Telephone: (281) 445-4380

GRIFFIN FINANCIAL MORTGAGE LLC
1701 River Run Suite 308
Fort Worth, TX 76107
Telephone: (817) 338-1708

HIBERNIA NATIONAL BANK
2318 Richmond Road
Texarkana, TX 75504
Telephone: (903) 838-2800

HOMECORP MORTGAGE INC
518 Main Street
Marble Falls, TX 78654
Telephone: (830) 693-1840

JUDITH O SMITH MORTGAGE GROUP
INC
6125 Interstate 20 Ste 140
Ft Worth, TX 76132
Telephone: (817) 294-7887

LEWALLEN MORTGAGE INC
10701 Montgomery NE—Suite A
Albuquerque, NM 87111
Telephone: (505) 293-9300
Fax Number: (505) 294-1974

MAJOR MORTGAGE
1421 Luisa Street, Suite N
Santa Fe, NM 87501
Telephone: (505) 989-7050
Fax Number: (505) 989-7057

MERCANTILE FUNDING
CORPORATION
300 North Coit Road Suite 235
Richardson, TX 75080
Telephone: (972) 661-9988
Fax Number: (972) 661-9989

MILDOR CORPORATION
5001-C John Stockbauer Drive
Victoria, TX 77904
Telephone: (361) 574-8800
Fax Number: (361) 574-8906

PLAINSCAPITAL MCAFEE MORTGAGE
COMPANY
1008 Central Parkway South
San Antonio, TX 78232
Telephone: (210) 495-2677
Fax Number: (210) 495-7485

REALTY MORTGAGE CORPORATION
1014 W. Broadway
Ardmore, OK 73401
Telephone: (580) 223-1948
Fax Number: (580) 223-2646

REALTY MORTGAGE CORPORATION
3660 Warick Dr
Dallas, TX 75229
Telephone: (214) 654-0011
Fax Number: (214) 654-0047

RELIANCE MORTGAGE CO
8115 Preston Rd Ste 800
Dallas, TX 75225
Telephone: (214) 360-9000
Fax Number: (214) 853-4130

REVERSE MORTGAGE OF TEXAS INC
13455 Noel Road Suite 1000
Dallas, TX 75240
Telephone: (214) 418-7924
Fax Number: (972) 407-0534

SECURE FINANCIAL SERVICES
2500 West Loop South Ste 350
Houston, TX 77027
Telephone: (713) 355-9955
Fax Number: (713) 355-9999

SGB CORPORATION
1 S 660 Midwest Rd. #100
Oakbrook Terrace, IL 60181
Telephone: (630) 916-9299
Fax Number: (630) 916-1299

SOUTHSIDE BANK
1201 South Beckam
Tyler, TX 75701
Telephone: (903) 531-7111

SOUTHWEST FUNDING LP
10501 Central Expwy #303
Dallas, TX 75231
Telephone: (972) 739-1056

STEPHEN TAYLOR JOHNSON INC
8800 Business Park Dr Ste 200
Austin, TX 78759
Telephone: (512) 241-3197
Fax Number: (512) 502-0835

SUPERIOR MORTGAGE AND EQUITY
160 Dowlen Road
Beaumont, TX 77706
Telephone: (409) 866-7743

WR STARKEY MORTGAGE LLP
1705 S. Cap of Texas Hwy, Ste
Austin, TX 78746
Telephone: (512) 329-9040
Fax Number: (972) 329-9043

Utah:

ACADEMY MORTGAGE CORPORATION
4055 South 700 East Suite 200
Salt Lake City, UT 84107
Telephone: (801) 261-4860

ACCESS MORTGAGE LLC
7070 S Union Park Center S-220
Midvale, UT 84047
Telephone: (801) 208-5220
Fax Number: (801) 208-5221

AMERICA FIRST FEDERAL CREDIT
UNION
4646 S 1500 W Suite 140
Riverdale, UT 84405
Telephone: (801) 778-8487
Fax Number: (801) 778-8427

ASPEN HOME LOANS LC
315 S 500 E
American Fork, UT 84003
Telephone: (801) 642-0070
Fax Number: (801) 642-0071

ENCORE MORTGAGE INC
301 N 200 E Ste 3B
Saint George, UT 84770
Telephone: (435) 652-9898
Fax Number: (435) 656-2224

FSI MORTGAGE LLC
5373 Green St #550
Salt Lake City, UT 84123
Telephone: (801) 281-0205
Fax Number: (801) 606-2780

IRELAND BANK
33 Bannock Ave
Malad City, ID 83252
Telephone: (208) 766-2211

MOUNTAIN AMERICA CREDIT UNION
660 South 200 East Suite 250
Salt Lake City, UT 84111
Telephone: (801) 325-6241

SUN AMERICAN MORTGAGE CO
386 E. Sandy Woods Lane
Midvale, UT 84047
Telephone: (801) 256-0802
Fax Number: (801) 256-0731

SUN VALLEY FINANCIAL OF UTAH INC
9176 South 300 West Suite 3A
Sandy, UT 84070
Telephone: (801) 256-1153
Fax Number: (801) 256-1155

ZIONS FIRST NATIONAL BANK
255 N Admiral Blvd Rd
Salt Lake City, UT 84116
Telephone: (801) 273-3000
Fax Number: (801) 273-3035

Vermont

AMSTON MORTGAGE
711 Middletown Road Suite 8
Colchester, CT 06415
Telephone: (800) 625-8633
Fax Number: (860) 365-0001

BNY MORTGAGE COMPANY LLC
57 Jefferson Street
Milford, MA 01757
Telephone: (508) 422-9589
Fax Number: (508) 422-9592

CONTINENTAL FUNDING CORP
7 Cabot Place 2nd Floor
Stoughton, MA 02072
Telephone: (781) 344-4846
Fax Number: (781) 344-1841

EAST WEST MORTGAGE COMPANY
189 Hartford Ave Ste 1
Bellingham, MA 02019
Telephone: (508) 966-5250
Fax Number: (508) 966-5251

EQUITY AMERICA MORTGAGE SVCS
INC
340 Granite St
Manchester, NH 03102
Telephone: (603) 625-2820

FAIRFIELD COUNTY BANK CORP
374 Main Street
Ridgefield, CT 06877
Telephone: (203) 438-6518

FREEDOM CHOICE MORTGAGE
30 East Main Street
Avon, CT 06001
Telephone: (203) 677-0127

GMAC MORTGAGE CORPORATION
3 Executive Park Dr Ste 310
Bedford, NH 03110
Telephone: (603) 668-0778

HOME MORTGAGE LOAN COMPANY
393 Center Street
Auburn, ME 04210
Telephone: (207) 946-2820

M AND T MORTGAGE CORPORATION
Northway 10 Executive Park
Clifton Park, NY 12065
Telephone: (518) 877-3500

MORTGAGE FINANCIAL SERVICES INC
170 Main St Suite 108
Tewksbury, MA 01876
Telephone: (978) 863-9555

PROVIDIAN NATIONAL BANK
295 Main Street
Tilton, NH 03276
Telephone: (603) 286-4348

WEBSTER BANK
609 West Johnson Avenue
Cheshire, CT 06410
Telephone: (888) 681-7788

Virginia:

AAKO INC
3569 Bristol Pike Bldg No 2
Bensalem, PA 19020
Telephone: (215) 633-8080
Fax Number: (215) 633-8088

ACADEMY MORTGAGE LLC
5602 Baltimore National Pk 401
Baltimore, MD 21228
Telephone: (410) 788-7070

ALBION FINANCIAL INC
1873 Route 70 East Ste 302-D
Cherry Hill, NJ 08003
Telephone: (856) 424-4367

CARDINAL FINANCIAL COMPANY
444 Jacksonville Road
Warminster, PA 18974
Telephone: (215) 293-6800
Fax Number: (215) 293-6807

CENTURA BANK
133 S Franklin Street
Rocky Mount, NC 27804
Telephone: (919) 454-6053

COMMERCE BANK NA
17000 Horizon Way
Mt Laurell, NJ 08054
Telephone: (732) 747-1999

EAST WEST MORTGAGE COMPANY
1568 Spring Hill Rd Ste 100
McLean, VA 22102
Telephone: (703) 442-0150

EVERBANK
4010 Jefferson Woods Drive
Powhatan, VA 23129
Telephone: (804) 403-3380

FIDELITY AND TRUST MORTGAGE INC
115-22 Aikens Center
Martinsburg, WV 25401
Telephone: (304) 260-9433
Fax Number: (301) 260-9434

FIRST MARINER BANK
3301 Boston Street
Baltimore, MD 21224
Telephone: (410) 558-4118
Fax Number: (410) 342-0489

FIRST MONEY GROUP INC
1777 Reisterstown Rd Suite 230
Baltimore, MD 21208
Telephone: (410) 653-6909

GLL AND ASSOCIATES INC
4550 Country Club Road
Winston Salem, NC 27104
Telephone: (336) 760-4911
Fax Number: (336) 760-6338

HOME CONSULTANTS INC
661 Northern Boulevard
Clarks Summit, PA 18411
Telephone: (570) 586-7863
Fax Number: (570) 586-7865

LUMINA MORTGAGE COMPANY INC
219 Racine Drive Suite A
Wilmington, NC 28403
Telephone: (910) 452-3555
Fax Number: (910) 452-9929

M AND T MORTGAGE CORPORATION
2270 Erin Court
Lancaster, PA 17604
Telephone: (717) 397-5548
Fax Number: (717) 397-2643

MORTGAGE CAPITAL INVESTORS INC
6571 Edsall Road
Springfield, VA 22151
Telephone: (703) 941-0711
Fax Number: (703) 256-3118

MORTGAGE MOBILITY LLC
1094 Second Street Pike
Richboro, PA 18954
Telephone: (215) 357-4900
Fax Number: (215) 364-1927

NEW JERSEY HSNG MTG FIN AGEN
637 South Clinton Avenue
Trenton, NJ 08650
Telephone: (609) 278-7400

OCEANFIRST BANK
975 Hooper Avenue
Toms River, NJ 08753
Telephone: (732) 240-4500

PEOPLES TRUST MORTGAGE LLC
3920 Plank Road Suite 200
Fredericksburg, VA 22407
Telephone: (540) 548-8749

SAVINGS FIRST MORTGAGE LLC
100 Painters Mill Road Ste 800
Owings Mills, MD 21117
Telephone: (410) 654-8800

SENIORS FIRST MORTGAGE COMPANY
LLC
4525 South Avenue Suite 301
Virginia Beach, VA 23452
Telephone: (757) 671-6000

SUPERIOR MORTGAGE CORP
1395 Route 539
Tuckerton, NJ 08087
Telephone: (609) 294-2854
Fax Number: (609) 294-0620

THE MORTGAGE MALL INC
615 South New Hope Rd Ste 100
Gastonia, NC 28054
Telephone: (704) 866-4089

UNITED FIRST MORTGAGE INC
1503 Santa Rosa Road Ste 109
Richmond, VA 23229
Telephone: (804) 282-5631

Washington:

ALLIANCE GUARANTY MORTGAGE
CORP
505 East Gem Lane
Colbert, WA 99218
Telephone: (877) 766-4742

AMERIFUND FINANCIAL INC
8833 Pacific Ave. Ste. G
Tacoma, WA 98444
Telephone: (253) 535-4770
Fax Number: (413) 556-7432

BANK OF THE CASCADES
1070 NW Bond St Ste 100
Bend, OR 97701
Telephone: (541) 385-9933
Fax Number: (541) 385-9936

CAPSTONE INC
1313 NE 134th St Ste 220
Vancouver, WA 98685
Telephone: (360) 574-3599

EAGLE HOME MORTGAGE INC
34709 9th Avenue South #A-600
Federal Way, WA 98003
Telephone: (253) 874-2520
Fax Number: (253) 874-2606

FINANCIAL ADVANTAGE CORP
2709 Wetmore Avenue
Everett, WA 98201
Telephone: (425) 953-4021
Fax Number: (425) 303-8164

FRONTIER BANK
332 SW Everett Mall Way
Everett, WA 98204
Telephone: (206) 514-0798

GOLDEN EMPIRE MORTGAGE INC
25 West Main Street
Walla Walla, WA 99362
Telephone: (509) 525-4344
Fax Number: (509) 525-4359

HOMESTREET BANK
601 Union Street
Seattle, WA 98101
Telephone: (206) 623-3050
Fax Number: (206) 389-6306

INVESTORS WEST MORTGAGE
814 N 8th Street
Boise, ID 83702
Telephone: (208) 345-8153

JUSLYN ENTERPRISES INC
10906 East 17th Avenue
Spokane, WA 99206
Telephone: (509) 991-2129

LANDMARK MORTGAGE COMPANY
10415 SE Stark Ste D
Portland, OR 97216
Telephone: (503) 255-3995

LOAN SERVICES INC
451 SW 10th St Ste 201
Renton, WA 98055
Telephone: (425) 793-8880
Fax Number: (425) 793-8888

MERIT FINANCIAL INC
13905 NE 128th Street
Kirkland, WA 98034
Telephone: (425) 605-1350
Fax Number: (425) 605-6406

NORMANDY MORTGAGE INC
15525 1st Ave So Suite 1
Seattle, WA 98148
Telephone: (206) 242-3900

NORTHERN MORTGAGE INC
11020 South Tacoma Way #A
Lakewood, WA 98499
Telephone: (253) 512-1169
Fax Number: (253) 512-1125

PROGRESSIVE LENDING LLC
605 E Holland Suite 204
Spokane, WA 99218
Telephone: (509) 465-5363
Fax Number: (509) 464-0175

REAL ESTATE FINANCIAL SERVICES
INC
5400 Carillon Point
Kirkland, WA 98033
Telephone: (425) 576-4114
Fax Number: (425) 806-0046

SUNSET WEST MORTGAGE
5400 Carillon Point
Kirkland, WA 98033
Telephone: (425) 576-0502
Fax Number: (425) 576-0907

U S FINANCIAL MORTGAGE
CORPORATION
34004-B Texas Street
Albany, OR 97321
Telephone: (541) 928-5579
Fax Number: (541) 928-2196

UNITED FINANCIAL MORTGAGE CORP
2020 SW Fourth Avenue
Portland, OR 97201
Telephone: (360) 423-9032
Fax Number: (360) 423-9093

UNITED MORTGAGE CORP OF
AMERICA
328 N Olympic Avenue
Arlington, WA 98223
Telephone: (360) 403-9378

WAUSAU MORTGAGE CORPORATION
3025 112th Ave NE
Bellevue, WA 98004
Telephone: (425) 216-2979
Fax Number: (425) 452-0089

West Virginia:

ACADEMY MORTGAGE LLC
5602 Baltimore National Pk 401
Baltimore, MD 21228
Telephone: (410) 788-7070

ALL PENNSYLVANIA REVERSE
MORTGAGE INC
4085 Route 8
Allison Park, PA 15101
Telephone: (412) 963-6062

AMERICAN MIDWEST MTG CORP
6363 York Road
Parma Heights, OH 44130
Telephone: (216) 884-5000

AMERICAN MORTGAGE SERVICE CO
415 Glensprings Dr. Suite 203
Cincinnati, OH 45246
Telephone: (513) 674-8900
Fax Number: (513) 674-8906

AMERICAN REVERSE MORTGAGE CORP
2101 South Hamilton Road, #110
Columbus, OH 43232
Telephone: (614) 577-1440
Fax Number: (614) 577-1442

AMERISTATE BANCORP INC
7925 Graceland St
Dayton, OH 45459
Telephone: (937) 434-9900
Fax Number: (937) 434-9922

CENTURA BANK
133 S Franklin Street
Rocky Mount, NC 27804
Telephone: (919) 454-6053

CUSTOM MORTGAGE INC
6161 Busch Blvd Ste 323
Columbus, OH 43229
Telephone: (614) 840-1600

EAST WEST MORTGAGE COMPANY
1568 Spring Hill Rd Ste 100
McLean, VA 22102
Telephone: (703) 442-0150

EVERBANK
4010 Jefferson Woods Drive
Powhatan, VA 23129
Telephone: (804) 403-3380

EXCEL MORTGAGE CORPORATION
6100 Rockside Woods Blvd 225
Independence, OH 44131
Telephone: (216) 573-8090

FIDELITY AND TRUST MORTGAGE INC
7229 Hanover Parkway, Suite C
Greenbelt, MD 20770
Telephone: (301) 313-9100
Fax Number: (301) 313-0900

FIDELITY AND TRUST MORTGAGE INC
115-22 Aikens Center
Martinsburg, WV 25401
Telephone: (304) 260-9433
Fax Number: (301) 260-9434

FIRST COMMUNITY MORTGAGE INC
9352 Main Street
Montgomery, OH 45242
Telephone: (513) 791-3429
Fax Number: (513) 791-3547

FIRST FEDERAL SAVINGS AND LOAN
601 Clinton Street
Defiance, OH 43510
Telephone: (419) 782-5015

FIRST MARINER BANK
3301 Boston Street
Baltimore, MD 21224
Telephone: (410) 558-4118
Fax Number: (410) 342-0489

FIRST MONEY GROUP INC
1777 Reisterstown Rd Suite 230
Baltimore, MD 21208
Telephone: (410) 653-6909

MORTGAGE CAPITAL INVESTORS INC
6571 Edsall Road
Springfield, VA 22151
Telephone: (703) 941-0711
Fax Number: (703) 256-3118

MORTGAGE CORP OHIO
110 E. Wilson Bridge Rd #220
Worthington, OH 43085
Telephone: (614) 431-3499
Fax Number: (614) 431-2697

MORTGAGE NOW INC
750 W. Resource Drive, #300
Brooklyn Hts., OH 44131
Telephone: (216) 635-0000
Fax Number: (216) 635-1111

PARK NATIONAL BANK
50 North Third St
Newark, OH 43055
Telephone: (614) 349-8451

PEOPLES TRUST MORTGAGE LLC
3920 Plank Road Suite 200
Fredericksburg, VA 22407
Telephone: (540) 548-8749

REAL ESTATE MORTGAGE CORP
20325 Center Ridge Road,
Rocky River, OH 44116
Telephone: (440) 356-5363
Fax Number: (440) 356-3633

S AND T BANK
800 Philadelphia Street
Indiana, PA 15701
Telephone: (800) 325-2265

SAVINGS FIRST MORTGAGE LLC
100 Painters Mill Road Ste 800
Owings Mills, MD 21117
Telephone: (410) 654-8800

SENIOR REVERSE MORTGAGE LTD
4935 Dorr St
Toledo, OH 43615
Telephone: (419) 537-0015
Fax Number: (419) 537-0737

SENIORS FIRST MORTGAGE COMPANY
LLC
4525 South Avenue Suite 301
Virginia Beach, VA 23452
Telephone: (757) 671-6000

SIGNATURE MORTGAGE CORP
4194 Fulton Rd NW
Canton, OH 44718
Telephone: (330) 491-1986

SOUTHERN OHIO MORTGAGE LLC
912 Senate Dr
Dayton, OH 45459
Telephone: (937) 435-7277
Fax Number: (937) 435-5707

THIRD COMMUNITY MORTGAGE CORP
112 S. Water St. Suite C
Kent, OH 44240
Telephone: (330) 346-0380
Fax Number: (330) 346-0870

UNITED FIRST MORTGAGE INC
1503 Santa Rosa Road Ste-109
Richmond, VA 23229
Telephone: (804) 282-5631

Wisconsin:

AAA MORTGAGE CORP
717 N McCarthy Road
Appleton, WI 54913
Telephone: (920) 830-0600

AMERICAN DEBT REDUCTION
211 S Central Ave Ste 101
Marshfield, WI 54449
Telephone: (715) 384-7878

AMERICAN HOME MORTGAGE CORP
915 West 175th Suite 3W
Homewood, IL 60430
Telephone: (708) 647-7909

ASPEN MORTGAGE CORPORATION
651 N Washington
Naperville, IL 60563
Telephone: (630) 983-3600

CLA MORTGAGE INC
7280 S. 13th Street #103
Oak Creek, WI 53154
Telephone: (414) 570-8811
Fax Number: (414) 570-8822

COLE TAYLOR BANK
5501 West 79th Street
Burbank, IL 60459
Telephone: (800) 613-7778
Fax Number: (630) 801-8580

CSMC
10425 W North Ave Ste 100
Wauwatosa, WI 53226
Telephone: (414) 977-8660
Fax Number: (414) 977-8661

DOW MORTGAGE COMPANY
1600 Plainfield Rd
Crest Hill, IL 60435
Telephone: (815) 730-9400
Fax Number: (815) 730-0800

EVERBANK
2550 West Golf Road #100
Rollingsmeadows, IL 60008
Telephone: (847) 439-5500

EVERHOME MORTGAGE COMPANY
8100 Nations Way
Jacksonville, FL 32256
Telephone: (904) 281-6000

FIRST CENTENNIAL MORTGAGE
11 North Edgelawn Avenue
Aurora, IL 60506
Telephone: (630) 906-7315

FIRST MIDWEST BANK
300 Park Blvd—Suite 400
Itasc, IL 60143
Telephone: (815) 774-2165
Fax Number: (815) 774-2070

GSF MORTGAGE CORPORATION
999 N Plaza Dr Ste 710
Schaumburg, IL 60173
Telephone: (847) 605-8244
Fax Number: (262) 373-1641

METRO MORTGAGE CO INC
6657 Odana Road
Madison, WI 53719
Telephone: (608) 829-3000

MORTGAGE SERVICES INC
20510 Watertown Court
Waukesha, WI 53186
Telephone: (262) 796-3900
Fax Number: (262) 796-3911

OSWEGO COMMUNITY BANK
10 N Madison St
Oswego, IL 60543
Telephone: (630) 554-3411

SGB CORPORATION
1 S 660 Midwest Rd. #100
Oakbrook Terrace, IL 60181
Telephone: (630) 916-9299
Fax Number: (630) 916-1299

Wyoming:

ACADEMY MORTGAGE LLC
4502 E 115th Avenue
Thornton, CO 80233
Telephone: (303) 280-0356

ALLIANCE GUARANTY MORTGAGE
CORP
2821 S Parker Rd #605
Aurora, CO 80014
Telephone: (303) 785-2800
Fax Number: (303) 785-0089

CAPITAL ACCESS MORTGAGE
7900 E Union Ave Ste 150
Denver, CO 80237
Telephone: (303) 691-0691
Fax Number: (303) 691-0791

CLARION MORTGAGE CAPITAL INC
9034 East Easter Place Ste 204
Englewood, CO 80112
Telephone: (303) 843-0777

ENT FEDERAL CREDIT UNION
7250 Campus Drive
Colorado Springs, CO 80920
Telephone: (719) 574-1100

EPMC LLC
4779 N Academy
Colorado Springs, CO 80918
Telephone: (719) 260-7777

FARWEST MORTGAGE BANKERS INC
4940 Lakeshore Drive
Littleton, CO 80123
Telephone: (303) 795-9329

FIRST MAINSTREET
401 Main Street Suite 2
Longmont, CO 80501
Telephone: (303) 678-5551

GENERATION V INC
91 E. Dartmouth Ave
Englewood, CO 80113
Telephone: (303) 409-0111
Fax Number: (303) 409-0113

INTERMOUNTAIN MORTGAGE CO INC
3333 2nd Avenue North Ste 250
Billings, MT 59101
Telephone: (406) 252-2600
Fax Number: (406) 237-0187

LIBERTY FINANCIAL GROUP INC
2121 S Oneida Street Suite 470
Denver, CO 80224
Telephone: (303) 691-2626
Fax Number: (303) 691-2298

MOUNTAIN PACIFIC MORTGAGE CO
375 Horsetooth, Bldg. 6, #201
Fort Collins, CO 80525
Telephone: (970) 204-4509
Fax Number: (970) 204-1068

ROCKY MOUNTAIN MUTUAL
MORTGAGE INCORPOR
7550 West Yale Ave Ste B100
Denver, CO 80227
Telephone: (303) 989-3299

UNIVERSAL LENDING CORPORATION
6775 E Evans Avenue
Denver, CO 80224
Telephone: (303) 758-3336

Index

Urban Institute, 15

U.S. Department of Housing and Urban Development (HUD):
development of reverse mortgage program, xvi–xvii, 80, 84–86
reputation of, 81–83

Uses of reverse mortgage funds, 1, 42, 61–62, 168–169
airplane purchase, 65–67
by Boom Generation, 16
business development, 79
car purchase, 78
credit card debt, 62–63
foreclosure prevention, 67–69
by GI Generation, 9
home purchase, 56, 77–78
home repair, 63–65
residential elevator, 74–77
by Silent Generation, 12

supplement to monthly income, 5, 73–74
travel, 69–72

Use Your Home to Stay at Home program, 114

Visitability of home(s), 140–142

Wealth accumulation in home, 166–167

Web sites:
counseling agencies, 52
Fannie Mae Home Keeper Program, 54
Financial Freedom Senior Funding Corporation, 58
for modifications of home, 146–147
reverse mortgage calculator, 27
Title 1 loans, 88
U.S. Department of Housing and Urban Development (HUD), 83

Weicher, John, 32, 84–86, 165